CASTLES IN THE FAR EAST

The U.S. Army Corps of Engineers
Okinawa and Japan Districts
1945 - 1990

Foreword

Castles in the Far East is a public affairs publication, based on a command information initiative, that hopefully will provide needed background to past, present, and future employees of the United States Army Engineer District, Japan. This publication is not a historical document and is totally independent of the United States Army Corps of Engineers' history program.

Despite its limitations to some folks, the publication can truly be categorized as an effort emanating from a feeling of togetherness and need. For me as the Commander, United States Army Engineer District, Japan, watching the project unfold was poignant since I lived in Japan during the mid 1950's with a father who wore castles. For many employees, the absence of a command information publication describing our roots has represented a serious shortcoming. Our public affairs staff, Gretchen Greeson, Cindy McGovern, and Doyal Dunn, accepted the task and forged a togetherness with all our employees in reaching this milestone — a celebration of the accomplishments of this district and its people. Their efforts have been superb.

As the events of the last decade of this century unfold, it is apparent that change is imminent in the Far East from many vantages — economic, overseas military commitments, and political vantages are just a few. Our beloved Japan Engineer District will invariably undergo transformation too. So, let us dedicate this effort to all the employees of the district, past, present, and future, and simply state we kept faith with the Corps' motto — Essayons!

LEON R. YOURTEE III
Colonel, EN
Commanding

Acknowledgements

For a great deal of the past two years, I have worked to complete a project which began over ten years ago when district engineer Colonel Ralph A. Luther hired Ms. Grania Davis to write a history of this district. She was assisted in her efforts by Mr. Ray Corlett, a district employee and member of the JED History Committee, who was working on a history brochure when Ms. Davis was hired. These two district employees left invaluable research for our historical files although a manuscript did not result from their efforts. Division Engineer Brigadier General Robert Bunker made the decision to produce an official history of the Japan District. Not only would it be a record of the accomplishments of the district but also a celebration of the employees responsible for those accomplishments.

Dr. Ev Ma was contracted to write the history. Her work on the project, while extensive, did not meet the needs of three consecutive JED commanders. It did, however, provide the district with a wealth of research sources which are included as an appendix to this work.

To my horror, I was recruited to finish the task begun by Dr. Ma. That has now been accomplished and I am pleased to leave JED knowing that there is a record of as many of our accomplishments in this wonderful JED family as possible. I do not, however, deserve credit for everything in this work; my main function was editing the work of others. A great deal of the credit, and many of the words in this manuscript, belong to Mr. Erwin N. Thompson, author of POD's history, <u>Pacific Ocean Engineers, History of the Pacific Ocean Division, Corps of Engineers, 1905-1980</u>. I have made every effort to site each source taken from Mr. Thompson's exceptional historical account of the division and state unequivocally that this effort does not attempt to compare with the work of this highly regarded historian. I am grateful that we were blessed with his document as a major source.

No matter how smoothly words flow or how accurate the facts, much of the pleasure for a reader comes from the design of the pages and the photography. Ms. Cynthia McGovern spent endless hours typesetting each page of this history. In addition, she researched facts in every chapter. Her work as editor of the *Bamboo Bridge* made much of the final chapter possible. By writing meticulous articles about the district's projects over the last four years, she created an accurate history of that time. Many of the words in the final chapter were originally her's. Mr. Doyal Dunn, the district photographer, provided outstanding photography for much of the final chapter of this book. I am grateful for their professionalism and their invaluable assistance.

Many JED employees, especially those in the field, spent long hours providing numbers, facts, dates, names and places. They were responsive, helpful and supportive and deserve our thanks. Mr. Don Bleibtrey should have edited this project; his record of the work at our Northern Area Office is exceptional.

The driving force behind this project, however, has been the district engineer, Colonel Leon R. Yourtee III. His insistence that this work be completed in spite of what I considered insurmountable odds is the reason there is a record of JED in print. I feel grateful to have been a part of this district and of this project. After we've all seen how difficult it can be to resurrect a past that dates back to 1945, I challenge each of you to remember the importance of recording each footprint you leave now. By understanding and remembering where we've been we can continue forward with vision. Essayons.

Gretchen Charles Greeson
Chief, Public Affairs
October 1990

Table of Contents

星谷寺観音堂の浮世絵　安藤広重と三代目豊国の合作で、天保（1830〜1844）ごろの作といわれている。上部が広重、下部が豊国の手によるもので、観音堂の縁起も書かれている。

Zama Temple

Zama Temple, August 1990

The woodblock print on the front of this page was a joint effort of two of Japan's most famous ukiyo-e artists, Utagawa Hiroshige and Utagawa Toyokuni. The upper portion of the print shows the famous Zama Temple. The work is believed to have been completed between 1830 and 1844.

Chapter One

The Engineers Come to the Far East
1945 - 1957

In August 1945 at the height of the war in the Pacific, United States planes dropped the first atomic bombs ever used in warfare on the Japanese cities of Hiroshima and Nagasaki. With Japan's surrender on September 2, hostilities ended. But months before, Army engineers were at work on the island of Okinawa carrying out a legacy that would one day belong to the United States Army Corps of Engineers' Japan District.

During the war, the Ryukyu Islands were unfortunately situated on the main approaches to Japan; they were attacked, and defended, vigorously. Casualties were high, not only among the military on both sides but also in the civilian community.

The Iron Typhoon swept through Okinawa on L Day -- the name given to landing day that was hoped to be the last day of the war.

The Okinawan child in the arms of this American soldier was rescued by troops of the Seventy-seventh Infantry Division. The Division was shocked by an attempted mass suicide of civilians during the early stages of the battle in the Keramas.

American troops first landed on the Kerama Islands, 15 miles west of Okinawa, in March 1945. Into the devastation of an already war torn Okinawa, the U. S. Tenth Army began an assault on Okinawa on L Day, April 1, 1945, in what was to become the last major battle of World War II. They met with little resistance on the beaches but Okinawa was defended fiercely from inland positions. Aircraft from the Japanese mainland, suicide planes among them, assisted in the defense, sinking 36 Allied ships, damaging 368 more. American casualties were 12,500 men killed. More than 110,000 Japanese men were killed. The invasion, dubbed the Iron Typhoon, continued through the turbulent spring and summer and Okinawa remained the key to the invasion of Japan. No one dreamed at that time that within a few years Okinawa would become the key to the defense of the free world — including Japan — in the entire Pacific Area and that its importance in this respect would have a profound effect on its future. Most of all, no one dreamed that the terrible tragedy of Iron Typhoon would eventually lead to the greatest period of peace, growth, and prosperity that the people of the Ryukyus had ever known.

In support of the assault, engineers began repairing and enlarging air fields on Okinawa and near Ie Shima for American fighters and bombers. The southern end of the island and the principal city of Naha were in ruins. The Okinawans, stunned and left homeless by the bitter fighting, struggled to reestablish their families and their lives.

The American Army of Occupation, eventually designated as the Ryukyus Command, Army of Occupation, began establishing bases and rebuilding the ruins that were Okinawa. Over 30,000 engineer troops constructed camps, built roads and bridges and established communications systems.

By September of 1945, just days after the war officially ended, a petroleum storage tank farm and a major naval base had been completed in addition to the work at Naha. Army engineers were engaged in constructing hospital facilities, troop housing, water supply facilities, storage areas, recreational facilities and additional aviation facilities to support the 15 new runways that were in the process of being constructed since the initial landings. [1]

Then, on October 9, 1945, a typhoon struck the island, leaving in its wake major destruction to both the island and to the recent construction work by the engineers. The winds also destroyed newly completed communications, shredded Quonset huts, and ruined all water supplies.[2] A large number of ships anchored offshore were sunk or driven ashore. Four dredges from the Honolulu Engineer District, the *Pacific, San Joaquin, MacKenzie* and *Sacramento*, were heavily damaged. The dredges had arrived earlier in the summer as an HED initiative to follow combat forces and assist in the construction of forward bases in the captured islands. The *Sacramento* had received a wound stripe after she was shelled by a Japanese submarine in December 1941. During the typhoon, the *MacKenzie* was struck by two ships and was put out of action. A liberty ship crashed into the *Pacific* almost sinking the dredge. Two vessels rammed the *San Joaquin* but she too escaped major damage. The *Sacramento* managed to survive the storm intact. When the storm subsided, the engineers found the

Typhoons hammered at the work of the Occupation's engineers during the summer and fall of 1945 destroying a significant amount of work.

island almost as devastated as when they had landed. All they could do was begin again.

Engineers and the Army of Occupation on Mainland Japan 1945-1949

Unlike the military situation on Okinawa, the Army troops did not occupy mainland Japan and its adjacent islands until after the formal surrender on August 15, 1945. The Army of Occupation force was primarily composed of the United States Sixth and Eighth Armies with several large contingents from the Navy and Army Air Corps. In addition, there was a relatively small force under the command of the British, Indian and Australian Armies.

On August 29, 1945, one day prior to the initial landing of the principal Army units, General Douglas MacArthur, commander of the Army of Occupation, sent Brigadier General Bernard L. Robinson ashore with a small staff to evaluate the situation from a military engineering point of view.

What Brigadier General Robinson found in that first twenty-four hours would later be confirmed by more extensive investigations once the occupation was underway. There was adequate electrical power and generally adequate potable water. At least two airfields near Tokyo could be used immediately, although both soon would need repairs and additions. Housing would be a problem because of the extensive bombing of the island — especially the Tokyo area where the Army would be stationed. The vast differences in American and Japanese standards for housing complicated the situation. General MacArthur decided, based on Brigadier General Robinson's findings, that the Occupation Army would initially live in tents with flooring.

In addition, Brigadier General Robinson found that Japan's railway system was excellent and virtually untouched by the war. The roads, however, were in poor condition. Questions concerning the possible mining of the harbors and adequate storage space for fuel also plagued the Army.

With these conditions in mind, General MacArthur and his chief engineer, Major General Hugh J. Casey, began establishing priorities and developing an engineer master plan. Occupation requirements and their related engineering ramifications were not the only important considerations, however. The poor condition of the Japanese infrastructure placed severe constraints on the engineers. To complicate the situation, Japan's industrial capabilities were at a standstill; American bombers had dropped large quantities of incendiary bombs on most of Japan's urban areas leaving tens of thousands of Japanese homeless. In most cities a minimum of half of the residential housing had been totally destroyed. The country was so devastated by the war that mass starvation was a very real possibility without outside aid. The situation was so serious that the United States realized it would have to commit massive amounts of aid to Japan in order to avoid social chaos and tremendous loss of life. Under these circumstances, General MacArthur and his staff decided construction for the Occupation forces would have to be kept at a level which would not overtax the Japanese economy. In addition, local materials would be used whenever possible.

General MacArthur and Brigadier General Casey devised a very basic initial construction plan and set a 135 day timetable for its completion. Army engineer units were to engage in extensive repair and development of two or three airfields; other airfields would get only minor improvements and additions. The harbors in which Occupation forces would operate needed little initial modification. Mines, however, posed a problem. Most of the northern harbors were free of mines However, pressure mines made shipping impossible in Kyushu and Central to Southern Honshu, as well as the narrow Shiminoseki Straits between Honshu and Kyushu Although most of the clearing took place before the end of 1945, the Osaka-Kobe Harbor and the Straits were not cleared until early 1946.

Army engineers also constructed access roads to the airfields and harbors, maintained and repaired the country's few main roads, and repaired or reinforced many of her bridges. Providing hospital space for the Occupation Army meant renovation of existing facilities rather than new construction. In addition, General MacArthur soon saw that far fewer than the originally estimated 12,000 hospital beds would be needed. The engineers also provided more warehousing space and performed minor repairs and maintenance to petroleum storage tanks.

As the winter of 1945 approached, it was clear that tents would no longer be acceptable housing for the troops. Army engineers were instructed to convert houses, hotels, factories, Japanese Army barracks, and even the former Japanese Ministry of War headquarters into troop housing. The Sanno Hotel in Tokyo was included in this list of buildings taken over by the Occupation forces. By January 1946, local housing had been provided to take care of seventy-five percent of the 300,000 man Occupation force. Most of the remaining twenty-five percent lived in Quonset huts sent from the United States. Some personnel, however, toughed it out in the tents for a few of the coldest winter months in Japan until better quarters were available. During the first winter, heating for the housing was a serious problem. Many of the troops had to rely on inadequate and hazardous fuel-oil burning stoves.

By mid-1946, most of the major originally planned projects had been completed. One exception was airfields which required continued enlargement and improvement throughout 1946 and beyond. Another exception involved housing for dependents. To make the tour of duty in Japan more attractive, the Department of the Army ruled, in December 1945, that soldiers could bring their dependents to Japan in an accompanied tour status. This decision prompted planning for major housing projects initiatives.

Responsibility for construction in Japan during the Occupation fell principally to the Supreme Command Allied Powers, Headquarters, Army Forces Pacific, Tokyo, under the command of Major General Hugh J. Casey. The Eighth Army had charge of northern and eastern Japan, including the vital Tokyo area, while the Sixth Army had southern Honshu, as well as all of Kyushu and Shikoku. In January 1946, the Sixth Army returned to the United States, leaving the Eighth Army as the principal Occupation force and its engineer, Colonel David M. Dunne, as the second key player in the construction arena. Headquarters, Army Forces Pacific and the Eighth Army were responsible for all Army and Army Air Corps construction while the Navy and the British Occupation Forces managed their own, far smaller projects. When the British forces left Japan, Eighth Army took over their construction mission, leaving the Navy in charge of construction only on naval bases.

From the start of the Occupation, Headquarters, Army Forces Pacific formulated general policy, executed certain design duties — especially in the area of housing — and managed construction in the Tokyo area, including several airfields and major projects at Haneda and Tachikawa. Beginning in late 1946, their authority was extended to cover all engineering projects throughout Japan. In 1947, more budget control was exercised by the command over engineering projects. Engineering and construction responsibility remained with the field commanders and their engineers, under the general supervision of the Sixth, and later, the Eighth Army Engineer.[3]

Major Construction Activities: 1946-1949

Army engineers were also dismayed at the imbalance between the large number of workers and lack of mechanization employed by Japanese construction firms. Quality and standards were a problem. Concrete placement for airport runways, for example, had to be carefully monitored to be sure it would withstand repeated use. Many needed items were in short supply. In the case of some smaller items like space heaters and refrigerators, the Engineer Supply Division provided standards to Japanese companies who then manufactured them. To provide heavy construction equipment, the Eighth Army took over a former Japanese arsenal at Sagami in 1949, converting it into an Engineer Rebuild site and stockyard for the Far East Command. Bulldozers and other heavy equipment abandoned in areas throughout the Pacific at the close of World War II were repaired or rebuilt at Sagami. This facility eventually became the United States Army Engineer Supply Center, Far East.

The most important projects the Occupation Army managed were air fields and housing. Although Atsugi was the first airfield used in the early days of the Occupation, Major General Casey and others soon determined that Haneda airfield, located on Tokyo Bay, should be developed into the Occupation forces' major airbase. In addition to Haneda, Eighth Army engineers engaged in major airfield construction at Iruragawa and Yokota airfields, the later becoming the base for long distance B-29s. Minor construction projects were carried out on several other airstrips.

To provide troop housing, General MacArthur relied primarily on reconditioning housing requisitioned from the Japanese, He also ordered replacement centers at Zama and Tachikawa and base camps in Tokyo and at Yokohama. The replacement centers and base camps together provided quarters for over 6,000 men.

In addition to troop housing, thousands of family housing quarters were needed as a result of the decision to change the tours of duty in Japan from unaccompanied to accompanied tours. Between 1946 and 1949, approximately one-third of all design drawings produced by Army Forces Pacific's Engineer Section Design Branch was for dependent housing. Over the same period, a total of 12,000 units were completed; more than two-thirds of which were new construction. These units, mostly single family dwellings and duplexes, were far more elaborate than standard troop housing having significantly more floor space alloted than to dependent housing in the United States. Much of the new construction consisted of housing communities complete with support services, such as commissaries, chapels, schools and fire stations. These self-contained communities were similar to government housing built in the United States near factories important to the war effort.

Major General Casey's Engineer Section prepared nine basic housing floor plans which were used for all the U. S. housing communities in Japan. Some of these communities contained over 1,000 sets of quarters. At the Quartermaster's request, Army Forces Pacific's Engineer Section also designed the furniture for the housing, which was then built by Japanese contractors under the supervision of the Engineer Section.

The surge in housing needed to support the military presence in Japan continued to drive the engineering mission during the early years of the Occupation. It was the beginning of an engineering and construction phenomenon — support to an increase in forces buildups on Japan and Okinawa — that would, time and again, form the basis of the work done by military engineers as the government of Japan continued to support the American military presence necessary in the strategically volatile Far East.[4]

The 1950s - A Peace Treaty and the Korean War

In April 1952, President Truman signed a Peace Treaty with Japan. The Japanese nation, no longer regarded as a defeated, occupied nation, became an ally in Asia. In addition to restructuring international relationships, the treaty profoundly changed the military construction program in Japan. The treaty ended both the requirement for Japan to pay for American military construction and the Procurement Demand System. The old system was replaced by the Military Construction Program (MCP) under which the U. S. government paid its own bills, awarded contracts directly to Japanese contractors, used American designs and specifications, and procured materials from America and Japan.

By way of background, at the beginning of 1949 American troop strength was at a low point. There were approximately 130,000 troops and the engineer units, equally as understrengthed, who were continuing the peacetime tasks of completing and maintaining American bases and housing areas in Japan. Major General Casey returned to the United States in the summer of 1949 after eight years as MacArthur's chief engineer. He was replaced by Major General James G. Christiansen, who supervised the reduced engineer units in what had become rather routine tasks.

With the outbreak of hostilities in Korea on June 25, 1950, the engineer mission underwent a rapid transition from post-war activities to active support of the United Nations forces in Korea. However, this increased pace was accompanied by a considerable loss of staff as personnel were transferred to combat units in Korea. Department of the Army civilians were difficult to recruit during the Korean war which placed added stress on all personnel, including the newly hired Japanese nationals.

American military bases in Japan were vital links in the Korean War effort. Vastly increased funding was appropriated for a tremendous buildup of forces, facilities, equipment and support activities, including relief efforts for Korean civilians. Supplies were shipped regularly from Japan to Korea to prevent disease, starvation, and unrest among the Korean civilian population. Iwakuni Air Base in Southern Honshu was a center of activity as troops and equipment were shuttled daily to the front lines in Korea and the base became known as the "gateway to Korea".

The war pumped considerable funds into the Japanese economy for construction, material, and the manufacture of support items. All of these assisted the process of postwar recovery. Cities and towns were beyond the point of needing critical reconstruction; shopping sectors were beginning to reappear once again while housing was still in short supply. By the mid-1950s, much had been accomplished to alleviate the problem. With contracts being let by the engineer units to construction companies, shipping companies, factories and major commercial concerns like Mitsubishi, American money was helping restore the Japanese economy.

Yokota Air Base took on an important role in supporting the Korean conflict. Between 1950 and 1955, the B-29 base was upgraded for jet aircraft. Much of the work, accomplished by the 43rd Engineer Battalion (Construction), consisted of reinforcing the runway landing areas and improving aircraft hangers. In addition to runway improvements, Yokota Air Base received a major fuel oil storage and dispensing system. Barracks and airmen's dormitories, troop and support facilities and more sophisticated maintenance shops were part of the base buildup.

Engineer supply operations were expanded considerably and crews at the Sagami Depot worked overtime to overhaul and repair thousands of pieces and millions of dollars worth of World War II equipment for the war. Microwave communications systems were constructed by Nippon Telegraph and Telephone Company. Roads were improved and communications systems were built at Camp Zama and other bases throughout Japan. Utilities were expanded to keep pace with the buildup of forces. Storage warehouses were increased. Medical units were improved to provide care for combat victims. The Far East Radio Network was expanded; administrative offices, post offices and map production facilities throughout the island were improved. More dependent housing, schools, exchanges and commissaries were built to handle the influx of personnel. Virtually every American military base in Japan was enlarged and improved during the war; dozens of Japanese contractors were awarded the construction contracts to accomplish this work.

By the mid-1950s, American bases in Japan had reached a new level of operational efficiency, the Japanese economy was recovering and the engineer units were moving toward consolidation under the United States Army Corps of Engineers' Far East District. In less than a decade, a tremendous amount of work and restoration had been accomplished on mainland Japan by the Army engineers.[5]

The Okinawa Engineer District

While the engineers from the Army of Occupation were busy rebuilding the devastation they found on mainland Japan, Okinawa was cleaning up after the typhoon of October 1945. Shortly thereafter, the Office of the Chief of Engineers published General Orders No. 2 on February 18, 1946, establishing the Okinawa Engineer District (OED) under the Western Ocean Division. The new district's operating area included all of the Ryukyu Islands, but the bulk of its work was confined to Okinawa. Housed in the abandoned U. S. Navy Construction Battallion (Seabee) Camp Boone, in the village of Machinato and supplied with equipment and construction materials left behind by other engineer units, the new district began operations with a staff of six officers, 20 enlisted men and 197 civilians. The Ryukyus Command Staff Engineer, Colonel Lee B. Washbourne, a combat

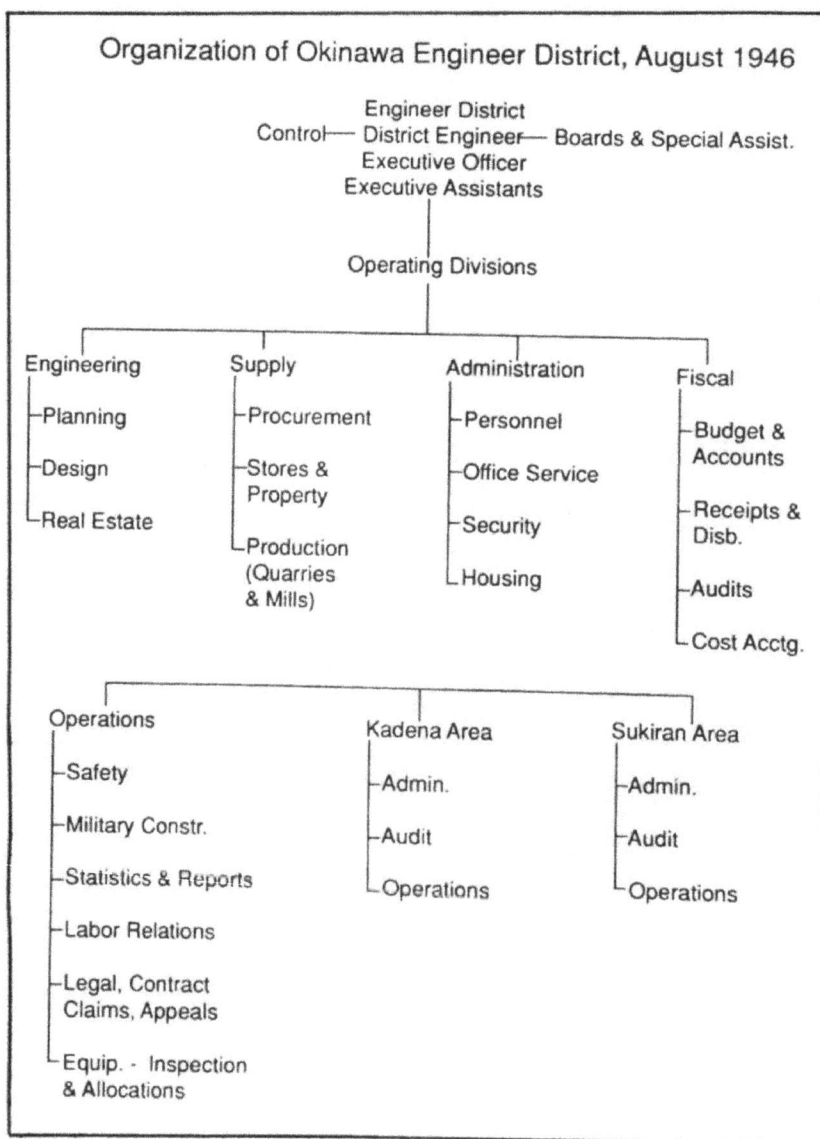

Organization of Okinawa Engineer District, August 1946

Control — Engineer District — District Engineer — Boards & Special Assist.
Executive Officer
Executive Assistants

Operating Divisions

Engineering
- Planning
- Design
- Real Estate

Supply
- Procurement
- Stores & Property
- Production (Quarries & Mills)

Administration
- Personnel
- Office Service
- Security
- Housing

Fiscal
- Budget & Accounts
- Receipts & Disb.
- Audits
- Cost Acctg.

Operations
- Safety
- Military Constr.
- Statistics & Reports
- Labor Relations
- Legal, Contract Claims, Appeals
- Equip. - Inspection & Allocations

Kadena Area
- Admin.
- Audit
- Operations

Sukiran Area
- Admin.
- Audit
- Operations

engineer officer who had landed on Okinawa with his regiment in June 1945, became the first district engineer in the Far East.

OED consisted of five operating divisions: engineering, supply, administration, fiscal, and operations, with two field offices at Kadena and Sukiran.

OED contracted with two American firms, Atkinson and Jones, for construction and Holmes and Narver for design and inspection. Working under the district's direction on a cost-plus-fixed-fee basis, these two firms were tasked with adding to and improving military facilities on Okinawa.

Colonel Washbourne's initial organizing efforts were complicated by problems in two areas: personnel and budgeting. U. S. civilians were not anxious to come to Okinawa so soon after the war. Washbourne solved the resultant worker shortage by hiring many Filipinos to fill clerical positions on Okinawa His district was troubled by small budgets; $25 million was allocated for OED's budget during its first year and only $20 million worth of construction was placed between 1947 through the fall of 1949. This was considered only a fraction of what would be needed to build modern Army and Air Force bases on Okinawa. He was dealing with the reality that the United States was a war weary nation, anxious to cut back on military expenditures.

In 1947, Colonel Washbourne was equally anxious to find a new facility to house the district and, it moved from Camp Boone at Machinato, to Camp Kue, located between Kadena Air Base and Naha. He had hoped to see the construction begin on adequate barracks to house troops stationed on Okinawa. In his exit interview, Washbourne expressed optimism for the district's future predicting that work on family quarters would extend through 1948.

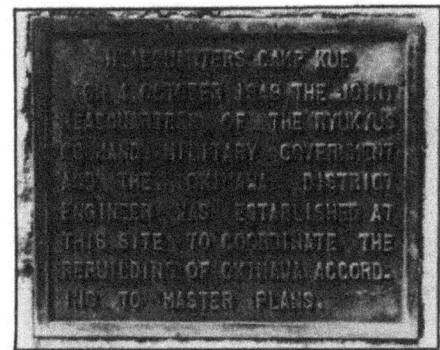

In 1947, OED moved to their new location at Camp Kue

11

Colonel Lee B. Washbourne
Okinawa District Engineer
May 1946-May 1947

Colonel James L. Green
Okinawa District Engineer
May 1947-May 1949

Colonel Washbourne's predictions would eventually come true. In the years following the arrival of OED's second district engineer, Colonel James L. Green, in May 1947, the district experienced lean budgets and more typhoon devastation. Because Congress was reluctant to provide sufficient money for the construction of permanent barracks and family housing in a foreign country cheaper, temporary facilities were constructed. The district was, however, able to use nonappropriated funds to construct theaters, libraries, and recreation centers, as well.

In 1948 and 1949, three deadly typhoons hit the island. Typhoon Libby, which struck Okinawa in October 1948, left damages of over $10 million in her wake; Typhoon Della, in June 1949 left another $5 million in damages. On Della's heels came Typhoon Gloria, smashing into the island with winds exceeding 175 miles per hour. Gloria ripped apart Quonset huts, destroyed family housing, toppled chapels and theaters, destroyed military aircraft, wiped out communications, and killed and injured many Americans and Okinawans. There was over $80 million in damage to military installations which were less than four years old.

By the time Gloria hit Okinawa, the district had its third commander, Colonel Warren N. Underwood, who plunged the district into the rigors of recovering from Gloria's devastation. The district shared its offices at Camp Kue with the staff of the Ryukyus Command whose own offices had been destroyed. The Commanding General's personnel office was reduced to one typewriter, one table and a tent.

Typhoon Gloria's destruction finally forced Washington D.C.'s, attention on Okinawa. The U. S. government, concerned over the recent triumph of the Chinese Communists on mainland China, the Nationalist Chinese government's subsequent exile to Taiwan and the withdrawal of American troops from South Korea, decided to continue the occupation of Okinawa and rebuild it into a major element in the Nation's Far East line of defense. Undersecretary of the Army Tracy S. Voorhees, followed by a team sent by the Office of the Chief of Engineers headed by Major General George J. Nold, Assistant Chief of Engineers, recommended a stop to the building of temporary facilities on the island; to construct typhoon and earthquake proof facilities; to encourage Far East contractors to enter into competitive bidding on contracts as a means of lowering U. S. government costs; and to transfer the Okinawa Engineer District from the Western Ocean Division to General Headquarters, Far East Command, Tokyo. When this transfer was carried out in late 1949, the Far East Command Engineer acquired contract authorities similar to those given to division engineers. The Okinawa District established a small suboffice in Tokyo to coordinate paperwork. [6]

With the transfer, the district gained an important new responibility. A real estate division was established in recognition of its growing rsponsibilities in that field. The district was now organized and prepared to begin the permanent base construction mandated by the State Department. The district, however, still needed to obtain funding from Congress and make important decisions concerning a labor force and equipment.

The Far East command proposed the following alternatives to solve the district's labor and material problems:

1. Use Japanese contractors and primarily Okinawan labor, supplemented by mainland Japanese workers if necessary. Use Japanese manufactured goods except where they are obviously inferior to American products.

2. Use American contractors with Okinawan, and possibly some mainland Japanese technicians and laborers. Use Japanese manufactured goods except for major electrical items such as transformers and generators.

3. Use American contractors with Okinawans only as laborers, with either Americans or Okinawans as technicans. Use American manufactured goods almost exclusively.

The first of these alternatives was expected not only to be the cheapest, but also the most beneficial, acting as a stimulant to the economies of both Okinawa and mainland Japan. The command recognized, however, that the Okinawans felt resentful of the Japanese, and some difficulties could be anticipated if Okinawan laborers were put under the supervision of Japanese contractors and technicians.

While sensitive to these concerns, the Department of the Army, equally concerned about the efficient use of funds, decided to adopt the first alternative, calling for maximum use of Okinawan and Japanese personnel and resources.

Having addressed the problems of labor and equipment, the district still faced the lack of sufficient appropriations. The Army and Air Force hoped for $73 million in emergency funds and an additional $25 million for housing. It was the duty of the Nold group to prepare a detailed plan justifying the need for these funds, as well as outlining what construction projects would be completed in a specified time frame.

The Nold group completed its work and the Army presented its case. Congress granted most of what the Army requested; $48 million in authorized construction plus $20 million in relief funds which could

Colonel Warren N. Underwood
Okinawa District Engineer
May 1949–January 1950

Colonel Thomas A. Lane
Okinawa District Engineer
January 1950-June 1952

also be used for construction. Only $28 million, however, could be used during what remained of fiscal 1950 and 1951. This seemed to be a more realistic way of handling the funds since the district could only place $20 million worth of construction during that period. Housing had the highest priority of the authorized construction. Other important items were electrical power plants and transmission lines, the water supply including sewage treatment facilities, harbor rehabilitation and road repair and construction. Operating on an under-developed, recently devastated island, the basics of housing, utilities and communications received high priority.[7]

In order to ensure the smooth development of its program, the Army made several important revisions in the way OED operated. The earlier cost-plus-fixed-fee contracts were terminated in 1949 in an economizing effort. The district began operating on a force account basis and hiring the laborers needed for construction, as well as hiring the contractors. OED also supervised the work performed by the contractors, and provided many of the supplies needed. All of these changes resulted in the need for an increase in district personnel. The outbreak of the Korean War served to accelerate this trend, making the development of Okinawa even more important.

In January 1950, Colonel Thomas A. Lane, another veteran of the war in the Pacific, became the District Engineer. It was his responsibility to oversee expansion resulting from the Korean War. In February, the Far East Command authorized the district to increase its manpower strength to 50 officers and 75 enlisted men. By the end of the fiscal year a few months later, OED was employing close to 600 civilians evenly divided between Americans and Okinawans. The military personnel, and most of the American civilians, held supervisory or technical positions while most of the 300 Okinawans were laborers.

The Korean War created a constantly expanding workload for the district. The islands' strategic location, especially as a base for heavy bombers, made it a vital part of the American Far East defense posture. During the next two years, the number of district employees increased at an exceptional rate. By December 1952, personnel strength had reached its peak: 52 officers, 74 enlisted men, and 3,498 civilians. The large number of civilian employees included 396 Americans, 472 Filipinos, 285 Japanese, and 2,345 Okinawans. The number of employees hired by contractors also peaked with 28,000 on the payrolls, 80 percent of whom were Okinawan.[8]

When the first invitations to bid were issued in 1950, American, Japanese, and Filipino firms were encouraged to submit bids. However, it soon became apparent that the Japanese could outbid the competition because of their low wage scale. The Americans and Fili-

14

pinos, therefore, quickly withdrew from bidding on projects. In 1951, all but four of the forty-two construction contracts were with Japanese contractors. Americans were able later to reenter the market; among the American contractors working on Okinawa in the early 1950s were Skidmore, Owings and Merrill of Chicago who had a major design contract from 1952 to 1954; Morrison-Knudsen International who operated the division shops for the repair and rebuilding of equipment; and Chester Clark, a road contractor.

In 1950, a major concern was that necessary construction supplies and equipment were not readily available on Okinawa. The district had hoped to obtain supplies and machinery from Japan, but several factors thwarted that effort. The Ryukyus were administered separately from mainland Japan. While Japan was controlled, at least nominally, by an Allied army the United States exercised direct control in the Ryukyus. General MacArthur, as Supreme Commander, still kept the Japanese economy under tight control, preventing goods from passing freely between Japan and Okinawa. In addition, although General MacArthur first intended to supply OED with construction equipment from the stockpile being developed at Sagami, the outbreak of war in Korea ended that plan. OED was then forced to rely on whatever sources it could develop on its own.[9]

Since Okinawan contractors lacked contacts and had little experience in undertaking large, technically demanding projects, the district devised a plan to provide them with both supplies and equipment. The district itself began using island resources to produce basic materials such as asphalt, cement, and aggregate. Between 1950 and 1953, they established and operated nine plants to produce these materials.

The Okinawa Engineer District constructed this maintenance hangar at Naha Air Base in the 1950s.

OED opened a repair and overhaul facility similar to the one in Sagami where it stocked everything from heavy equipment to nuts and bolts. From 1950 until July 1952, Morrison-Knudsen undertook the responsibility, doing some $6 million worth of business for the district At its peak, the stockyard carried 21,000 line items including earthmovers and mobile cranes, and maintained a workforce of 1,600.

With the exception of road building, which was under the exclusive all-island contract to Chester Clark, the district had primary responsibility for the new building program. In 1950, the United States Civil Administration, Ryukyus (USCAR) was established. This organization then assigned responsibility for all real estate dealings of the United States government agencies, principally, the military, USCAR, and the State Department. This task, which required the district to resolve the claims of all involved parties, was a complicated matter. The amount of arable land in the Ryukyus is very small in proportion to the population. The majority of the population was involved in farming and land was traditionally kept within the family being passed down generation to generation. As the occupying force since 1945, American forces had confiscated whatever land they wanted. To add to the problem, since land had changed hands so infrequently prior to the coming of the Americans, and since Okinawa and the other Ryukyus had been devastated by the war, few accurate land registers were available. Determining a fair market value for land was also a matter of real difficulty.

In December 1950, the General Headquarters, Far East Command, directed USCAR to begin paying rent for private land occupied by American forces, retroactive to July 1, 1950. In addition, land needed on a long-term basis by American military forces was to be acquired, preferably by purchase but if necessary, by condemnation. USCAR was further directed to have OED handle these real estate functions, including: determining a fair rent or purchase price, ascertaining ownership of the land, disbursing the rent or purchase money and, where necessary, initiating condemnation proceedings.

However, due to the dearth of real estate appraisers in the Ryukyus and the lack of records of ownership and property boundaries, OED had to seek outside help. They contracted with the Hypotech Bank of Japan, which had extensive dealings with Okinawan land in the years prior to the war, to determine fair land values. Once the bank had finished its work, rent was set at six percent of the appraisal value and offered to those Okinawans whose land was being used by the American government. The owners, however, were not satisfied either with the American use of their land or the amount of rent being offered. When the district approached the land owners and attempted to negotiate 25 year leases, the owners refused.

In spite of these real estate problems, the district's construction proceeded in a satisfactory manner. OED did not require bonds because of the distance between Okinawa and the United States, the relative inexperience of Okinawan contractors and the difficulty that Japanese contractors had in getting adequate credit. During this early period, Japanese contractors were almost always able to underbid competitors of other nationalities. Fortunately, however, the Japanese contractors got the job done. Credit in Japan became increasingly tight as the impact of the Korean War grew. As a result OED found it necessary to pay up to 30 percent of the value of a contract in advance in order to enable the Japanese contractors on Okinawa to begin a job. Once the project was underway, district personnel had to exercise close supervision over each stage of construction to stress the differences between American and Japanese construction standards and working methods.[10]

The episode of the 1952 command inspection of the district by the Far East Command is described thusly by Erwin Thompson in his history of the Pacific Ocean Division. In 1952, in the middle of Colo-

In 1953, OED paved 21 miles of four-lane and 130 miles of secondary two-lane highways replacing muddy byways common in the 40s and early 50s throughout the island.

nel Lane's tour as district engineer, a command inspection team made up of three officers from the Far East Command conducted a management survey of his operations. Almost entirely negative, the results of the inspection caused Colonel Lane to react with a vengeance. He felt that the team came to Okinawa with a preconceived vision of the district's work and spent their time inspecting the district looking for proof of what they believed to be the truth — that the district was not healthy. Of the greatest concern to Colonel Lane was the fact that none of the members of the team had any idea of the role and responsibilities of a district engineer or of the district mission on Okinawa. Dur-

Colonel Clarence Renshaw
Okinawa District Engineer
August 1952-August 1954

ing the week-long visit, the team gathered a stunning amount of misinformation and Colonel Lane was indignant. The team stated that several post commanders had refused to accept a great number of projects due to serious deficiencies. Colonel Lane countered with the fact that the only deficiencies were the result of products being unavailable on the island. Certain features were ordered but were unavailable for installation in the otherwise completed facilities. He also offered proof of very favorable comments on the facilities from both Air Force and Army commanders.

When the team learned that the members of the Ryukyus Command headquarters were complaining that they had be forced out of their headquarters as the district continued to grow, Colonel Lane was quick to point out that the building belonged to the district and that, when Typhoon Gloria ravaged the island, the district had given the homeless command space in the building. More serious was the accusation by the team that the American employees suffered from serious morale problems because of the high number of Filipinos in the district office. Colonel Lane hit back with the observation that the Filipinos had been employed since 1946 and that a general condemnation of them was nothing short of narrow prejudice.

The survey report also expressed a less than favorable impression of the work output of civilian employees from the United States. The solution, they submitted, was to assign engineer construction troops to the district. While Colonel Lane didn't oppose the military units under certain conditions, he pointed out that the type of construction the district was able to provide in Okinawa was considerably cheaper than troop construction — the most expensive type of construction He also made it clear that the district could not afford it. In addition to this recommendation, the inspection team made several recommendations for the reorganization of the district. Colonel Lane's most common, always frustrated, response was: The recommendation does not fit the requirement. He managed to prove that the attacks on his district, the employees, and their work were weak.

The dramatic rise in the district's rate of construction started during Lane's command and would continue through the tours of three subsequent district engineers: Colonel Clarence Renshaw (1952-54); Colonel George B. Summer (1954-56); and Colonel George A. Finley (1956-57).

Colonel Lane passed a healthy district to Colonel Renshaw in the summer of 1952, the same summer that Japan and the United States signed a peace treaty. The treaty had very little effect on the district since the United States retained exclusive authority of the Ryukyus. The treaty did, however, make several reorganizations within the Army in the Far East including the transfer of OE to the United States Army Forces, Far East, Tokyo.

Of greater impact to Colonel Renshaw, however, was the Civil Administration of the Ryukyu Islands which was now providing the majority of the work of the district.

Projects completed from 1950-1953 were varied in nature and complexity. A great deal was accomplished in the area of base development including more than $15 million worth of work at Naha Air Base to provide facilities for a fighter wing. At Naha harbor, OED built the Executive Branch Building, the first of three buildings for the joint use of the Ryukyuan government and the U. S. Civil Administration. On Kadena Air Base OED added a $1 million two-story base operations building, 13 reinforced concrete barracks, 425 permanent family housing units, a swimming pool, and a telephone exchange to the existing base facilities. By 1951, a $1.2 million refrigerated warehouse had been constructed at Machinato and twenty-one 165-man barracks at Sukiran.

One of the district's most ambitious projects began in 1952. Although Colonel Lane started providing better electrical and water systems for Okinawa, it was under Colonel Renshaw that these programs actually came to fruition. While the primary aim of these two projects was to provide adequate utilities to military installations, a secondary aim was to benefit the civilian population and the economy of the Ryukyus. The two most important elements of the water were a distribution system from central to southern Okinawa, and water treatment plants at Naha and Kadena Air Bases. In 1950, the district began constructing the electrical power system consisting of a 46,000-KW steam turbine power plant, and a 25 mile distribution system funded by an appropriation for aid and relief in occupied areas. The plant provided power for the local economy and revenue for the Okinawa government by selling it to the American forces. Seventy percent of the power was utilized by the military forces on Okinawa, ten percent was purchased by commercial activities, and, 20 percent was used by private consumers.

The $4.7 million construction contract was awarded to Tokyo Shibaura Electrical Company of Japan and most of the plant equipment was manufactured in Japan. The structure housing the plant was typhoon proof with insulation prohibiting the growth of fungus on the motors. Heaters in outdoor equipment rooms reduced humidity and prevented erosion. The engineers trained the Okinawans to operate the plant and the transmission system. To minimize damage from Okinawa's frequent typhoons, the transmission lines were mounted on four-legged steel towers. The system was supplemented by floating power plants — the *Impedance*, 300,000 KW, anchored in Naha Port and tied in with the land system and the *Jacona*, 10,000 KW, anchored off Sukiran and used for emergency power.[11]

Colonel George B. Sumner
Okinawa District Engineer
August 1954-February 1956

Colonel George A. Finley
Okinawa District Engineer
March 1956-December 1957

The *Impedance* (below) and the *Jacona* (right)) played an integral part in Okinawa's electrical power network.

While the construction program was progressing at a rapid pace, the real estate branch was experiencing some difficulties. The 1952 OED reappraisal of the property then in use by the United States had resulted higher property values and, subsequently, rents. The land in question consisted of some 75,000 acres, of which 25,000 had belonged to the Japanese government prior to the arrival of the American forces. The other 50,000 acres were privately owned. The land previously owned by the Japanese government presented no problem since the United States was paying rent for its use. However, the land owned by 38,000 private owners was presenting the United States with difficulties.[12]

With higher rents proposed as the basis for negotiation, OED approached the newly organized Government of the Ryukyu Islands (GRI) — a democratically elected government serving under the United States High Commissioner and USCAR — and asked it to help arrange leases with the land owners. The United States was particularly anxious to execute long-term, 20 year leases. Land owners, however, still objected to both the long-term leases and the low rental rates. Their objection was based on the traditional Okinawan view that land was hereditary, and with few exceptions, they refused to sign the leases. While desiring to uphold property rights and promote democracy in the Ryukyus, the United States also felt it imperative to establish its right to use the land it then occupied — mostly in the form of military bases. Seeking a solution, the district, along with assistance from the Office of the Chief of Engineers, reappraised the value of the U.S. controlled land as of the date of the peace treaty, April 28, 1952. Although the appraisal resulted in a substantial increase in rent, Okinawans still remained adamant. At that point, GRI withdrew totally from any land negotiations.[13]

In April 1953, the U. S. Civil Administration established condemnation procedures and created the U. S. Land Acquisition Commission to hear appeals and make the final determination of adequate and fair compensation. The district engineer felt this move would assist in future acquisition of land but would not help in acquiring leasehold interest in lands then in U. S. possession. The district was also pressured by the need to acquire the leasehold interests quickly since all funds on hand in the district at the end of FY 1954 would have to be returned to Washington. To solve this problem, the Civil Administration issued a proclamation in December 1953, giving the United States an implied leasehold interest — in effect, a mass condemnation — on all lands that it held, retroactive to the date of the signing of the peace treaty on April 28, 1952. The district engineer filed certificates of condemnation of lands held which also provided for the purchases of improvements in the lands. By filing these certificates the government's interest was officially established. Almost all of the land holders readily accepted 75 percent of the rent offered, which surprised everyone involved in the leasehold issue. Later, however, the Okinawan land owners filed an appeal with the Land Acquisition Commission for what they considered the fair and full rental. [14]

In July 1955, the district reappraised the land, resulting in another increase. The land owners once again accepted only 75 percent of the rent and filed new appeals. Meanwhile, in 1954, the United States had announced its intention to make a single payment for the land it required indefinitely, as opposed to annual rent. This announcement was met with furious protests. The chief executive of the govern-

The opening of this bridge in June 1953 at Sukuda Village on Okinawa's Highway 1 signified the completion of a $475,000 road rehabilitation project from Onna to Okuma.

ment of the Ryukyus traveled to Washington, D. C., voicing his protests to the single payment plan to the Armed Services Committee. As a result a subcommittee led by U. S. Representative Melvin Price, traveled to Okinawa in October 1955 to investigate the entire land issue.[15]

In 1956, the Price Committee announced its findings and the Okinawans were outraged. The committee's major recommendation was that the United States acquire free title or maximum interest in

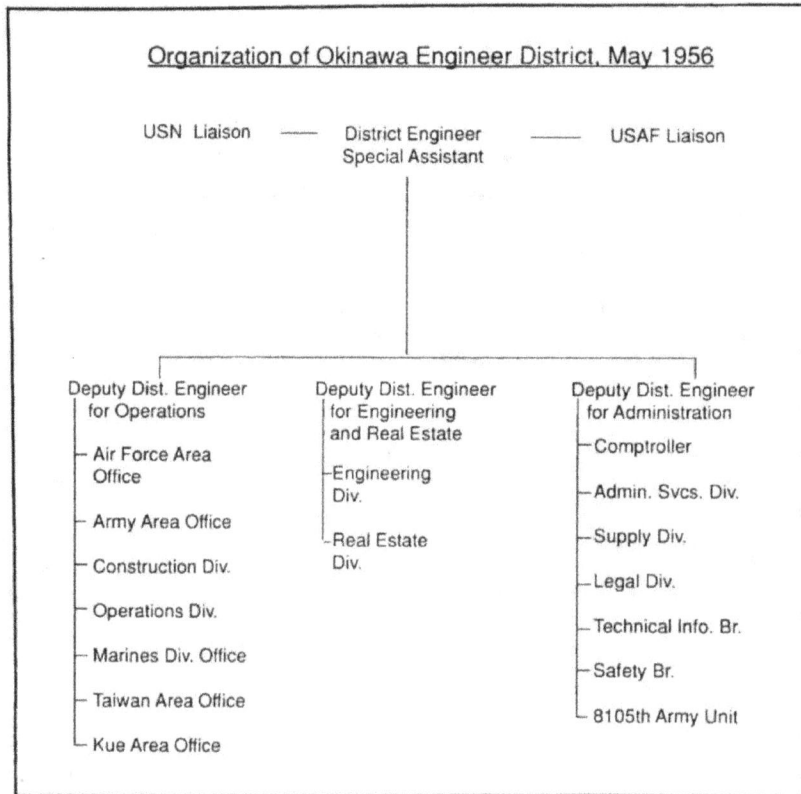

Organization of Okinawa Engineer District, May 1956

USN Liaison —— District Engineer Special Assistant —— USAF Liaison

Deputy Dist. Engineer for Operations
- Air Force Area Office
- Army Area Office
- Construction Div.
- Operations Div.
- Marines Div. Office
- Taiwan Area Office
- Kue Area Office

Deputy Dist. Engineer for Engineering and Real Estate
- Engineering Div.
- Real Estate Div.

Deputy Dist. Engineer for Administration
- Comptroller
- Admin. Svcs. Div.
- Supply Div.
- Legal Div.
- Technical Info. Br.
- Safety Br.
- 8105th Army Unit

land required for an indefinite period of time. Government officials at all levels threatened to resign and the protests continued well into 1957. Officials didn't resign; the governor of the Ryukyu Islands, General Lyman L. Lemnitzeer, announced that the U. S. would not take title to any land in the Ryukyus. Although fierce protests continued, the U. S. Civil Administration once again promulgated an ordinance in February 1957 providing the legal basis needed for the United States to acquire indefinite interest in any lands held by making a one-time payment based on 16 2/3rds years rental at the rental rates in effect on July 1, 1955. The ordinance also established a Land Court to replace the U. S. Land Acquisition Commission. Although the Okinawans continued to protest, the United States did acquire the indefinite interest, now called "determinable estate," in land by single payment. Finley and his real estate division were besieged by continuous delegations of Okinawans; newspapers were filled daily with voices opposing the arrangement, and a steady stream of petitions arrived at the district.[16]

OED constructed Stilwell Hall in 1956 for the Army. Indoor troop use was the primary function but the 80,000 square foot, $1.7 million building was also used as a sports arena.

In July 1957, the Okinawa Engineer District, burdened by land problems that seemed to have no solution in sight, came under administrative supervision of the newly established Pacific Ocean Division. In 1958, Lieutenant General James E. Moore, High Commissioner of the Ryukyu Islands, took the first step to settle the land problems by directing district engineer Colonel Hamilton W. Fish to suspend the acquisition of land under the existing system. The district had gathered a wealth of information concerning real estate and the ancient traditions of the Orient concerning land. The Americans had come to realize that, during the seven years they were battling for real estate which they considered little better than bombed out, war destroyed

U.S. Army Hospital, Okinawa

land, the Okinawans were tenaciously holding onto their heritage — no matter how battered and wasted.

But, just as they met the real estate challenges, the engineers and civilians working at OED met the construction challenges on Okinawa over the years from 1945 through 1957. Okinawa could not have bounded back from devastation without the help of Army engineers who came ashore on L Day. In a 1958 summary of OED projects completed during the first 12 years of operation, the numbers are staggering. Included in that list are accomplishments such as these: One hundered and twenty barracks buildings, 193 sets of officers' quarters, 3,824 units of family housing, a 250-bed hospital, highways, schools, dormitories, warehouses petroleum and electrical powers systems, ports and harbors and miscellaneous facilities which included things like chapels and milk plants.[17]

A tribute to the success of the district engineers' efforts were the buildings that were left standing, time and again, as typhoons hit the island. When damage did occur, it was usually to projects still under construction The devastation that occurred during Gloria did not happen again; the typhoon proof construction proved its worth.

Colonel Sumner's responsibilities as district engineer increased in 1955 with two important developments. The Formosa (later, Taiwan) Area Office was established during his tour and the Defense Department moved the U. S. Marine Division, Fleet Marine Force, from Japan to Okinawa.

In the early years of the Korean War, the United States and the Republic of China on Taiwan signed a Mutual Defense Assistance Agreement for the United States to construct military installations on Taiwan if required for defense purposes. The U. S. Military Assistance Advisory Group was stationed on Taiwan at the time and when

Typhoon Faye's winds of 145 miles per hour slammed across the island on September 26, 1957.

24

District cars were tossed around and temporary buildings were destroyed but typhoon resistant construction stood up to the winds.

the Peoples' Republic of China on the Asian mainland shelled Quemoy and other offshore islands and made threats against Taiwan, a crisis resulted. General Orders No. 12, published by the Okinawa District on May 23, 1955, established the Formosa Area Office. By late 1956, Washington and Taipei agreed to construct an airfield at Kung Kuan (Quan) in conjunction with the development of Chinese Navy projects at Tsoying Harbor and at three other naval facilities. Twenty-five million dollars were authorized for the largest of these projects — the airfield at Kung Kuan, and the contract to construct the airfield was awarded in early 1957.[18]

While deeply involved with the work on Taiwan, the district was preparing to support the Marines who were moving into the Army's facilities at Sukiran and into eleven temporary camps. The 20,000 men of the Third Marine Division needed typhoon proof facilities. Camp Schwab was to be the first home for the division and, in 1957, plans were completed and a contract was awarded for work to begin after the Pacific Ocean Division was established.[19]

In late 1956, Brigadier General Philip F. Kromer, Engineer, U. S. Army Forces, Far East, predicted that Korea would become the scene of considerable post-war construction. He noted that requirements for construction in FY 1957 in Okinawa, Taiwan, and Korea could amount to $132.5 million, with the possibility of an additional $30 million being authorized. He felt that Korea needed a district of its own or, at least, a Korea Area Office should be established there under the Okinawa Engineer District. Brigadier General Kromer's ideas were met with opposition by the commander of Korea's Eighth Army who did not want to relinquish construction responsibility to an organization on Okinawa. He wanted, and got, a construction agency in Korea directly under his control. Brigadier General Kormer did not give up his ideas, and in November 1956, he wrote to Finley in Okinawa that a letter had been sent to the Chief of Engineers recommending that Okinawa become a Division and that it be reassigned to the Office of the Chief of Engineers. He anticipated that these changes would be approved.[20]

Okinawa would not become a division. In December 1956 the district was renamed — the United States Army Engineer District, Ryuku Islands. However, this only lasted six months and, in the summer of 1957, the organization became, again, the Okinawa Engineer District.

Airfield at Kung Kuan, Taiwan. (Later renamed Ching Chuan Kang Air Base.)

Iwakuni Castle

Iwakuni Castle was completed in the spring of Keicho year 13 (1608) after six years of construction. It was then destroyed seven years later. For over 300 years, this castle remained in ruins. In March 1962, the castle tower was rebuilt. The castle is very rare because of its architecture and construction.

Chapter Two
A New Division and a Diversified Construction Program
1957 - 1972

In 1957, the definition of the Corps of Engineers' role in the Pacific was refined when the Pacific Ocean Division (POD) and its districts in Honolulu and Korea were established. The Okinawa Engineer District became a part of the Pacific Ocean Division. With its three districts, POD became, and remains today, the largest geographic division in the Corps of Engineers. Major world events would effect the work of Corps' Pacific engineers: Hawaii would see statehood, the war in Southeast Asia would begin, and North Korea would seize a United States Naval intelligence ship and hold her crew captive. Each of these situations created new missions for the Corps and, with each mission, the engineers increased their skills and competence to meet volatile international situations and the often bitter wrath of Mother Nature as she played out her own uneasy alliance with the Pacific Islanders year after year.

Colonel Hamilton Fish
Okinawa District Engineer
January 1958 - June 1959

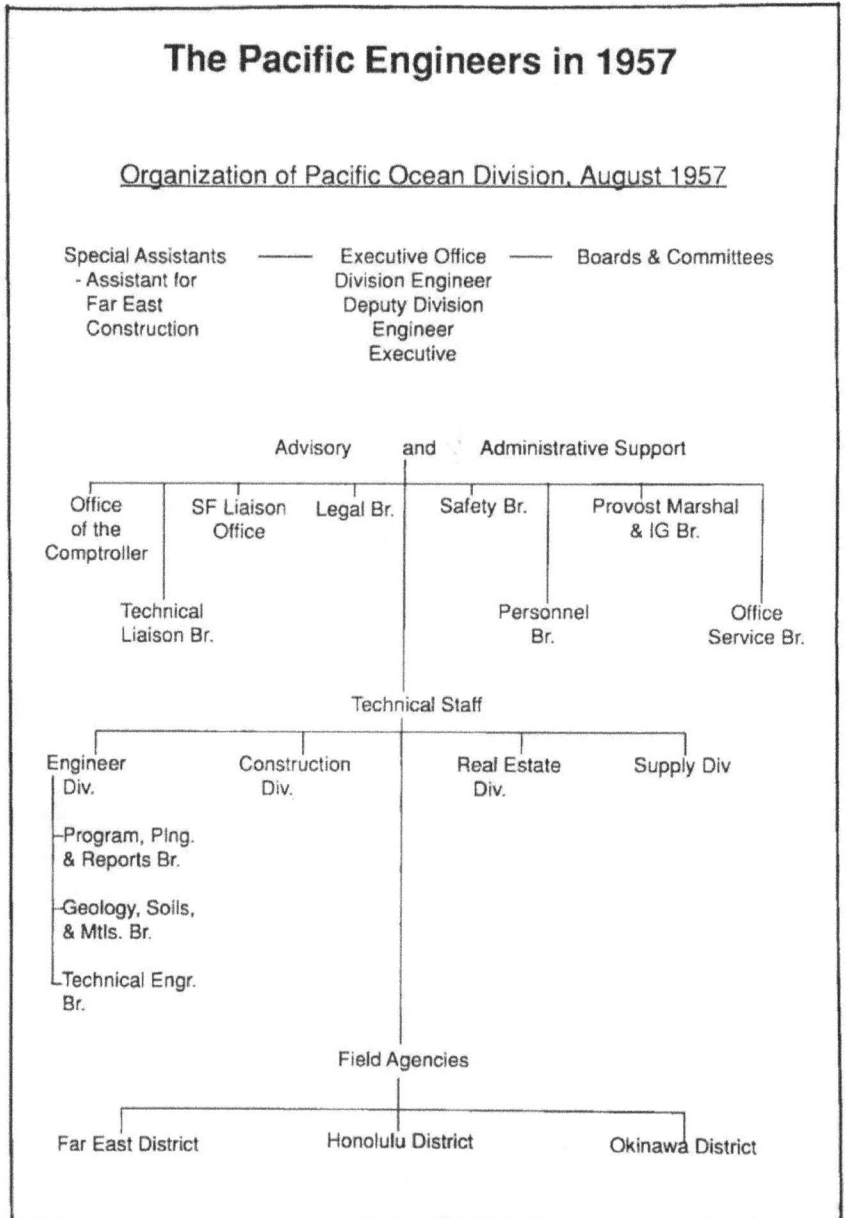

The Pacific Engineers in 1957

Organization of Pacific Ocean Division, August 1957

```
Special Assistants  ——  Executive Office  ——  Boards & Committees
- Assistant for         Division Engineer
  Far East              Deputy Division
  Construction          Engineer
                        Executive

                Advisory   and   Administrative Support

Office      SF Liaison   Legal Br.   Safety Br.   Provost Marshal
of the      Office                                & IG Br.
Comptroller

Technical                            Personnel              Office
Liaison Br.                          Br.                     Service Br.

                        Technical Staff

Engineer         Construction        Real Estate      Supply Div
 Div.             Div.                Div.

-Program, Plng.
 & Reports Br.

-Geology, Soils,
 & Mtls. Br.

-Technical Engr.
 Br.

                        Field Agencies

Far East District      Honolulu District         Okinawa District
```

In the fall of 1956, Chief of Engineers Emerson C. Itschner sent Brigadier General Ellsworth I. Davis, deputy commander of the Engineer Center at Fort Belvoir, Virginia, to the Far East to determine the feasibility of establishing an engineer organization in the Pacific Ocean area for Army and Air Force construction missions. A 1932 West Point graduate, Brigadier General Davis had served as a combat engineer in both World War II and the Korean War and had been the district engineer of the Galveston District in Texas where he gained extensive knowledge in the Corps' civil works mission. When Brigadier General Davis and his team left for the Pacific, they knew of the impending reorganization of the Army and Air Force in the Far East and the plan to move the major commands located in Tokyo to Hawaii. In the spring of 1957, Brigadier General Davis toured the Far East and Hawaii on his fact finding mission. [1]

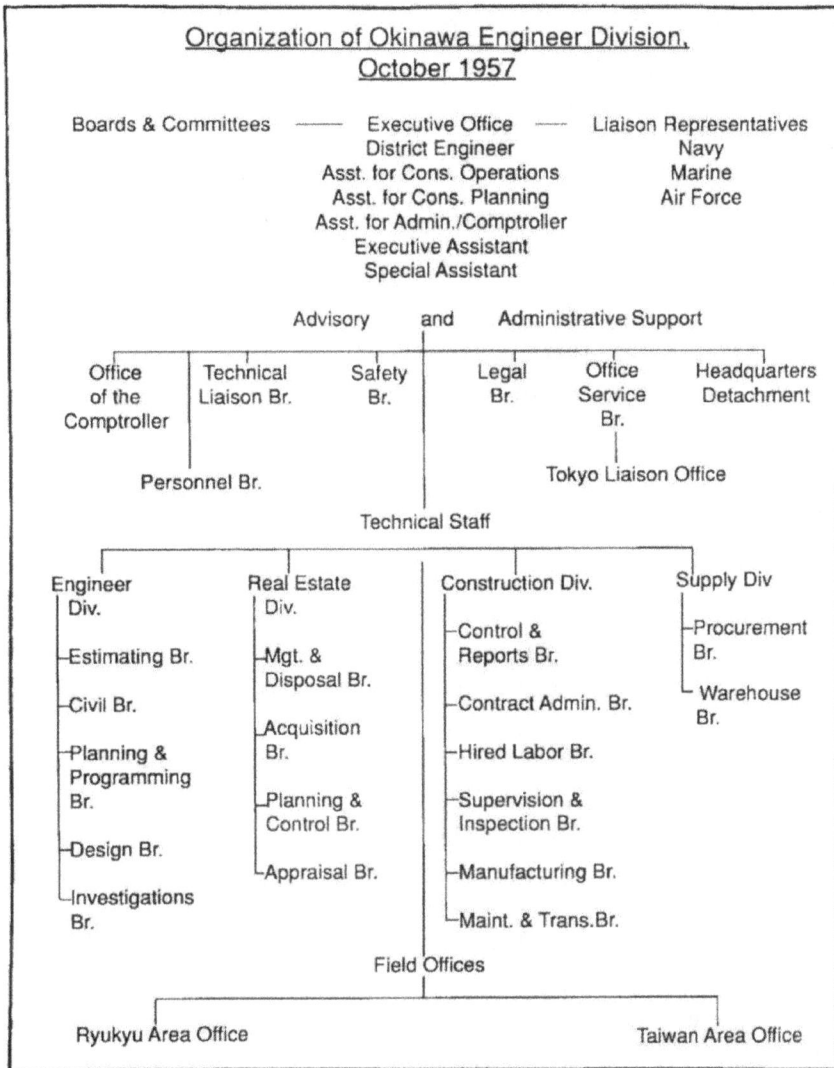

Organization of Okinawa Engineer Division, October 1957

Boards & Committees —— Executive Office —— Liaison Representatives
District Engineer — Navy
Asst. for Cons. Operations — Marine
Asst. for Cons. Planning — Air Force
Asst. for Admin./Comptroller
Executive Assistant
Special Assistant

Advisory   and   Administrative Support

Office of the Comptroller | Technical Liaison Br. | Safety Br. | Legal Br. | Office Service Br. | Headquarters Detachment

Personnel Br.   Tokyo Liaison Office

Technical Staff

Engineer Div.
—Estimating Br.
—Civil Br.
—Planning & Programming Br.
—Design Br.
—Investigations Br.

Real Estate Div.
—Mgt. & Disposal Br.
—Acquisition Br.
—Planning & Control Br.
—Appraisal Br.

Construction Div.
—Control & Reports Br.
—Contract Admin. Br.
—Hired Labor Br.
—Supervision & Inspection Br.
—Manufacturing Br.
—Maint. & Trans.Br.

Supply Div
—Procurement Br.
—Warehouse Br.

Field Offices

Ryukyu Area Office   Taiwan Area Office

Colonel Menon W. Whitsitt
Okinawa District Engineer
June 1959 - March 1961

The Honolulu Area Office, under the command of Lieutenant Colonel McGlachlin Hatch and assigned to the San Francisco District, was experiencing gradual growth in both military construction and its civil works program. In 1957, the Honolulu Area Office was the only engineer organization in the Pacific Ocean under the control of the Chief of Engineers. The U. S. Army Engineer District, Ryukyu Islands was under the command of the United States Army Forces, Far East/

Colonel Alvin D. Wilder
Okinawa District Engineer
March 1961 - June 1962

Lieutenant Colonel Elmer M. Regn
Acting Okinawa District Engineer
June to July 1962

Eighth United States Army in Tokyo. Under the terms of the United States-Japan Mutual Defense Treaty of 1951, the United States was the sole administering authority of the Ryukyus and had developed Okinawa into a strong military base during the years from 1946 through 1957.

In Korea, three U. S. construction programs were underway in 1956. Family housing and support facilities for the Provisional Military Assistance Advisory Group, family housing for the United States Office of Economic Coordination, and non-appropriated funds projects for the construction of libraries, gymnasiums, service clubs and other recreational facilities. Together these projects amounted to $14 million dollars. An additional $6 million dollars had been approved by Congress to improve living standards for American troops stationed in Korea. When Brigadier General Davis arrived in Korea in 1957, he found the Korea Construction Agency, under the command of Eighth Army, facing severe difficulties with this $20 million construction mission. His immediately made the resources, procedures, and expertise of the United States Army Corps of Engineers available to Korea with the establishment of a district.

In Japan, Brigadier General Davis encountered an almost non-existent construction program but he wanted Japan included in any plan to reorganize the construction effort in the Pacific. There were almost 50,000 military troops stationed on the island at the time of Brigadier General Davis' visit and, under the 1951 Mutual Security Treaty and the 1952 Peace Treaty, these forces would stay in Japan for years. By 1957, American military advisors were in Vietnam training troops of the South Vietnamese Army and Brigadier General Davis recognized the impact that the unrest in Southeast Asia would have on the military stationed in both Korea and Japan.[2]

In April 1957, Brigadier General Davis completed his fact-finding tour of the Far East and proposed an Engineer District for Hawaii, Okinawa and Korea. He also recommended the establishment of an Engineer Division in Hawaii to work with the relocating Pacific commands and to provide a Pacific-wide construction capability there. Brigadier General Davis' recommendations resulted in the establishment of the Pacific Ocean Division on June 3, 1957 in Honolulu, Territory of Hawaii. The Division consisted of three districts which became operational on June 1. The Honolulu Area Office became the Honolulu District (HED). The U. S. Army Engineer District, Ryukyu Islands took back its original name — the Okinawa Engineer District (OED). It retained responsibility for the Ryukyu Islands and Taiwan. The new Far East District (FED) was located in Seoul and replaced the Korea and Japan Construction Agencies as the responsible agency for military construction on Korea and on Japan. Lieutenant Colonel Hatch retained command of the Honolulu District as did Colonel

Finley in Okinawa. Colonel Stephen E. Smith, a close friend and West Point classmate of Colonel Finley's, became the district engineer in Korea. In Washington, Chief of Engineers Itschner selected Brigadier General Davis to be the first division engineer for the Pacific Ocean Division.

The Okinawa and Honolulu districts closely followed the organizational structure of the division. Colonel Finley established a Ryukyu Area Office and a Taiwan Area Office. The Far East District, with less manpower than either Honolulu or Okinawa, had no technical liaison branch or real estate office but it had four resident offices in Korea and an area office in Japan. Over the next 13 years, the group of people working for FED in Japan would be known by three different names — the Japan Area Office, the Far East District, Rear and the Japan Resident Office. And the mission of the organization would change as the needs of the American military forces stationed in Korea and on Japan adjusted to changing world conditions being played out in the Pacific setting.[3]

Concern for contractor safety eventually stopped contractors from using local material, such as the bamboo shown below, for scaffolding on construction sites.

Colonel Henry C. Schrader
Okinawa District Engineer
July 1962 - August 1964

Colonel Richard G. Rhodes
Okinawa District Engineer
August 1964 - July 1965

The Okinawa Engineer District, 1957-1970

The establishment of the Pacific Ocean Division in 1957 caused no interruption of construction projects on Okinawa. Colonel Finley served as district engineer until the completion of his tour in December when he was replaced by Colonel Hamilton J. Fish. The work of the Okinawa Engineer District during this period can be divided into two categories — military construction for the United States armed forces and work performed to benefit the civilian population of Okinawa under the direction of the U. S. Civil Administration of the Ryukyus (USCAR).

As a district under the Pacific Ocean Division, OED increasingly attempted to follow the normal Corps' policy of supervising rather than executing construction. The amount of work fell sharply; in fiscal year 1958 the district's work force fell to 1,480 people and the district was forced to close its Hired Labor Branch in July. By 1961, the district employed only 484 people — a stark contrast to the 1955 work force of 4,132. The vast majority of those people who left the district during this seven year period were laborers who had worked in the district-operated stockyard, quarry, or batching plants or had been directly employed on the district's many construction sites.

In addition to a declining work force, the district accelerated the process of eliminating those items from its stockyard which contractors could readily obtain elsewhere. By July 1959, the district stocked only 32 specialty items such as Nike missile equipment as opposed to the 21,000 items stocked in 1952. Some of the district's remaining plants for producing construction material were closed by the end of 1959. And in a conscious attempt to benefit the Okinawan construction industry, the district adopted the policy that encouraged Okinawan construction firms to submit bids for district offered projects, accelerating the entry of Okinawan firms into the district dominated construction market. By January 1959, one-third of the 21 contractors working for the district were Okinawan.

Although at a reduced rate, base construction did continue during this period. By 1959, over $350 million in construction for the military had been accomplished including the major items originally planned at the time of the Nold group visit in 1949 — all earthquake and typhoon resistant. However, as the military construction needs were decreasing, the U. S. Civil Administration of the Ryukyus (USCAR), called upon the district to perform important activities to benefit the civilian population as well as military forces stationed on Okinawa. These programs included not only construction but planning, and boosted the district's dollar placement. Even so, with the exception of a $41 million workload in 1959, it would be the war in

OED constructed the Machinato milk plant (right) during its first years as a district. The replacement, below, a permanent facility, was completed in 1958.

Vietnam that finally raised the workload for OED from the $15 - $25 million range to nearly $50 million.[4]

Due to the shrinking workload and declining work force, Brigadier General Davis sent the following message to the Chief of Engineers in 1957 after the division established the Okinawa District which addressed a problem that would plague the Corps of Engineers into the 1990s — the cost of doing business:

> Declining workload and the prospects of increasing government costs continue to be the major area of concern in the Okinawa District . . . . The situation is made more painful in Okinawa because a substantial portion of their work is for non-captive customers, the Marines and USCAR, who are most critical of our costs. The District and we have explained the basis for the costs to our customers and will continue to do so in the future, but the fact remains that they like to see 100 cents out of every dollar spent on design and construction.[5]

Despite fiscal problems and reductions in construction, district engineer Hamilton W. Fish began a visionary training program. The district began hiring Okinawan engineer graduates from the University of the Ryukyus in 1958. The project suffered a lapse until 1961 when the new district engineer, Colonel Alvin D. Wilder, enforced the pro-

Colonel George A. Austin, Jr.
Okinawa District Engineer
July 1965 - August 1967

gram. By 1963, with the district under the command of Colonel Henry C. Schrader, the training program made a quantum leap with the establishment of a formal three-year program for graduate engineers financed by USCAR. By 1966, a total of 21 Ryukyuan engineers had enrolled in the program and each year seven new graduates were hired as others completed their training.   That year district engineer Colonel George A. Austin, Jr., presented a certificate to Mr. Misuo Uechi, the first Ryukyuan engineer to complete the "Professional Engineer Training Program." [6]

The district's civil mission for USCAR was varied and provided some of the most interesting projects for the engineers in the district. In 1957, Okinawa faced a critical water shortage which effected all inhabitants on the island. In early 1958, USCAR organized the Ryukyu Domestic Water Corporation and designated the various elements of the island's water system as the Integrated Island Water System. As the construction agent for USCAR, the district constructed $3 million worth of new facilities including the large Tengan water treatment plant, the Zukeyama dam and reservoir and the Camp Hansen dam and reservoir built for the Marines at Camp Hansen between 1958 and 1962.

OED called upon the pool of Corps engineering talent to assist with the Zukeyama dam work by recruiting the assistance of an expert soils engineer from Washington's Walla Walla District. On temporary duty to OED, the Walla Walla engineer reviewed hydraulic data which had been collected by Okinawa engineers. He discovered adverse foundation conditions at the projected dam site and a more feasible site was selected on the Fukuji River in northern Okinawa. The drought of 1957 resulted in the construction of the Zukeyama dam; the Fukuji

The Zukeyama dam and reservoir was an OED project for the Ryukyu Domestic Water Corporation.

OED's work for the Ryukyu Domestic Water System

Ryukyu domestic water system plan

The drought situation on Okinawa prompted many different forms of providing water. OED drilled over 60 test holes on Kadena in 1960 and 14 became permanent wells adding an immediate source to the raw water supply and greatly reducing the need for water rationing.

Construction of Tengan Dam and Reservoir.

Pipeline under construction in 1968 for the island-wide water system.

A $2.7 million water treatment plant constructed between 1964 and 1968 provided a 20 million gallon per day capacity to the RDWS.

Camp Hansen dam and reservior.

Site of the $104 million Fukuji dam and reservoir.

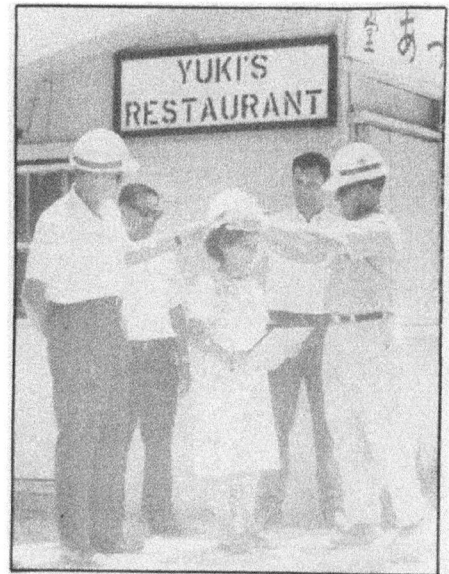

River site for a dam and reservoir was the result of the most severe drought ever to plague the island — the drought of 1963.

Because of that drought, the Ryukyu Domestic Water Corporation authorized a $795,000 program involving survey, exploration and design of water system facilities. This work involved two dams, a well field, a hydrological study, a water treatment plant, several pumping stations and pipelines. Over the next several years, the Okinawa District enlarged and improved existing water systems. In 1967, the Tengan dam and reservoir were completed and supplied eight million gallons of water per day to the Tengan treatment plant. The East Side Transmission System, a 24-inch pipeline completed in 1966, well fields in the Tengan area and at Kadena Air Base and a ten million gallon water tank at Naha were among the most significant projects undertaken in the water system program. [7]

The lack of a sufficient electrical system throughout the island was another major concern for the Ryukyus and, as Okinawan industry continued to develop in the post war years and the islanders learned that there were modern amenities that could increase the value of their lives, the problem became critical. The influx of United States forces and their dependents increased the burden on existing power sources.

At the time of the district's assignment to the Pacific Ocean Division, the integrated power system on Okinawa was operated by the United States Army which sold power to the Navy, the Air Force and

On July 16, 1969 Miss Yuki Nakamura was presented with a certificate of appreciation and a personalized hard hat by Lieutenant Colonel William S. Cutler, acting district engineer. For over two years, Miss Nakamura cooked and served OED construction representatives and acted as an unofficial vehicle dispatcher and welcoming committee to VIP's at the Fukuji dam site in Kawata Village. The certification included these words: ". . . from this day forward, Miss Yuki Nakamura will be tendered the honorary title of Inspector - Okinawa Engineer District, Corps of Engineers."

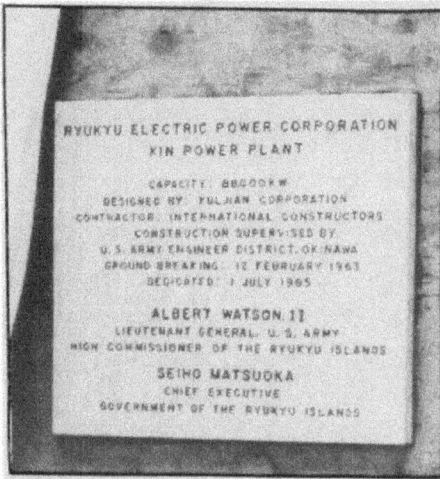

RYUKYU ELECTRIC POWER CORPORATION
KIN POWER PLANT

CAPACITY: 88000KW
DESIGNED BY: KULJIAN CORPORATION
CONTRACTOR: INTERNATIONAL CONSTRUCTORS
CONSTRUCTION SUPERVISED BY
U. S. ARMY ENGINEER DISTRICT, OKINAWA
GROUND BREAKING: 12 FEBRUARY 1963
DEDICATED: 1 JULY 1965

ALBERT WATSON, II
LIEUTENANT GENERAL, U. S. ARMY
HIGH COMMISSIONER OF THE RYUKYU ISLANDS

SEIHO MATSUOKA
CHIEF EXECUTIVE
GOVERNMENT OF THE RYUKYU ISLANDS

There was a shortage of qualified welders for high pressure type work at the Kin Power Plant. In order to qualify the 40 welders required for the job, International Constructors, prime contractor for the project, conducted a welding school. Mr. Walter D. Manis, shown here with some of the students, conducted the training. Manis was a technical representative from Babcock and Wilcox Corporation, the U.S. firm which manufactured the four boilers. Graduates of the class received certification in welding of all steel, except stainless, regardless of the thickness. The training was conducted during National Engineers' Week. The 1964 Engineer Week slogan was "Creative Engineering . . . Design for Tomorrow."

the Ryukyu Electric Power Corporation. Power came from several inadequate sources: The old Machinato Power Plant, constructed by OED in the early 1950's; two power barges, the *Impedance* anchored at Naha Port and the *Jacona* moored off Suiran; and a 5,000 kilowatt power train and some smaller diesel plants. The lack of natural heating sources such as coal and water added to the power problems.

At the request of USCAR, the district supervised the construction of the Kin Power Plant, a $14.7 million facility which took three years to complete. The plant, designed by the Kuljian Corporation of Philadelphia and constructed by International Constructors, was dedicated on July 1, 1965. It included four 22,000 kilowatt turbo-generators which almost doubled Okinawa's permanent electrical power capacity. A low-interest, long term United States Treasury loan financed the project and the Ryukyu Electric Power Corporation took over production of electric power from the Army. In 1965 the government of the Ryukyu Islands issued a three-cent stamp commemorating the construction of this power plant on the eastern side of the island in the village of Kin.[8]

District engineers soon determined that the electrical power generated at the Kin plant would be insufficient after 1970 and began planning for the enlargement of the Machinato Power Plant. In December 1965, the district awarded the A-E contract for a plant addition to Burns and Roe of New York. Construction of two 80-MW steam-turbine generators began in the fall of 1968 and the $19.4 million addition was completed just prior to reversion in 1972 when the Okinawa District merged with the Japan Engineer District.[9]

At the same time, electrical power production was transferred from the United States Army to the Ryukyu Electric Power Company (REPC). The company began selling power to the armed forces with the district engineer serving as contracting officer for REPC. It was shortly after this transfer that enlargement plans for Machinato began.

To meet the increasing demands of the military on the island's power supply, the Corps of Engineers purchased the *Inductance*, a 30-MV floating power plant, from the city of Jacksonville, Florida. The Jacksonville District overhauled the power barge and the Chief of Engineers loaned it to the United States Army, Ryukyu Islands (USARYIS). REPC leased the plant from the Army. In January 1968, *Inductance* was connected to the Okinawa Electric Power System via mooring facilities constructed at Naha Port. OED monitored the contract for this work. The utilization of this additional floating power plant enabled REPC to release power from its other island generators for use by the military. OED's role expanded as the district developed

This photo shows the method used for testing a butt weld.

Manis shows results of training to Mr. Nagamine, Vice President, Ryukyu Electric Power Corporation and personnel from the government of the Ryukyu Islands and OED.

The aerial photo at the right shows the Kin Power Plant. It was an OED project for USCAR. The photo above shows a 75-ton steam turbine manufactured for the power plant by General Electric in Lynn, Massachusetts.

Okinawa's electrical power system with the installation of floating power sources and constructed permanent facilities at Kin and Machinato.[10]

In addition to these two major projects, the district undertook several smaller jobs for the island government. In the early 1960s, the district built the Bank of the Ryukyus and made additions to the Naha airport to allow service to commercial airlines. The district also completed an island-wide population survey and master plan for Okinawa. Both to satisfy USCAR and in accordance with its own

The Okinawa District constructed the Bank of the Ryukyus for USCAR.

policy, it developed a training policy for aspiring Okinawan engineers to allow them to train at the district. Selected engineering graduates could find temporary employment with the district and the district offered scholarships to send talented Okinawans to the United States to study engineering.[11]

OED Support to United States Military Forces

The development of bases and camps, the construction of communications and missile facilities, and the building of piers and airfields were among the most important military projects supervised by the Okinawa District between 1957 and 1967.

Several Marine Corps bases on Okinawa were either constructed from the ground up or enhanced with the addition of quality of life projects. In 1958, the district completed work at Camp Schwab, a 3,000 man permanent Marine Corps Base. Marines at Camp Courtney

Two 166-man barracks (left) provided 20,539 square feet each for Navy personnel at Naha Air Base. The dental clinic (below) at Naha, also completed in October 1962, had a reinforced concrete roof and floor, central air conditioning and X-ray and dentistry labs.

The 50-man BOQ (right) used the same concrete frame and block wall structure as the enlisted men's barracks and consisted of units of four bedrooms, two each connected by a bathroom and all four bedrooms opening onto a living room and kitchen. Each apartment had its own balcony and the total square footage was 28,939. All billets were completed in October 1962 at a cost of $1.2 million. Phase I of the Naha Elementary School (below), constructed in four wings, provided 12,600 square feet of space for students and faculty. Phase II added 8 additional wings, a cafeteria and an administration building adding another 30,326 square feet. The school was open for the fall classes in 1962. At a cost of $477,000, the school was constructed to withstand typhoon winds. All Naha construction was completed under the supervision of the Kue Resident Office.

Headquarters Building, 3rd Marine Division, Camp Schwab.

benefited from a $2.7 million construction effort on the base. In 1959, OED installed special ammunition storage facilities at Henoko for the Marines at Camp Schwab at a cost of $2.3 million; another $2.7 million construction contract resulted in additional Marine facilities at Camp Courtney. An even larger project in 1959-1960 was the development of Camp Hansen, a project to construct a regimental camp for 5,000 Marines totalled almost $11 million and additional projects by the same contractor totalling $4 million were added in 1964.

Camp Hansen, the largest pre-cast, tilt-up constructed camp of the United States Marine Corps was completed on October 20, 1962 at Kin-son, 30 miles north of Naha on the Pacific Coast. Prime contractor on the project was Kokuba Gumi. Over 2,000 Ryukyuan construction workers provided $11.4 million of construction -- 218 buildings, 251,320 square yards of asphalt concrete pavement for a network of roads and parking areas, 22,935 feet of varying sizes of concrete pipe culverts, 39,160 feet of various sizes of direct burial electrical cables, 57,260 feet of electric copper wire, 52,290 feet of cast iron water pipes, 46,590 feet of concrete sewer pipes and lesser quantities of many other construction items. An underground radiant heating system was used throughout the contract for living, working and recreation facilities. (Radiant heating was believed to be used as long

ago as 500 A.D. in Korea.) The photographs on this page, represent some of this massive construction effort.

Construction on Camp Hansen included the Staff NCO Club (left), a 1000 man mess hall (below), enlisted men's barracks (middle), and theater (bottom photo).

Army base improvements during this period included a milk reprocessing plant at the Machinato Service Area. OED constructed barracks, bachelor officers quarters and a dining facility for the Air Force at Naha Air Base for a total cost of $1.2 million in the early 1960s.

The American development of Kadena Air Base which began in 1946 was still flourishing. During the 1960s, the construction program for the air base totalled over $8 million in the second half of 1963 alone and included the Corps of Engineers design award winning 1,000-seat theater. The precast concrete and coral theater, at $443,000, was a winner in the competition for its use of local materials.[12]

Several district projects served more than one branch of the service. A number of tri-service family housing units were built in the mid-1960s: The Matsumura International Construction Company constructed $2.6 million worth of quarters at RYCOM Plaza and Futenma, the joint venture of Alcan and JHW, Inc., built tri-service units for $7.9 million at Kadena, and the Tokai International Installation Company completed a similar project for $2.8 million at Naha. Other contracts with local firms between 1964 and 1966 resulted in the construction of approximately $4.8 million worth of Army Housing at RYCOM Plaza, Machinato, Naha, Futenma, and Camp Kue. Okinawan owned camps and bases were the recipients of housing: Kokuba Gumi built enlisted men's barracks and dining facilities at Machinato for $1.7 million while the United States firm of Stolte, Inc. added more BOQ's at Machinato as well as Kue for approximately $2 million.[13]

Sukiran Army Chapel. This typhoon resistant chapel provided seating for 300 people. This same design was used for a chapel at Kadena Air Base.

This $1 million automatic voice network and digital network was constructed for the Army.

A series of earthquake and typhoon resistant chapels designed and constructed in the early 1960s also served families of all branches of the service. Department of Defense Dependent Schools (DoDDS) were among these. Between 1962 and 1965, Kubasaki High School was built at Sukiran. To meet the needs of the students, portions of the school were completed and made available in 1964. Construction of the school should not have been complicated; however, it was one of the district's most frustrating projects to complete. The contractor experienced serious financial difficulties before the work was completed. In order to keep the project on schedule, OED helped negotiate a loan with First National City Bank of New York for the contractor. As more time passed, the contractor's financial condition worsened and the bank threatened foreclosure. With additional intervention from OED, the bank was convinced to provide interim financial assistance. Close to the end of the project, however, the contractor voluntarily ceased work and the district, despite efforts to keep the contractor on

46

Kubasaki High School serves 1,500 students.

Six hundred twenty-five foot tower for the United States Coast Guard Station, Gesashi.

the job, was left with $11,000 worth of work to contract out in order to add finishing touches to the high school. A three-wing, 66 room school built in the Machinato Housing Area between 1967 and 1969 incorporated features of United States educational facilities and became a part of the DoDDS network on Okinawa.[14]

Projects more directly involved with the island's defense were communications facilities built for several agencies. A 1961-1963 project for the Navy involved the construction of a $1.6 million Radio Direction Finder (RDF) facility at Sobe; a Long Range Navigation (LORAN) station was added for the Coast Guard. Operated under the jurisdiction of the Defense Communications Agency and funded by the United States Army, a $1 million automatic voice network (AUTOVON) and automatic digital network (AUTODIN) were constructed in the mid-60s In addition to these special projects, the Army, Navy and Coast Guard enjoyed communications improvements throughout the Okinawa area.[15]

The Taiwan Area Office

Work done by the OED engineers on Taiwan was the direct result of the May 1955 Chinese Communist shelling of Quemoy and Matsu Islands which were controlled by the Republic of China. On May 23, 1955 the Okinawa District issued General Orders Number 12 establishing the Formosa Area Office. In the fall of 1956, Washington, D.C., and Taipei reached a mutual agreement to allow the district's Taiwan Area Office — renamed from Formosa Area Office — to construct an airfield at Kung Quan and develop naval facilities for the Chinese Navy at Tsoying Harbor and three other navy sites. Kung

Kuan had the highest priority and $25.5 million was authorized for the construction of the air base.

Funded by the Military Assistance Program (MAP) and MAAG, "KQ502" as the air base project was called, included a 12,000 foot rigid pavement runway, taxiways, aprons and access roads. Vinnell Corporation of Alhambra, California, was the key contractor on KQ502.

Pier development, in addition to missile site construction, took place on both Taiwan and Okinawa during the ten years beginning in 1957. OED prepared several studies for MAAG on Taiwan in 1958 and 1959 for enlarging a dock at Keelug, executing a MAAG-proposed site plan for Koohsiung ammunition pier, and extending a quay wall at Koohsiung Harbor. In 1960, development of the Chinese Naval Harbor at Tsoying required dredging of 11 million cubic yards of material to reach a depth of 36 feet.

Concern over the bombings also created a need for the rapid construction of Nike batteries with launching pads and underground control systems on the northern end of Taiwan. OED sent its chief of engineering division to serve as a technical advisor to the United States

$18.3 million in construction was placed at Ching Chuan Kang (CCK) Air Base as part of the 1966 Supplemental Military Construction Program in support of the war in Vietnam.

Military Assistance Advisory Group (MAAG), Taipei, Nike siting team. In addition, OED contracted with a United States A-E firm to design four battery sites. In September 1958, with the district still under the command of Colonel Fish, OED awarded a $1.4 million contract to Vinnell Corporation to construct two of the sites with Chinese engineers responsible for building the other two sites.

Design and construction were handled concurrently for both MAAG and the United States Taiwan Defense command. Included in this construction effort were concrete pads and aprons, underground

shelters, revetments, fencing and utilities. Construction of the Phase I
tactical readiness facilities and design of Phase II support facilities
were completed by late-spring of 1959, two months before Colonel
Fish would relinquish command of OED to Colonel Manon W.
Whitsitt. The need for speed, coupled with the varied labor forces —
district engineers, civilian contractors and United States and Chinese
labor troops — made this one of the most interesting projects in OED's
history.

In 1966, the OED engineers returned to Kung Quan Air Base.
By this time the base had been renamed Ching Chuan Kang (CCK) Air
Base and was an important focus of the district's work under the 1966
Supplemental Military Construction Program. This supplement to the
appropriated MILCON program for 1966 funded important construc-
tion activities in support of the United States military mission in
Southeast Asia and included projects on Japan as well as Air Force
projects on Taiwan and Okinawa.

For CCK, the district contracted Lyon Associates and Henning-
son, Durham and Richardson as A-Es. Vennell Corporation was the
contractor. By this time, May 1966, with the district under the command of Colonel George A. Austin, Jr., the Taiwan Resident Office
was in place to administer the cost-plus-fixed-fee (CPFF) contract.
CPFF contracts, originally terminated in 1949, had been restored as
viable contracts.

By October 1967, OED's employees on Taiwan were administering a total construction workload of $20.4 million. Of this, $19.9
million was work for the Air Force. The majority of Air Force construction, $18.3 million, was the construction of CCK.

One of the largest CCK projects was a $6 million POL complex
including a mooring system, a pipeline and fuel storage facilities.
When the project was completed, KC-135 tanker planes flew from this
site to support troops in Vietnam.[16]

Outgoing district engineer Colonel George
Austin passes a hardhat to the new DE,
Colonel Vernon T. Loesing. Colonel
Loesing served as district engineer from
August 1967 to June 1970.

The Okinawa District Builds for a Strong Defense During Troubled Times

Similar Nike facilities were being constructed on Okinawa
during this same time period with one major difference. The launching
pads on Taiwan were temporary; those on Okinawa were permanent.
Five years later, the emergence of the new Hawk missile system
created the need for additional facilities totalling $4 million.

Missile sites constructed on Okinawa during the 1960s were
even more challenging than those for the Nike systems. Matsumura
Gumi developed Mace operational facility sites One and Two for the
United States Air Force for $2.4 million, while International Construc-

Mace missile launch site, Okinawa, 1960.

One of eight Hawk missile batteries constructed on Okinawa between 1962 and 1969.

(Above) The plastic covered "bubble" contains highly sensitive radar instruments. Although the cover supplied by the manufacturer would withstand winds of 60 miles per hour, on Okinawa nearly triple this protection is required. (Below) All four segments begin rising together and are "dropped off" as they reach proper elevation.

tors build sites Three and Four for another $3.2 million. When facilities were constructed, these missile systems — the Nike, Hawk and Mace — represented an extremely important segment of the United States defense system in this forward deployed area. These facilities provided underground areas from which the survivors of an atomic bomb could launch retaliatory weapons.

An additional benefit of the projects was the challenge to our engineers' ingenuity. OED engineers developed new engineering techniques when they designed clamshell domes to protect the Nike radars from typhoons and when they adapted stationary Hawk designs from the United States in order to create mobile equipment at fixed installations.

Concurrent 66-S work for the Air Force took place at Kadena Air Base on Okinawa where Pomeroy-M-B constructed a $6 million project for airfield improvements between 1966 and mid-1968. These improvements included fuel storage facilities, hangers and support facilities as well as new paving, and provided operational projects for the Strategic Air Command's B-52 bombers and military air lift command flights to and from Vietnam.[17]

The Chief of Engineers' Design Award, Honorable Mention, was captured by an important OED project in 1968 at Machinato which completed the Army's primary storage depot area on the island. New general purpose warehouses, at a cost of $5 million, doubled the storage space for the 2nd Logistical Command. The district used the warehouse rooftops for additional storage. Designed to hold 200 pounds per square foot and to sustain winds in excess of 180 miles per hour, the rooftop storage became a major site for artillery pieces, bulk cargo containers and vehicles returning from Vietnam. The design award noted the economical use of limited space in the storage depot.

OED received additional commendation as a result of the 66-S program on Taiwan and Okinawa and several district officers and employees won praise for their supervision of the CPFF contracts at CCK and Kadena. These awards (shown on the next two pages) culminated in 1969 with the award of the Meritorious Unit Commendation to the district for its design and construction of the projects at Kadena, Machinato and CCK. All of these combat facilities had aided in the United States military mission in Vietnam.

Top photo: Trailers, loaded one on top the other for maximum utilization of storage space, being towed up the ramp to the roof for storage.
Center photo: Portion of Machinato Service Area showing roof top storage warehouses beginning to be utilized and maximum utilization of space in the depot area.

DEPARTMENT OF THE ARMY

THIS IS TO CERTIFY THAT THE

MERITORIOUS UNIT COMMENDATION

HAS BEEN AWARDED TO THE

THE UNITED STATES ARMY ENGINEER DISTRICT, OKINAWA

FOR MERITORIOUS SERVICE IN SUPPORT OF MILITARY OPERATIONS

IN THE REPUBLIC OF VIETNAM, 1 JANUARY 1966 TO 31 DECEMBER 1968

GIVEN UNDER MY HAND IN THE CITY OF WASHINGTON
THIS 18TH DAY OF SEPTEMBER 1969

Stanley R. Resor

SECRETARY OF THE ARMY

The Meritorious Unit Commendation is awarded by direction of the Secretary of the Army to

THE UNITED STATES ARMY ENGINEER DISTRICT, OKINAWA

with citation as follows:

The United States Army Engineer District, Okinawa distinguished itself by exceptionally meritorious conduct in the performance of outstanding services in support of military operations in the Republic of Vietnam during the period 1 January 1966 to 31 December 1968. Demonstrating outstanding organizational talents and professional competence, the District's personnel were instrumental in the design and construction of combat support facilities for the military services in the Republic of China, Taiwan, and the Ryukyu Islands. The determined resourcefulness and initiative which characterized their performance enabled them to accomplish this additional emergency construction program and to continue their normal construction program in an exemplary manner. In addition to their normal responsibilities, the District personnel programmed, designed, contracted and supervised the construction on three major projects. Because of the emergency nature of these projects and the critical completion date, two projects were built using cost-plus-a-fixed-fee contracts. These projects gave Kadena Air Base on Okinawa the facilities to support the SAC B-52 operation and MAC airlift requirements, and Ching Chuan Kang Air Base in Taiwan the facilities for KC-135 tankers, critically needed in the Armed Forces operations in the Republic of Vietnam. At the same time, the District provided support in the doubling of storage areas and troop support facilities for the 2d Logistical Command on Okinawa, furnishing them the means to perform their vital role in the logistical support of operations in Southeast Asia. The technical expertise and managerial talent exhibited by the District members not only gave the United States Air Force and the United States Army facilities for the critical daily needs of combat support in the Republic of Vietnam, but also for the future requirements in protecting the western wall of the free world. The remarkable proficiency and devotion to duty displayed by the members of the United States Army Engineer District, Okinawa are in keeping with the highest traditions of the Corps of Engineers, and reflect distinct credit upon themselves and the Armed Forces of the United States.

Mr. Masayasu Saito, JED's Safety/Value Engineering Officer, headed the team that translated the Corps' Safety Manual into Japanese in 1967 in an effort to improve safety on construction sites.

Unfortunately, there was a dark shadow over the district's laudatory accomplishments. On both Okinawa and Taiwan, a serious collapse of the district's safety program resulted in a report to the Chief of Engineers that there had been seven construction fatalities in the first five months of 1967. In an effort to alleviate the safety risks associated with construction projects, a team from Far East District, Rear led by Safety Officer Masayasu Saito, spent months working to translate the Corps' Safety Manual into Japanese.[18]

Prompted in part by the increased aggression of the North Koreans, in conjunction with the taking of the *Pueblo*, and the need for a few additional facilities to support the Vietnam conflict, an FY 68 Supplemental Military Construction Program much like the S-66 program was implemented. The Congressional appropriation provided over $100 million for projects ranging from paving improvements at air bases in Korea to ammunition pier complexes and the trans-Korea POL pipeline for the Army.

Projects funded under S-68 which were supervised by the Japan Area Office included the Atsugi Naval Air Station jet engine maintenance and sound suppression facilities. These were two of the last projects on Japan in support of the war in Vietnam. The placement of the jet engine maintenance facility lagged due to underestimation of the required funds. Initial bids in mid-1967 were $300,000 above the funds available. After a reduction in scope and redesign, the project was readvertised in June 1968 and the contract for $1.1 million went to Tekken Kensetsu Company, Ltd. A change in the scope of work postponed the sound suppression award until a few months after that of the maintenance facility. Tekken also built a commissioned officers' mess at Atsugi. This project, too, was underestimated and the result was an austere interior.

JAO supported the Navy at Sasebo by expanding an ammunition wharf and dredging the bay. These two insignificant projects created incredible problems. Review of the FED design was not done — the confusion resulting from shifting some district elements to Korea created an environment where the review was overlooked. This caused severe time delays. Citoh Company, Ltd. accepted the $147,000 contract on May 21, 1968 and began work. After Citoh had driven all the piles, the stability of the pier to resist the lateral forces of a moored ship subject to wind was questioned. A review of the drawings revealed an absence of seismic criteria requirements and an apparent error in the allowable tapering and diameter of the piles. JAO stopped construction, load tested two piles, and measured the deflections and settlement. The tests proved that the soft mud overlying the sandstone bedrock offered sufficient support and the piles were judged satisfactory.

Work for the Marines at Iwakuni Marine Corps Air Station included a $1.2 million enlisted men's barracks and additional aircraft maintenance hangers costing $434,000. The Air Force at Yokota Air Base continued to develop and expand the operational support facilities of the base. JAO placed more than 14 contracts valued at $4.1 million between July 1968 and June 1970. Projects included ammunition, jet fuel and open storage, housing, aircraft maintenance buildings, a storm drainage system, additions to the air passenger terminal and hydrant fueling, and the expansion of the taxiway and apron access. [19]

Even while OED was immersed in planning and construction programs, the district had to contend with the real estate problem left over from the time before the district was attached to POD. In addition, two new concepts, the value engineering program and the International Balance of Payments (IBOP) requirements, were introduced in 1962 and 1963. Because Okinawa was under American jurisdiction, IBOP requirements were interpreted somewhat differently than they were for mainland Japan. Many local goods were considered to be "American goods" for the purposes of IBOP. However, there was still a list of items which had to be imported from the United States and shipped on American carriers.

In a related measure, OED was required to hire more Americans and fewer local nationals, even though this actually raised costs due to American salaries being four times higher than salaries paid to Okinawans or Japanese. Using more Americans also lowered the morale of the Okinawans and other non-American employees, but the politicians in Washington considered it important enough to insist upon.

While the purpose of IBOP was to stop the gold drain from the United States even though it raised costs, the function of value engineering was to give contractors an incentive to devise less expensive methods of construction. Contractors finding cheaper ways of completing a project without sacrificing quality were rewarded with a percentage of the amount of money the suggestion saved the United States government.

To assist Japanese contractors in understanding and implementing the program, the Mr. Saito, the Safety Officer/Value Engineer who had already produced a Japanese version of the safety manual, prepared a pamphlet describing in detail how value engineering worked and what steps a contractor needed to take to prove he had a bona fide method of lowering costs on a project. Mr. Saito translated the work into Japanese and distributed it to contractors who worked on projects for the district. In addition, OED organized several meetings and gave presentations to further explain the program. Contractors who provided value engineering savings were publicly honored in awards ceremonies.

Value engineering program translated into Japanese.

Real Estate Problems

The real estate situation which existed as OED was removed from Eighth Army command and returned to the Corps of Engineers was highly volatile. Okinawa is densely populated; in 1958, the population density was 1,500 people per square mile. And land on Okinawa was in great demand as agriculture was the major industry on the island. As the United States proceeded with determinable estate claims and long-term rental payments charged to the military for use of land on Okinawa for American bases, the already serious opposition became more pronounced. Finally, in April 1958, the High Commissioner of the Ryukyus directed OED to suspend further acquisition of long-term leases according to determinable estate procedures. In response, a delegation of officials from the Government of the Ryukyus Islands (GRI) travelled to Washington, D. C., to address the Congress. The delegation suggested that the United States forego the long term leases and assured Congress that, under those conditions, a workable leasing system could be developed for the land the United States needed. Congress was favorably impressed and, as a result, an American negotiating team began discussions on Okinawa with the GRI designed to reach a permanent solution to the real estate problem.

By July 1958, the American representatives had reached an agreement with GRI which the majority of the Okinawan landowners were willing to accept. This agreement established two types of leases — indefinite and five year leases. The indefinite leases could only be revoked by the United States. Rent was paid annually except where the holder of an indefinite lease desired long-term rent in a lump sum.[20]

In 1963, the five year leases were subject to renewal. OED conducted another appraisal which resulted in a 16 percent raise in rents; the 1968 appraisal raised the rates even higher.

Besides coping with increasing rental fees for military residents and with the dismay expressed by commanders at each increase, the district also investigated encroachments on land leased by the military. Sometimes these encroachments were insignificant; landowners were using a portion of their leased land which was not being utilized by the leaser to plant a garden. Other times, encroachments were more noticeable — owners actually constructed permanent buildings on the land. OED's task was to investigate each suspected incident and determine its validity. A special effort was made not to antagonize land owners unnecessarily. If possible, farmers would be given time to allow any crops they had planted to mature and be harvested before vacating the land. If the United States truly wasn't using the land and had no projects for its use in the future, the leases might be terminated and the land returned to the owner. This became increasingly less probable during the mid- to late-1960s due to the war in Vietnam and additional land requirements that mission placed on the bases on Okinawa. By 1970, rent paid per year by the United States government had reached $10.4 million for approximately 51,191 acres of privately owned land in over 137,000 tracts and another 24,201 acres owned by the governments of Japan and of the Okinawa Prefecture.[21]

By the end of the decade, OED had served under eight commanders and three acting commanders: Colonel George A. Finley, March 1956 to December 1957; Colonel Claude P. Joyce, Jr. (Acting), December 1957 to January 1958; Colonel Hamilton Fish, January 1958 to June 1959; Colonel Manon W. Whitsitt, June 1959 to March 1961; Colonel Alvin D. Wilder, March 1961 to June 1962; Lieutenant Colonel Elmer M. Regn (Acting), June 1962 to July 1962; Colonel Henry C. Schrader, July 1962 to August 1964; Colonel Richard G. Rhodes, August 1964 to July 1965; Lieutenant Colonel Frank H. Armstrong (Acting), July 1965; Colonel George A. Austin, Jr., August 1965 to August 1967; and Colonel Vernon T. Loesing, August 1967 to June 1970.[22]

The Japan Area Office and Far East District-Rear A Reorganization

District operations in Korea got off to a tortuous beginning due to incredible labor shortages, the lack of trade relations with Japan due to Korea's distrust of her Japanese neighbor, and the conditions of a country torn by 30 years of continuous war. However, the Japan Area Office (JAO) experienced few of the problems suffered in Korea. The core work force was already in place, having transferred from the United States Army Construction Agency, Japan. The Area Office had no trouble recruiting additional qualified Americans to travel to Japan to work; exactly the opposite was true in Korea. In addition, there was a wealth of experienced Japanese engineers available for work.[23]

The area office took over the work of the Japan Construction Agency and gave a great deal of support to the district in Seoul. Besides procuring huge amounts of construction material in Japan for use in Korea, the area office supervised the district's design contracts awarded to A-E firms headquartered in Japan. From November 1957 to the close of the fiscal year, the district committed approximately $1.5 million for design in Japan. And, in FY58, over $2 million in engineering designs from A-E firms were completed.[24]

The area office handled these tasks so skillfully that the FED commander, Colonel Ellery W. Niles, transferred the engineering

Organization of Far East Engineer District, July 1957

```
                    Executive Office
                    District Engineer
                 Deputy District Engineer
                  Asst. for Engineering
                    Asst. for Supply
                  Asst. for Construction
                  Asst. for Administration

            Advisory    and    Administrative Staff

 Office      Legal    Security    Safety    Office     Military
 of the      Br.     Detachment    Br.      Services   Detach-
 Comptroller                                Br.        ment

                    Technical Staff

 Engineer        Construction         Supply Div.
 Div.            Div.
                                      Procurement Br.
 Design Br.      Contr. Admin.
                 & Control Br.        Property Admin.
 Estimating                           Br.
 Br.             Contr. Sv.
                 Br.                  Storage & Issue Br.
 Contract
 Control Br.

 Foundation &                  Supply      Supply     Supply
 Mtl. Br.                      Point       Point      Point
                              No. 1       No. 2      No. 3
 Service Br.
                    Flield Offices

 Seoul          Taegu       Japan Area    7th Div.     24th Div.
 Resident       Resident    Office        Resident     Resident
 Engr. Office   Engr. Office              Engr. Office Engr. Office
```

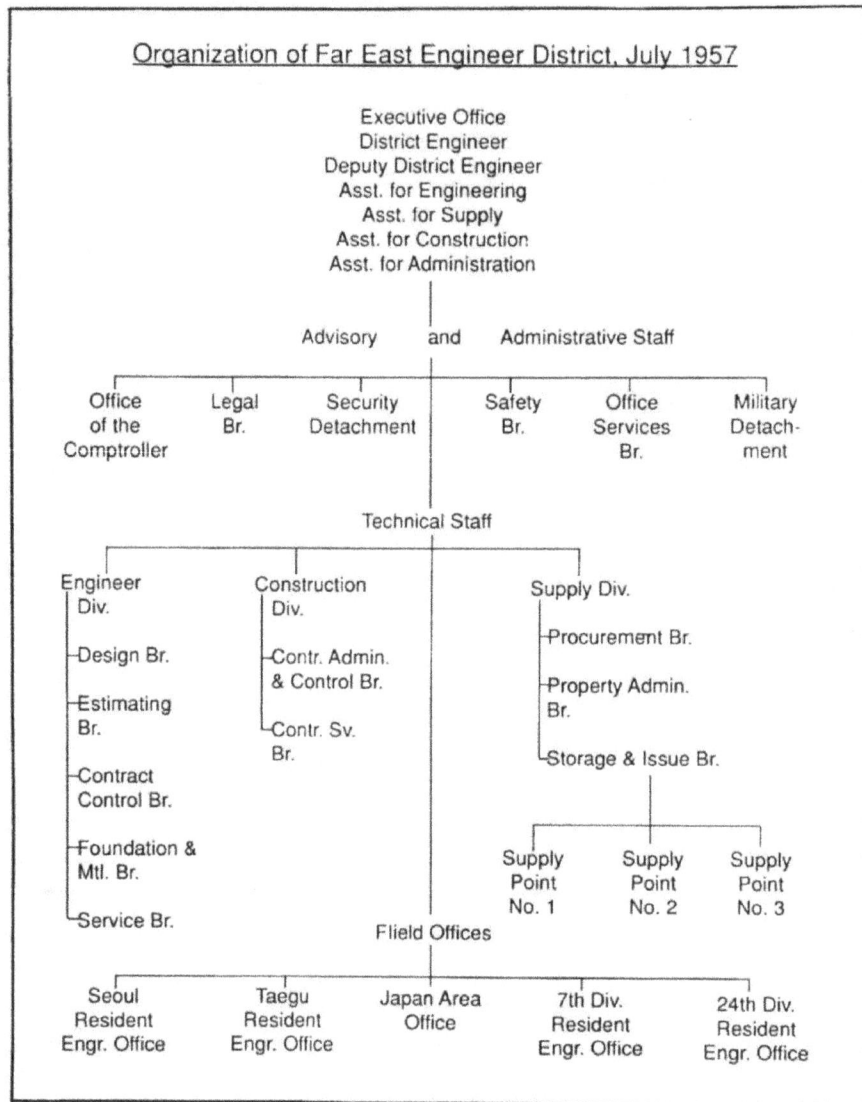

division's design branch to the JAO at Camp Oji, Tokyo, in December 1958. The JAO had been housed at Camp Burnett and at Hardy Barracks, both in Tokyo, but moved to Oji to accommodate the FED employees.

At this same time, Colonel Niles organized the JAO and other district elements in Tokyo under the title of Far East District, Rear (FED-R) to parallel the United States Army Forces, Far East/Eighth United States Army (Rear) already in Japan. These moves were financially advantageous to FED. A tour on Japan was 24 months in length rather than the 12 month tours in Korea. In addition, Japan-based Department of the Army civilians did not receive the 25 percent pay differential and separation allowance authorized in Korea.

Organization of Japan Area Office, August 1968

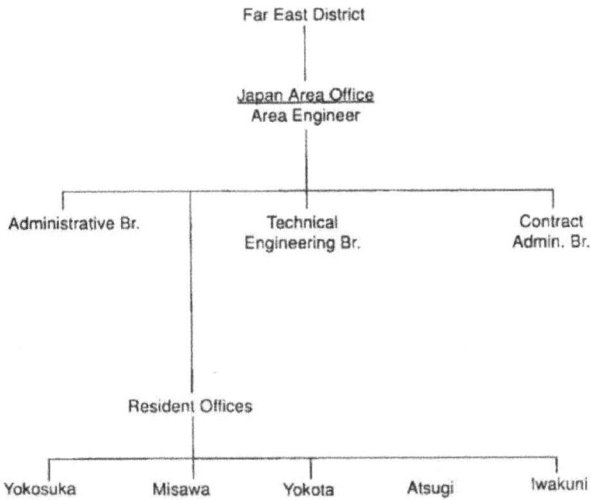

```
                    Far East District
                           |
                   Japan Area Office
                     Area Engineer
                           |
        +------------------+------------------+
        |                  |                  |
  Administrative Br.  Technical        Contract
                      Engineering Br.  Admin. Br.


                   Resident Offices
                           |
        +---------+--------+--------+--------+
        |         |        |        |        |
    Yokosuka   Misawa   Yokota   Atsugi   Iwakuni
```

In April 1959, JAO took on the duties of the Okinawa Engineer District's Tokyo Liaison Office.   After only 18 months in operation, the JAO was actively fulfilling its mission of supervising construction in Japan, assisting FED with procurement on Japan, aiding OED in a myriad of ways through the Liaison Office and managing A-E work done on the island. As early as 1960, Brigadier General Davis gave serious consideration to making FED-Rear a district. He presented his proposals to the Chief of Engineers in a detailed study but it would be

Hardy Barracks, the six-story building in the left of this photo, was the home of the Japan Area Office for a short time before the organization moved to Camp Oji.

Camp Zama's building 102 became the permanent home of the JAO in 1956 and was home to the Japan Engineer District until July 1989.

another 12 years before this became a reality.

Due to the confusion in Korea over the major changes anticipated in troop strength the JAO had little to do during the first few months of its existence. Early in 1958, the long-anticipated major reduction in Eighth Army troops began. The easing of military tension in Korea created the reductions-in-force and the cuts especially large for those troops stationed on mainland Japan. The Japanese had grown impatient with the large number of American military bases on the island and were glad to see the withdrawal. It had a drastic effect on engineering activities, however.

The cutback in the number of bases did not help to consolidate future engineering tasks. The huge United States Army Engineer Supply Center at Sagami Depot lost half of its work force and workload in August and September 1957. Cutbacks affected the entire Sagami Depot but not as drastically as the supply center. During this base reduction period, the JAO assisted the Department of Defense by executing plans to develop bases retained by the military.

By the end of its first year in existence, the office was supervising almost $750,000 in military construction projects. From 1957 to 1963, work consisted primarily of facilities for the 12th United States Army Security Agency Field Station at Chitose and for Public Law 480 projects: Family housing at Camp Zama and Chitose and a new junior high school at Zama.

One of the first projects constructed at Chitose in northern Japan was a bachelor officers' quarters and an officers' mess complex constructed by Ohki Construction Company, Ltd., for approximately

Middle School, Camp Zama, Japan 1958.

Above: The Sagamihara Dependent Housing Area. Left: Four-bedroom single unit typical of all housing at Sagamihara Housing Area.

Chitose Chapel.

Fire station, Chitose.

$95,000. In 1960 and 1961, Ohki also constructed similar facilities costing $681,000 for the enlisted men stationed at Chitose. Headquarters buildings and vehicle storage sheds totalled an additional $204,000; exterior utilities were constructed at a cost of $336,000. A series of negotiated contracts with Ohki in 1962 provided a fire station, a motor repair and ordnance field maintenance shop, a dispensary and dental clinic, and two warehouses. Additional facilities built at Chitose in the early 1960s included a non-commissioned officers' club and open mess, a library, a boiler plant and a heating distribution system. All facilities were built in support of the Army Security Agency and constituted FED-R's major workload.[25]

The next major reorganization of the Far East District was the move of the entire engineering division to Tokyo. In March 1960, Brigadier General Davis moved even more of the engineering division to Japan, leaving only the foundations and materials branch in Korea and Colonel Nile's FED-R title for this organization became official. By now, the components of the Far East District, Rear included JAO, the district's engineering division and smaller rear detachments of the budget and fiscal, supply and contract administration and office service staffs. Although the district engineer remained in Seoul, a considerable portion of his staff was now in Tokyo and within months, the construction division would join the already large Far East District- Rear team. Three years later, the Defense Department made a firm decision regarding construction responsibilities in the Far East. The Corps of Engineers became responsible for construction for all services on Japan, Taiwan, the Ryukyu Islands, Marshall Island and Korea.[26]

Construction gained for the Air Force and the Navy increased the work of the JAO dramatically. Facilities built for the 6986th Security Group, Air Force Security Service (AFSS) at Wakkanai included an operations building, antenna foundations, a heating plant, a commissary, school, post office and laboratory. Constructed of cast-in-place concrete and concrete block masonry, the items cost a total of $3 million and were turned over between 1963 and 1966.

Projects similar to those at Wakkanai were also constructed at Misawa Air Base and included an operations building, antenna foundations and concrete support structures — $3.4 million in projects which were turned over to the Air Force in 1965.

The construction activity that attracted the most attention at Chitose, Wakkanai and Misawa was the USAHOMES project and the assembly, placement and, later, removal of the homes. Developed by the Corps of Engineers between 1962 and 1965 in order to provide American military forces with pre-fabricated, easy to assemble housing, the easily transportable homes seemed ideal. Two contractors, Home Building Contractors of Sedalia, Missouri, and Knox Homes Corporation of Thompson, Georgia, assisted the Corps in development of the homes. Spurred on by the same forces that led to the passage of the IBOP program in 1962, USAHOMES were intended to lessen the gold drain from the United States.

Wakkanai Air Station: The school is in the foreground; housing in the center.

Between 1962 and 1965, the Corps of Engineers developed prefabricated housing in the U.S. for use on military installations overseas.

Although the Japanese contractors on the erection job were largely experienced companies — Mitsubishi and Ohki — and both had extensive experience with the district, the project experienced difficulties and serious delays. A major factor was the unforgiving northern Japan winter. Due to heavy snowfalls, the area was difficult to work in; due to the sparsely populated regions around Chitose and Wakkanai, there were few workmen available to attempt the work.

Assembly and placement of the homes in the mid-1960s was accomplished in four phases. In Phase I, 48 units were erected at Chitose. Phase II saw 39 units go in at Wakkanai; Phase III added another 66 sets at Chitose and, in Phase IV, another 41 units were added to Wakkanai for a total of 194. Because of recurring delays between contract award and the release of funds, the best months for installation of the homes were lost, putting the real installation periods in the middle of Hokkaido's 200 inch average snowfall season.

Additional problems occurred due to the requirement that the homes be shipped on American carriers. One shipment to Wakkanai included only half of each unit. The matching halves arrived several months later. Even more delays were the result of units damaged in transit.

The Wakkanai Project Office managed all construction in northern Japan.

The Corps and the manufacturers of USAHOMES anticipated that 20 men needed only one day to put up the framework on one home and two additional days to complete the trim and finishings. Due to the damaged condition of the homes when they arrived from the states, workers had to take some replacement parts from some units to repair others, adding more time to replace pirated material. Erection of USAHOMES took twice as long as originally expected; each group of homes took almost a year in country before it was ready to turn over to the using agency. The 1970s would bring USAHOMES and its legacy of problems back to the forefront when Chitose and Wakkanai were returned to the Japanese.[27]

Between 1966 and 1968, contractors completed a major project for the Air Force, the Kanto Plains Communication System, in central Japan. Communications buildings were constructed at Yokosuka Naval Base, Atsugi Naval Air Facility, Kamiseya Naval Security Group Activity and Totsuka Naval Radio Station. The project also included power facilities: A 350 foot steel microwave tower at Yokosuka and concrete buildings at Camp Zama, Sagami Depot and Camp Fuchinobe.

During this same period, a runway and taxiway costing $557,000 were completed for the Air Force at Yokota Air Base. Construction of a $470,000 air terminal air freight building cost and a $556,000 air passenger terminal, designed by OED, were included in this effort.

Major Air Force construction between 1966 and 1968 included a $470,000 air terminal/air freight building on Yokota Air Base.

The Air Force at Tachikawa needed housing. From 1964 to 1966, Japanese contractors built $624,000 worth of officers' quarters and a $308,000 airmens' dorm.[28]

After 1963, the Navy provided work for the Japan Area Office. Kamiseya's operations building was destroyed by a fire in September 1965 and the Navy asked FED-R to design and construct a replacement facility in 90 days. In an incredible effort, the district completed the design in two weeks, awarded the construction contract in late October and turned over two of the four steel buildings 65 days later.

Between 1966 and 1968, Atsugi Naval Air Facility was improved with construction projects monitored by the JAO. A mine facility, an airfield lighting system and airport parking aprons were a part of those improvements. Included in the $1.4 million contract was expansion of an existing power plant.

At Iwakuni Marine Corps Air Station three barracks were added for enlisted men stationed there at a cost of $641,000. With $828,000 in airfield and support work and another $412,000 in rehabilitation of storage and port facilities, the Navy's requirements further increased the workload.

In spite of these new construction requirements, the district's workforce in Japan continued its support to the Army. In addition to USAHOMES, 272 enlisted men and 59 officers got new billets and dining facilities were enlarged at Chitose. Additional construction included a post office, post exchange and a chapel. At a cost of $1 million, all of these facilities were designed and completed between December 1965 and August 1967.[29]

Although OED and JAO construction was almost totally in support of the military mission in the islands, an interesting project under the Federal Engineer category, later renamed "Work for Others", was undertaken on mainland Japan for the United States Information Agency (USIA). EXPO '70, a world's fair type scientific exposition to be held in 1970 in Osaka, required the construction of a USIA pavilion. The JAO was involved in negotiating and administering the contract and supervision and inspection of the pavilion.

Unique in appearance, the pavilion was designed by the New York firm of Davis, Brody, Chermayeff, Geismar, Deharak and Associates in consultation with the Japanese firm of Ohbayashi Gumi Construction Company. The first ever built anywhere in the world, the pavilion was an air-supported structure of cable and fabric. The roof was a super ellipse with a span of 465 feet by 274 feet. Three blowers maintained the air pressure necessary to keep the roof inflated and a concrete ring kept it anchored. The blowers were designed to permit the roof to support normal snow loads as well as compensate for changing air pressure in case of high winds or typhoons. Because the roof was translucent, little artificial light was needed during the day.

In addition to the roof, the pavilion provided other interesting features. The building was constructed partly above and partly below the ground. The above-ground section was buttressed by earthen berms which sloped up to the perimeters of the roof. Inside, the exhibition area was divided into two levels, the highest one extending into the roof area. The height of the structure at its lowest point was 59 feet; at the center of the inflated roof the height was 75 feet.

For political reasons, the district's connection with the pavilion could not be made public. This fact made overcoming numerous difficulties even harder. The problems which developed before construction included major cuts in the funding. The contractor ran into difficulties early in construction due to unseasonably heavy rains in early 1969. In addition, several crucial drawings were not made available to the contractor when needed. In spite of these situations and with JAO's encouragement, the Japanese contractor managed to compensate for lost time. By November, the roof was inflated and the scaffolding was removed and the $4.5 million pavilion was completed for the opening of EXPO '70 on March 15, 1970. The exceptional work done by the JAO would cause USIA to make another request in the 1980s for Tsukuba EXPO '85. [30]

Contract Construction and Engineering Efforts on Japan and Okinawa

By 1957, Japanese contractors were reasonably experienced in American construction methods and specifications. They had developed greater financial stability and resources and had obtained sufficient equipment and materials with which to perform construction jobs at increasingly complex levels. An adequate, skilled labor force with solid engineering talent was available in 1957.

Because of these improved conditions, FED experienced no major difficulties with construction on mainland Japan. Differences between Japan and the United States remained, however. As they do now, the Japanese used the metric system which required constant conversion. In addition, the standard size of certain furnishings such as kitchen and bathroom lavatories, doorways and windows were often different. A concerted effort was made by the contractors for each project to ensure that all of these things were taken into account. American and Japanese contractors who had been able to presume that "standard" meant standard to their industry in the past found themselves checking and rechecking material. This was especially true in the case of housing; Japanese contractors had to work more diligently to ensure that American servicemembers and their families were satisfied end users. [31]

The financial situation of Japanese construction firms had improved greatly by 1957, due primarily to the contractors' high rate of earnings during the previous decade. Borrowing capital, however, remained a problem; Japanese construction firms had difficulty in securing approval on their loan applications. Unfortunately, bank loans were the most common way for Japanese industries to raise money for capital improvements and equipment replacement. The availability of sufficient capital and the extent to which the Japanese government directed the country's economy were are the root of their financial difficulties. Limited capital dictated that medium and small-sized firms, which included almost all construction firms, could not easily compete with Japan's more stable, less risky large firms in the search for capital. At the same time, the Japanese government encouraged the growth of heavy industry, steel, and other import items to the detriment of industries such as construction. Construction firms could not expect government support to help tip the balance in their favor and two to three percent of all loan applications granted to industry during the mid-1950s went to construction firms. The contractors used these loans almost exclusively for current operations rather than for equipment replacement.

OED celebrated 20 years of engineering achievement in 1966 with these articles in the *Okinawa Morning Star.*

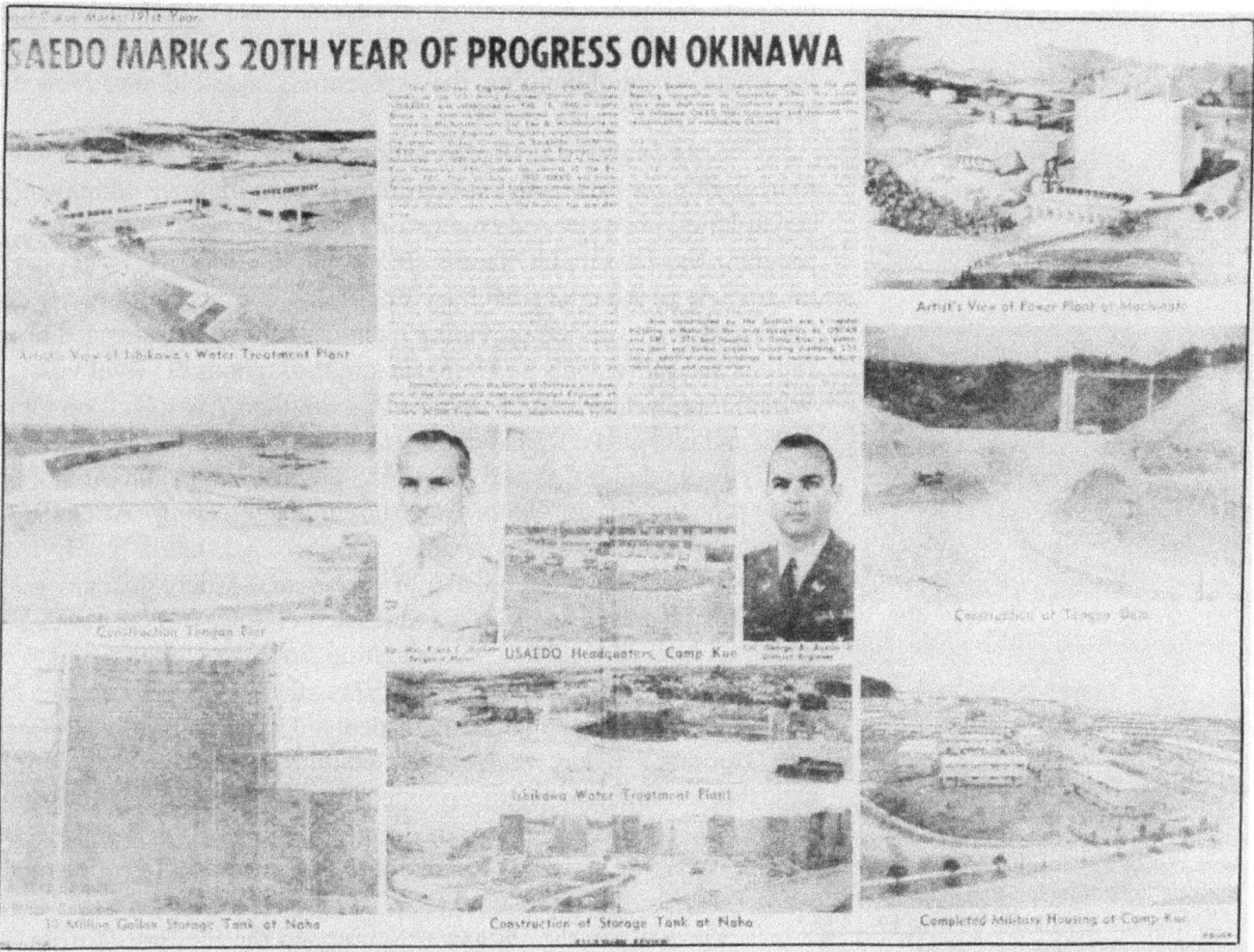

SAEDO MARKS 20TH YEAR OF PROGRESS ON OKINAWA

Artist's View of Power Plant at Machinato

Artist's View of Ishikawa's Water Treatment Plant

Construction of Tengan Pier

USAEDO Headquarters, Camp Kue

Construction of Tengan Dam

Ishikawa Water Treatment Plant

Million Gallon Storage Tank at Naha

Construction of Storage Tank at Naha

Completed Military Housing at Camp Kue

By 1957, there was no longer a shortage of either skilled laborers or heavy equipment operators. However, almost one-third of the construction laborers had been unionized. This meant that FED was faced with a greater potential for strikes. Japanese labor unions historically have been more inclined to left-wing politics and political activism than American unions, less concerned with political questions, but at times highly aroused and politically active. On several occasions in the late 1960s, major anti-American strikes and mass demonstrations organized by labor unions temporarily halted construction on district projects.[32]

On Okinawa, one of OED's first tasks as a Corps district was to close out all remaining force account work — work done for U. S. forces similar to the work performed by the Facility Engineers and, later, the Directorates of Engineering and Housing. Accordingly, Japanese and Okinawan contractors acquired a correspondingly larger share of the district's work. Individual Japanese firms were able to accomplish projects ranging in the hundreds of thousands of dollars and could tackle million dollar projects when several firms combined in a joint venture. Okinawan firms were not able to undertake projects as large in scale as the Japanese, but on medium-sized projects such as the island's capitol building, they sometimes underbid their Japanese competitors.

Shortly after POD's formation, the Okinawa District began a more highly organized and substantial effort to improve Okinawan construction potential and engineering expertise. One part of this program was informal in nature: Beginning in 1959, the local post of the Society of American Military Engineers, composed primarily of OED personnel, started providing technical advice to interested organizations and individuals on Okinawa and throughout the Ryukyus. Within three years, it had helped with more than 70 projects on Okinawa and received a formal commendation from the Government of the Ryukyu Islands. As early as 1955, the post had begun providing some scholarships for Okinawans studying engineering. After 1957, the number of scholarships awarded increased substantially. By 1962, the post offered eleven scholarships each year — more than any other post. The post even sponsored a Science Youth Day in the 1960s for which it received a public commendation from the United States Army High Commissioner in the Ryukyus. The district offered summer job training programs to engineering students. Under its Ryukyuan Engineer Training Program, it also provided on-the-job experience and exposure to American engineering techniques for recent engineering graduates. The district encouraged training programs undertaken by private American firms to provide more Okinawan skilled construction workers. [33]

The work of the Okinawa District and the Far East District-Rear from 1957 to 1970 brought a wealth of projects to Japan —

Home of the U.S. Army Engineer District, Okinawa, located in Kakazu on Route 5. The district moved to the new headquarters in February 1968 after spending more than 20 years in the familiar building at Camp Kue. The new headquarters building was constructed by a commercial firm and leased by the U.S. Army for the district.

projects which enriched the lives of not only military personnel and their families but also Japanese citizens, most particularly on Okinawa. But change was imminent. In the summer of 1969, President Richard M. Nixon ordered a 10 percent reduction in American forces overseas. In Vietnam, the number of troops committed to the war was declining although some of the fiercest fighting had yet to take place. And in Korea, FED had improved the south's ability to defend itself against the north and tensions, while still high, became more manageable.

On Okinawa, the district's major mission — to rebuild the Ryukyus after World War II — had been virtually completed. The Marines had moved into new camps and an air station, all constructed by OED. Okinawa's defenses had been strengthened with additional batteries for Nike-Hercules, Hawk and Mace missiles. A variety of projects highlighted the diverse talents within the organization: The Bank of the Ryukyus, a museum, navy piers, an ammunition depot, warehouses, runway repair on Okinawa and on Taiwan, and quarters for the troops in addition to electrical power plants, sewage and water treatment plants, dams, reservoirs, wells and pipelines gave expression to the work of our engineers.

USIA Pavilion, EXPO '70, Osaka, Japan.

Work on Japan during this period culminated with the opening of EXPO '70 in Osaka, Japan, where the USIA Pavilion stood as a testimony to the work done by the engineers on mainland Japan. It seemed, with its futuristic design, to predict the future of a new district and agreements between the United States and Japan which would result in billions of dollars in construction over the next two decades.

Hiroshima Castle

Hiroshima Castle, also known at the "Carp Castle," was originally constructed in 1589 by Terumoto Mori. The donjon (central tower) was registered as a National Treasure until 1945, when the atomic bomb explosion destroyed the entire castle. The five-story donjon was reconstructed for the Hiroshima Rehabilitation Exposition in 1958.

Chapter Three
Reorganization and the WESTPAC Era
1970 - 1972

T̲o understand the significance of the reorganization which effected the employees of the Okinawa Engineer District and the Far East District, Rear during the 1970-1972 period, it is vital to look at the reorganization efforts throughout the entire Pacific Ocean Division. Erwin N. Thompson describes that reorganization in his book, Pacific Ocean Engineers, History of the U. S. Army Corps of Engineers in the Pacific. Thompson explains the three-phased reorganization and the tremendous upheaval that accompanied it and as well as its impact on the division, its employees and the future this way:

"The Pacific Ocean Division entered the 1970s faced with a sharp reduction in its workload in the western Pacific and in Hawaii.

The result of this decline was a sweeping reorganization of the division . . . . About the same time, the United States Congress passed a number of laws that greatly affected the Corps of Engineers' responsibilities in terms of environmental protection, cultural resource preservation, and regulatory activities.

". . . Early in 1970, Division Engineer Brigadier General Curtis W. Chapman, Jr. observed that the trend in the workload was decidedly down. The Honolulu District's overhead costs could be contained only by a reduction in force. On Okinawa, military construction was almost nonexistent and only projects for the U. S. Civil Administration justified that district's continued existence. Even that work would be jeopardized when a 1969 agreement to return the Ryukyus to Japan was carried out. Only the Far East District continued to have ample work as construction continued on emergency projects resulting from the *Pueblo* affair. When these were finished, the workload in Korea would drop sharply. Nor were hard times restricted to the division. The United States in general was experiencing a recession. President Richard M. Nixon, exempting Vietnam and Korea, directed a ten percent reduction in American forces overseas, including civilian employees. And, as a result of the state of affairs, the Chief of Engineers ordered a Corps-wide retrenchment.

"As a first step (Phase I) toward retrenchment, Brigadier General Chapman consolidated the Honolulu District and the division by merging the two staffs. In addition to reductions in force already underway, the general predicted that consolidation would eliminate a further 25 spaces. To reduce uneasiness and confusion, Brigadier General Chapman proposed an all-at-once consolidation to be effective July 1, 1970. He established the position of Deputy Division Engineer, Mid-Pacific (DDEMP), with contracting authority for the Corps' work within the Honolulu District's existing boundaries. Because Hawaiians had become familiar with the term Honolulu District over most of the past 65 years, Brigadier General Chapman wished to retain it for the deputy's use when the latter dealt with the local community. When put into effect, this idea worked well as far as the public was concerned, but for a time it caused confusion among the division staff who remained uncertain which title to use under varying circumstances.

"The Chief of Engineers approved the plan of consolidation by early April and General Orders No. 25, June 25, 1970, announced the deactivation of the Honolulu Engineer District and the transfer of its functions and area of responsibility to the Pacific Ocean Division, effective July 1. In order to allow the old title to be legally used, the district remained in being at zero strength and without an assigned mission. District Engineer Colonel John A. Hughes now became the Deputy Division Engineer, Mid-Pacific, remaining in the new position three months before transferring in October 1970.

```
Organization of Pacific Ocean Division, February 1971


Special Assistants ————— Executive Office — Boards & Committees
                         Division Engineer
                         Deputy Division Engineer

            Advisory            and            Administrative Staff


Office        Office of      Safety      Personnel    Operating     Office of
of the        Counsel        Office      Office       Civ. Pers.    Admin.
Comptroller                                           Office        Sv.


                              Technical Staff


Engineering    Construction-Opns.      Real Estate         Supply Div.
   Div.            Div.                    Div.

-Technical        -Supv. &             -Acquisition        -Proc. & Sup.
 Review Br.        Insp. Br.            Br.                  Br.

-Service Br.      -Contract            -Plng. &            -Contracts Br.
                   Admin. Br.           Control Br.

-Prog. Plng.      -Office Engr.        -Mgmt. &            -SF Liaison Br.
 & Reports Br.     Br.                   Disposal Br.

-Fdn., Mtls., &
 Survey Br.

-Planning Br.

-Design Br.


                   Operating Elements


Deputy Div. Engr. for               Deputy Div. Engr. for
    Western Pacific                      Mid-Pacific
```

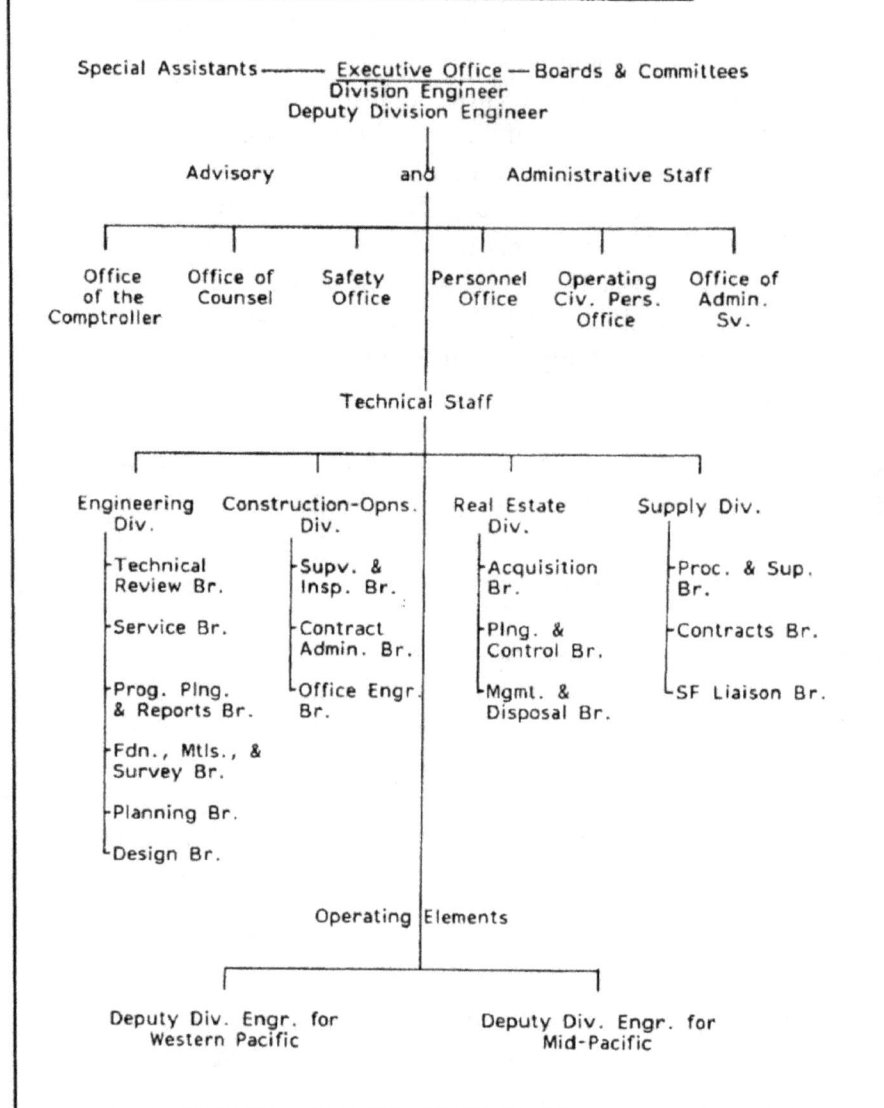

"The Pacific Ocean Division published its own General Orders establishing the office for Mid-Pacific and its field offices: Hickam, Schofield, and Waikiki Project Offices; and the Kwajalein Resident Office with its four Projects Offices at Kwajalein, Illeginni, Roi-Namur, and Majuro. The General Orders also announced the reorganization of the following division elements: Comptroller Office, Supply Division, Construction-Operations Division, and Engineering Division, all under the Deputy Division Engineer, Mid-Pacific. Reporting on the completed consolidation, Brigadier General Chapman said that the organization worked well; the only problems concerned precise areas of responsibility and coordination procedures.

"Meanwhile, Brigadier General Chapman's staff began detailed studies concerning reorganization in the western Pacific. This was Phase II for which the general selected a target date of October 1, 1970. These studies were more complicated than for Hawaii. In addition to two districts, there were four nations to be considered: Korea, Japan, Ryukyus, and Taiwan. Therefore plans required clearance from the Department of State. The overriding principle, however, was cost effectiveness. The division determined and evaluated no fewer than 26 alternatives for the western Pacific, reducing them to nine that appeared most feasible. These nine were subjected to cost effectiveness analysis out of which emerged a plan. The analysis showed that Okinawa was the most economical location for maintaining a staff to support a contracting officer; thus, it was chosen for the office of the Deputy Division Engineer, Western Pacific (DDEWP and WESTPAC) and his staff, which included a Comptroller Office, Real Estate Division, and centralized design and engineering services. The study proposals called for three Area Offices: Japan, Korea and Southern (Okinawa); and a Resident Office on Taiwan.

"Brigadier General Chapman supported the study's findings, saying he preferred it over such other alternatives as having the Okinawa District absorb the Far East District. He gave several reasons for his preference including its giving maximum authority to the Deputy Division Engineer on the ground, retention at his own office of adequate management and control, reduction of personnel unrest and morale problems by a one-time reorganization rather than several in succession, and achieving an operational parallel in the western Pacific to that approved for Mid-Pacific. He said that the Deputy Division Engineer concept 'is a bold but prudent and timely step toward the fully operating division in the Pacific area . . . which I foresee in the not too distant future.' Under the concept, he explained, 'the division engineer will be able progressively to reduce work forces in the Orient and absorb workload in Hawaii unilaterally and promptly'.

"Brigadier General Chapman proposed to the Chief of Engineers that in order to assure management continuity and to have an experienced contracting officer in the western Pacific, Colonel Franklin R. Day, the Far East District Engineer, be given the new job of Deputy Division Engineer, Western Pacific, and Colonel Wesley E. Peel replace Colonel Day in Korea. The Chief agreed and the two colonels moved to Okinawa and Korea that summer, before the reorganization took place. Colonel Peel looked forward to the challenge of military construction in Korea but when he learned that the proposed name of his organization was Far East Area Office, he protested that he had not spent a career only to become an Area Engineer. Assisting his views was the Chief of Engineers' desire 'to keep the flag flying' in

Korea by retaining the term Far East District. The wishes of both officers were met when the new organization was established as the Korea Office (Far East District).

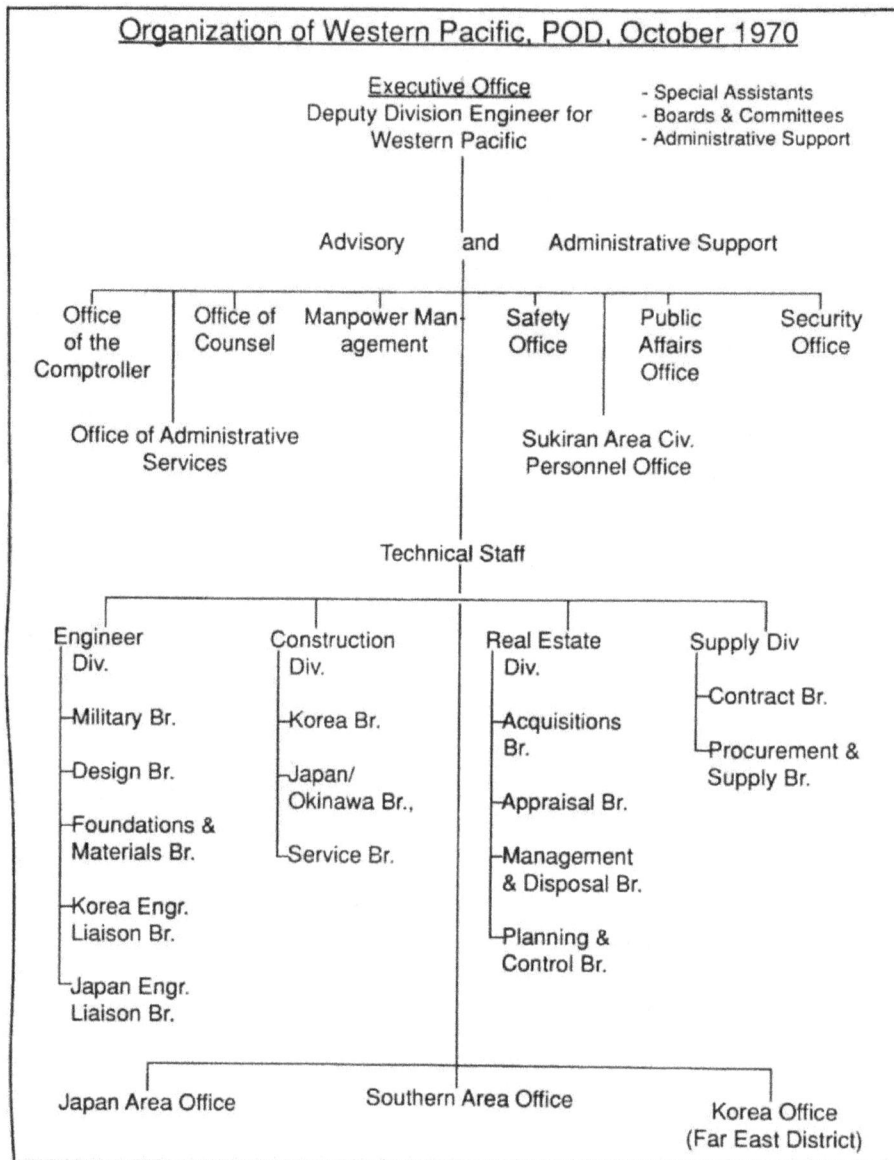

Organization of Western Pacific, POD, October 1970

Executive Office
Deputy Division Engineer for
Western Pacific

- Special Assistants
- Boards & Committees
- Administrative Support

Advisory and Administrative Support

| Office of the Comptroller | Office of Counsel | Manpower Management | Safety Office | Public Affairs Office | Security Office |

Office of Administrative Services

Sukiran Area Civ. Personnel Office

Technical Staff

Engineer Div.
- Military Br.
- Design Br.
- Foundations & Materials Br.
- Korea Engr. Liaison Br.
- Japan Engr. Liaison Br.

Construction Div.
- Korea Br.
- Japan/ Okinawa Br.,
- Service Br.

Real Estate Div.
- Acquisitions Br.
- Appraisal Br.
- Management & Disposal Br.
- Planning & Control Br.

Supply Div
- Contract Br.
- Procurement & Supply Br.

Japan Area Office   Southern Area Office   Korea Office (Far East District)

"The Office of the Chief of Engineers published General Orders No. 44 on September 21, 1970, reorganizing the Pacific Ocean Division in the western Pacific area. Effective October 1, the Okinawa and Far East Districts remained in being but at zero strength and without assigned missions. Similar to Honolulu, the district engineer titles were retained. A week later, the Pacific Ocean Division published General Orders No. 6 that provided the details of the reorganization. The office of the Deputy Division Engineer contained four divisions: Engineering, Construction, Real Estate, and Supply; and several supporting offices such as Comptroller, Counsel, Administrative Services, Safety, and Public Affairs. Although the organization of the three Area Offices was generally similar for all, each was tailored to its particular situation:

Japan Area Office:
Administrative Branch
Office Engineering Branch
Supervision and Inspection Branch
2 Resident Offices
7 Project Offices

Southern Area Office:
Office Engineering Branch
Supervision and Inspection Branch
3 Resident Offices

Korea Office
Administration Branch
Aviation Branch
Construction Branch
2 Resident Offices
10 Project Offices

"The reduction in personnel in the western Pacific as a result of the reorganization was indeed impressive. The January 1, 1970 total of 1,162 employees dropped to only 576 a year later. Yet, Colonel Day continued to experience a continuing high rate of supervision and administration costs. Part of this problem was caused by the one-time expenses for severance payments, lump-sum leave payments, travel and transportation costs of displaced persons and their household goods, and for moving government equipment. Together, these amounted to about $1,665,000. The pay raises for all Americans and Japanese and Korean nationals that were awarded in January 1971 also drained his supervision and administration account. Colonel Day was determined to cut costs further : 'I have delegated authority to the maximum, eliminated every unessential task . . . simplified tasks wherever possible, and cut out such nice-to-have items as trip reports, scheduled staff visits, and self-serving memoranda for the record.' He added, 'I'll try anything to save a dollar provided mission accomplishment is not adversely affected.'

"Phase III of the reorganization of the Pacific Ocean Division coincided with, and, in part, was brought about by the reversion of the Ryukyu Islands to Japan which became effective on May 15, 1972. As foreseen by Brigadier General Chapman two years earlier, the division moved further into operations as well as supervision. In Phase III, the two organizations, Deputy Division Engineer, Mid-Pacific and Western Pacific, were discontinued; and their command, control, contracting officer, and most other functions were transferred to the Division Office in Honolulu. The Japan Area Office became the United States Army Engineer District, Japan. The Southern Area Office on Okinawa was redesignated the Okinawa Area Office and placed under the Japan Engineer District. Colonel Peel in Korea must have been pleased that the Korea Office was now redesignated the United States Army Engineer District, Far East. Three division elements that had been in WESTPAC — the Engineering Division, Real Estate Office, and Counsel — remained on Okinawa at a reduced strength and were attached to the area office for administration and logistical support. In Hawaii, the discontinuance of Mid-Pacific had little effect. The Honolulu District continued to exist on paper only, and the Division's Deputy Engineer, now Colonel William D. Falck, continued to use the title Honolulu District Engineer for matters pertaining to civil works. Both the Kwajalein and Hawaii Resident Offices now reported directly to the Division. This phase of the reorganization allowed for the elimination of 41 positions in the division at an annual savings of $410,000.

"When Okinawa returned to Japanese jurisdiction [on May 15, 1972 in conjunction with the formation of the Japan District], the several construction contracts that the Corps administered for the former U. S. Civil Administration were transferred to the government of Japan, reducing the Engineers' workload by $15 million. Further discouraging the Engineering Division's remaining on Okinawa was the delay in the reversion construction whereby the Japanese government was to design and construct certain projects for the United States for which the Corps was to supply the criteria. At the end of 1972, this program had not yet started. On Taiwan, the existing construction was moving toward completion and, with the withdrawal of American combat troops from Vietnam, little future work was anticipated. In June 1972, the Taiwan Project Office closed and the remaining contract work as administered from Okinawa. Considering all these factors, it was clear to Division Engineer Brigadier General Fink that the Engineering Division on Okinawa would have to close down. This action was completed in January 1973, when the functions of the division were transferred at a reduced strength to the Japan and Far East Districts. Regarded as Phase IV of the reorganization that began in 1970, this transfer eliminated an additional 17 civilian positions.

"By August 1973, the Pacific Ocean Division and its two districts had reached a low point in the number of military and civilian personnel. In the four years since August 1969, reacting to changing missions and to the changing international situation, the division reduced its strength by over 60 percent. From a personnel high of

1,739 employees in 1973, POD dropped to 643 by August 1973. The breakdown in that years was POD 301, FED 255 and JED 87 employees." [1]

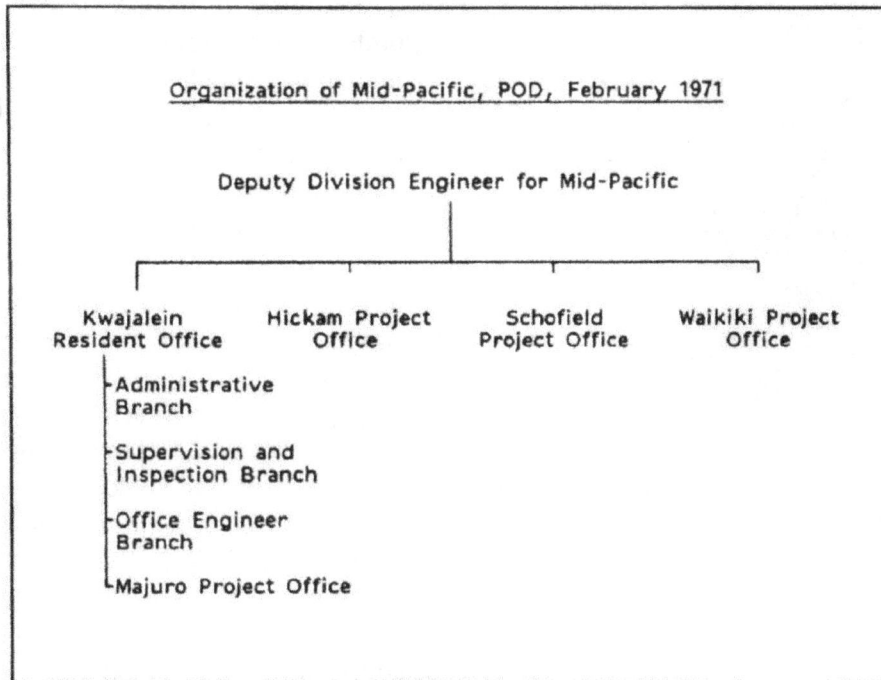

```
            Organization of Mid-Pacific, POD, February 1971


            Deputy Division Engineer for Mid-Pacific


    ┌──────────────┬──────────────┬──────────────┐
  Kwajalein      Hickam Project    Schofield     Waikiki Project
Resident Office     Office       Project Office      Office
  ├Administrative
  │Branch
  │
  ├Supervision and
  │Inspection Branch
  │
  ├Office Engineer
  │Branch
  │
  └Majuro Project Office
```

Japan Engineer District, WESTPAC, 1970 - 1972

Amid the frantic reorganization of the engineers in the Pacific Ocean Division, Colonel Day still had a construction program to manage along with WESTPAC's mandate to prepare for the return of Okinawa to Japanese administrative control and the closure of most military bases on the island. During this two year period he supervised three area offices: Far East (Korea), Southern (Okinawa), and Japan. He retained his engineering division in Okinawa where it provided design services for all three construction areas. Construction on Okinawa during this period was mainly confined to projects for US-CAR. Machinato Power Plant and the Fukuji Dam, projects undertaken for USCAR prior to 1970, were the major construction projects on the island.

The construction of Fukuji Dam for Okinawa's water supply was the largest project of its kind yet undertaken by POD. Work on the dam fell behind schedule in 1970 when highly jointed rock was encountered during tunnel excavation. A year later, however, Colonel Day reported that construction progressed well although the contractor did not exert himself as much as Colonel Day thought he should. As

Colonel Franklin R. Day
Okinawa District Engineer
June 1970 - June 1972

reversion day, May 15, 1972, approached, unusually wet weather hampered construction and Colonel Day estimated that the embankment would be completed to elevation 200 by that date. Also, all grouting, the spillway, and reservoir clearing would be finished by then. He was disappointed that the Southern Area Office could not see the job through to completion: "We don't like the idea of the (Japan) Ministry of Construction completing our embankment, but there is apparently nothing that can be done . . . except possibly to provide some U. S. assistance to them and keep book on them. But the Japanese officials did not need assistance; they were eager to complete the dam by themselves." [2]

Problems with the Machinato Power Plant were different in nature. WESTPAC's primary contribution to the power plant was to supervise part of the construction to the plant's second and third units. A constantly fluctuating yen-dollar rate required that Colonel Day make frequent requests for more funds from USCAR for the project. He finally asked USCAR to assume the risk of re-evaluation so that the firms involved in the construction of the power plant would know that their costs would be met. Unlike Fukuji Dam, the work on the power plant was completed prior to reversion in spite of the funding problems. [3]

Other construction during this period included a runway at Osan Air Base and an offshore petroleum unloading facility at Taegu, Korea; two elementary schools for the Department of Defense and more family housing units at Kadena Air Base. In addition, Naha Air Base on Okinawa was slated to become a civilian air base under Japanese control. To prepare for this, WESTPAC began a $1 million project at Naha which began with the runways. This project would be funded by the government of Japan. However, before the job could be completed, Japanese officials stopped the work while they contemplated a major redesign of the facility which would take place after they had regained control of the air base.

Although construction efforts on Taiwan had been considerable prior to 1970, the work there had diminished greatly. After President Richard M. Nixon's visit to Peking, China in 1972 and the subsequent return to normal of relations between the United States and China, military construction on Taiwan ceased although the island did remain within the geographical boundaries of the Japan District.

Military construction on Japan was at an all time low during this period. The Japan Area Office supervised the construction of $2 million worth of housing at at the Marines' installation at Iwakuni. In 1971, World War II oil storage tanks at Sasebo and Koshiba were rehabilitated at a cost of $6 million. The latter was the first scene of the first on-the-job fatality in six years when a workman was asphyxiated inside one of the tanks. The Sasebo project was not a complete success in other respects. The epoxy coating inside the concrete tanks failed and the manufacturer had to find a way to correct the problem.

The area office was involved in negotiations to move the USAHOMES from Chitose, which was marked for return to the Japanese, to an American base which was to be retained. Misawa Air Base was selected to receive the portable homes and moving the homes and installing them at Misawa proved no less of a problem than when the homes were installed at Chitose initially.

Finally, there was a lot of work left to do in the area of real estate on both Japan and Okinawa. On Japan, this effort primarily involved the Homeowners Assistance Program at Misawa Air Base. Five hundred thirty-seven homes of military employees went on the market due to the major reduction-in-force at the base and WESTPAC had the responsibility of seeing that the home owners received a fair price. On Okinawa, the real estate task was to arrange for the termination of leases, obtain fair property assessments of American-owned buildings and real estate, settle outstanding claims, and set things in motion for reversion. [4]

Thompson, "Pacific Ocean Engineers"

83

As May approached, Colonel Day prepared for the inevitable and progressed with plans for a major reduction-in-force in the Southern Area Office. Department of the Army civilians transferred to Hawaii while Okinawans were dismissed. In an effort to make reversion as confusion free as possible, Colonel Day stated, "We are meeting with USCAR, Corporation, and GOJ officials with a view towards making the transition in contract supervision and administration from the United States to the Government of Japan as smooth as possible under the circumstances." At the same time, WESTPAC's engineering division was engaged in design activity at the Marines' Futenma Air Station for the reception of aircraft from Naha. This design work was the first step in relocation construction: "This is primarily due to our having been designated as the Far East Representative for reversion related construction to be performed by the GOJ for the U. S. Forces in Japan and Okinawa." The effort was premature; the Japanese government was not yet prepared to undertake such construction.

Reversion Day, May 15, 1972, came on schedule. American military strength on Okinawa dropped from 52,000 to 40,000. WESTPAC's Real Estate Division prepared the documentation to transfer 46 military installations to Japanese control. The Pacific Ocean Division, in conjunction with reversion, abolished its advance office in the Western Pacific, created a new Japan Engineer District, and redesignated the Southern Area Office as the Okinawa Area Office under the Japan District. A country in the midst of reversion and a minor military construction program on mainland Japan with just the hope of a host nation construction program for the future were waiting for Colonel Edward M. Willis who arrived at Camp Zama in June 1972 to become the first Japan District Engineer.[5]

Osaka Castle

Osaka Castle was built in 1585 at the order of Hideyoshi Toyotomi. After the death of Hideyoshi in 1598, Ieyasu Tokugawa seized political power and the Toyotomi family realm was reduced to just the immediate Osaka area. Underground movements, however, worked to overthrow the Tokugawas and restore the Toyotomis. To crush these would-be rebels, Ieyasu's troops opened fire on Osaka Castle in 1614 and it was burned down in 1615. The present donjon (main tower) was reconstructed in 1931 and is a replica of the original.

Chapter Four
A New District, A New Era
1972 - 1979

Although employees of the Japan Area Office had been at Camp Zama since December 1966, there was still an atmosphere of new beginnings on May 15, 1972 when the JAO officially became the Japan Engineer District.

Camp Zama, located in central Honshu, is also home to U. S. Army Japan/IX Corps (USARJ). But in 1966 when JAO employees first moved here, the area around Camp Zama was still relatively rural. And prior to 1932, the area was only wooded hills and mulberry farms. In that year the War Ministry of the government of Japan began plans for the construction of a new military academy on the site. The school officially opened on September 30, 1937 when academy cadets marched from their old school at Ichigaya, Tokyo, to Zama, approximately 25 miles away.

In December 1942, Emperor Hirohito attended the first graduation ceremony at the new academy. The Zama area was so desolate at the time that a special road was constructed from the nearby town of Machida so the Emperor could attend the ceremony. During the graduation ceremony, the Emperor ordered that the name of the area surrounding the academy be called "Sobudai" which translates as "to observe the military from a prominent place."

The academy operated during the latter years of the Chinese-Japanese War of the 1930s and throughout World War II, graduating officers into the Imperial Army. In June 1945, as the war neared its

Above: Quarters 43A, now home of all of JED's district engineers, was the officer's club at the academy. Right: The main entrance to the Military Academy. Below: Emperor Hirohito reviewed the cadets during graduation ceremonies for the Class of 1942.

Left: The first class of cadets graduated in 1942. Above: Today's theater on Zama was used as the Grand Lecture Hall. Below: Sobu-dai monument, erected in 1939 to commemorate the Imperial gift of the name Sobu-dai, stands just inside the main gate of Camp Zama.

end, the academy moved farther inland to Nagano Prefecture. Camp Zama became the base for the portion of the Japanese 53rd Corps, which was assigned there to protect Sagami Bay against American invasion.

On September 5, 1945, a battalion of the U. S. 1st Cavalry Division assumed control of Camp Zama, using the old academy grounds as a cantonment area. In the more than 40 years since this first American use of the camp, numerous changes have been made. Military maneuver grounds were converted into a golf course. Some original academy buildings were torn down to make room for housing areas; some still remain. All monuments erected at the academy when it was in use remain on Camp Zama today.

JED's construction division occupied the building which stabled the Emperor's horses during the academy days; the Kanagawa Resident Office is still in that building. The new JED headquarters building is on the site of the old academy headquarters building and the Zama theater — still at the most prominent point on the base — is incredibly like it was when built for the cadets over 50 years ago. It is in these surroundings that JAO employees assumed the distinction and the responsibilities of a new district. [1]

Reversion - An Island Returns to its People

For both the Corps of Engineers and the residents of Okinawa, May 15, 1972 held great promise and ushered in a new era in post-war Japan. As important as that day was to the future of the Corps' work in Japan and the employees of the Japan Area Office (JAO), the sheer magnitude of events taking place on Okinawa cast a giant shadow on activities at Camp Zama and Lieutenant Colonel Dale Dobson's JAO.

Twenty-seven years of American sovereignty over Okinawa finally ended and Okinawa was returned to the Japanese on a day

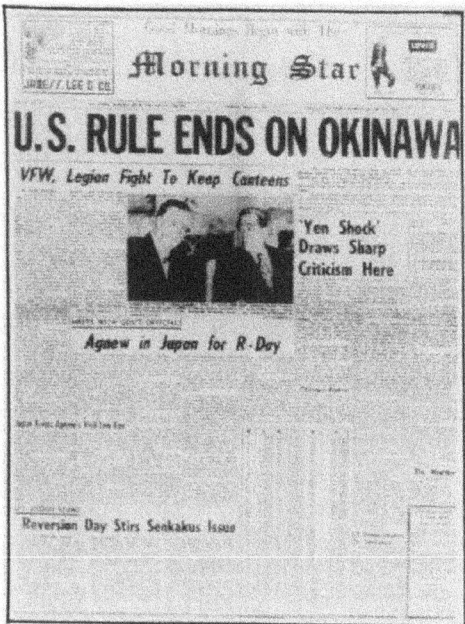

Okinawa Morning Star, May 14, 1972.

marked by a Reversion Day parade through the capital city of Naha and picnicers and festivals in Yogi Park celebrating the end of American Occupation. American troop strength dropped from 52,000 to 40,000 and 46 U. S. installations were targeted for return to the Japanese.

The climate in the Pacific provided an emotionally charged backdrop for the events of May 15. Six days before, on May 9, then United States President Richard M. Nixon announced his decision to mine North Vietnamese harbors in an effort to halt the flow of Soviet supplies into North Vietnam and hopefully bring an end to the Vietnam conflict. In addition, Japanese government officials were still reeling from what they called "Nixon shocks" — Nixon's visit to Peking without any notification to the Japanese and the consequent more open relations between China and the United States government.

While the mood on Okinawa was mostly one of revelry, concern was expressed in the form of a rally held by the Socialist Party in Yogi Park in conjunction with the celebrations. Their concerns involved the possibility of Nixon's mining policy bringing Okinawa into the Vietnam conflict. The Leftists also held their own rally: Their dissatisfaction over the terms of the reversion agreement centered on that part of the agreement allowing United States bases to remain on the island.

And, in spite of the excitement over reversion, the entire populace was rocked by the exchange rate set on Reversion Day — 305 yen to the U. S. dollar. Expecting a rate above 310 and anticipating the 360 rate that existed on mainland Japan on that day, the Okinawans felt cheated. For weeks before reversion, posters appeared all over the island predicting a rate equal to that of Japan's. [2]

In this climate of change and upheaval, many people lost sight of the fact that the movement to return Okinawa to the Japanese began over 20 years before R-Day and originated not only with Ryukyuan political leaders but with the U. S. government as well. As the United States/Japan peace treaty was being developed in San Francisco, some representatives of the powers that had been allied with the United States during the war urged that Japan be required to renounce its sovereignty over the Ryukyu Islands and hand them to the United States.

Ambassador John Foster Dulles, a member of the United States Peace Treaty mission opposed this idea saying that the United States felt the best formula would be to permit Japan to retain residual sovereignty, while making it possible for these islands to be brought into the United Nations trusteeship system, with the United States as administering authority. Residual sovereignty expressed exactly the basis of U. S. policy in regard to Okinawa and the Ryukyu Islands for the next 20 years. Although World War II had ended only five years before the peace treaty was written, the U. S. was already trying to reach a peaceable reconciliation with Japan and was ready to terminate its necessary postwar occupation. But the United States also had long term security interests in Asia, particularly in the strategically situated Ryukyu Islands. Complete peace and the need to keep a military force on guard in the Ryukyus were seemingly in conflict and residual sovereignty solved this conflict. The United States would retain temporary control of the Ryukyus but historic Japanese territory was not to be taken.

The idea of a United Nations trusteeship never materialized and the United States alone conducted the administration of the islands. But over the years, politicians from Japan and the United States continued discussions of reversion plans: President Eisenhower reaffirmed Japan's residual sovereignty with Prime Minister Kishi in June 1957; in 1961, Prime Minister Ikeda and President Kennedy restated this principle; in 1965, and again in 1967, President Johnson and Prime Minister Sato held meetings where reversion of the Ryukyus moved closer to reality. At the 1967 meeting they agreed to establish an Advisory Committee to the High Commissioner of the Ryukyus to promote the return of the islands to Japan and to help minimize any hardships caused by the reversion.[3]

Plans for reversion which would include the Corps began in October 1971 well in advance of R-Day. During the planning the United States Department of Defense assigned a major portion of reversion construction to the Corps of Engineers Pacific Ocean Division. In turn, that construction effort became the Japan Engineer District's responsibility. In the months before reversion, Corps em-

U.S. Army Engineer District, Japan

USARJ CIV PERS DIR Civ Pers Dir	**EXECUTIVE OFFICE**	**SPECIAL ASSISTANTS**
ZAMA AREA CIV PERS Civ Pers Off — POJEP	District Engineer — POJDE	Emer Ops Planner — POJOP
SUKIRAN AREA CIV PERS Civ Pers Off — POJOA-EP	Dep District Engineer — POJDD	Security Officer — POJCI
	Executive Officer — POJEX	Value Engineer — POJVE

ADMIN BRANCH POJAS	**CONSTRUCTION BR** POJCB	**#REAL ESTATE DIV (OKINAWA)** POJRE-O	**#OKINAWA AREA OFC** POJOA	**+ADMIN SUPPORT** OFC OF COUNSEL ENGR DIV OKINAWA
	SUPV&INSP SEC POJCB-S	**APPRAISAL BR** POJRE-OP	**CONSTRUCTION BR** POJOA-C	
	OFC ENGR SEC POJCB-O	**ACQUISITION BR** POJRE-OA	**ADMINISTRATIVE BR** POJOA-A	
		MGT&DISP BR POJRE-OM		
		PLANS&CONT BR POJRE-OC		

FIELD OFFICES

CHITOSE P.O. POJCP	**IWAKUNI P.O.** POJIP	**KOSHIBA R.O.** POJKR	**MISAWA R.O.** POJMR	**SASEBO P.O.** POJSP	**WAKKANAI P.O.** POJWP

YOKOTA R.O. POJYR

——— Administrative support

\# Duty Station Okinawa

\+ Duty Station Okinawa. Attached to OAO for admin support. Operational and technical responsibilities assigned to Chief, Engr Div, and Div Counsel, POD.

** Civ personnel management rendered under servicing agreement with USARJ.

Total Japan Dist	
Off - 10	
WO - 2	
EM - 6	
Total Civ	
GS - 21	
OPG - 2	
JN - 48	

August 1, 1972

ployees on Okinawa worked seven day weeks furnishing voluminous real estate data and maps to the Reversion Coordination Group, and completing and documenting disposal and transfer actions decided during negotiations." The work which began in these hectic months before reversion kept the real estate division busy through most of the 70s — something no one in the office predicted. [4]

For employees at the Japan Area Office, May 15 was a time for celebrating their new status within the division and their break from FED, but Lieutenant Colonel Dobson did not anticipate a heavy workload to accompany the name change. He was replaced as JED's acting district engineer in mid-June by Major Raymond F. Vachon. Colonel Edward M. Willis became JED's first district engineer at the end of July. The district's authorized strength consisted of 89 positions, 18 military and 71 civilians. This small number was based on existing and anticipated workload.

In terms of structure, JED's organization was simple and focused primarily on Okinawa and the work there. The district contained only two divisions: Engineering division and real estate, both on Okinawa under the Okinawa Area Office. The office of counsel was also on Okinawa. At Camp Zama there was the executive office, an administrative branch, a construction branch, and special assistants as well as a liaison office working with the USARJ Civilian Personnel

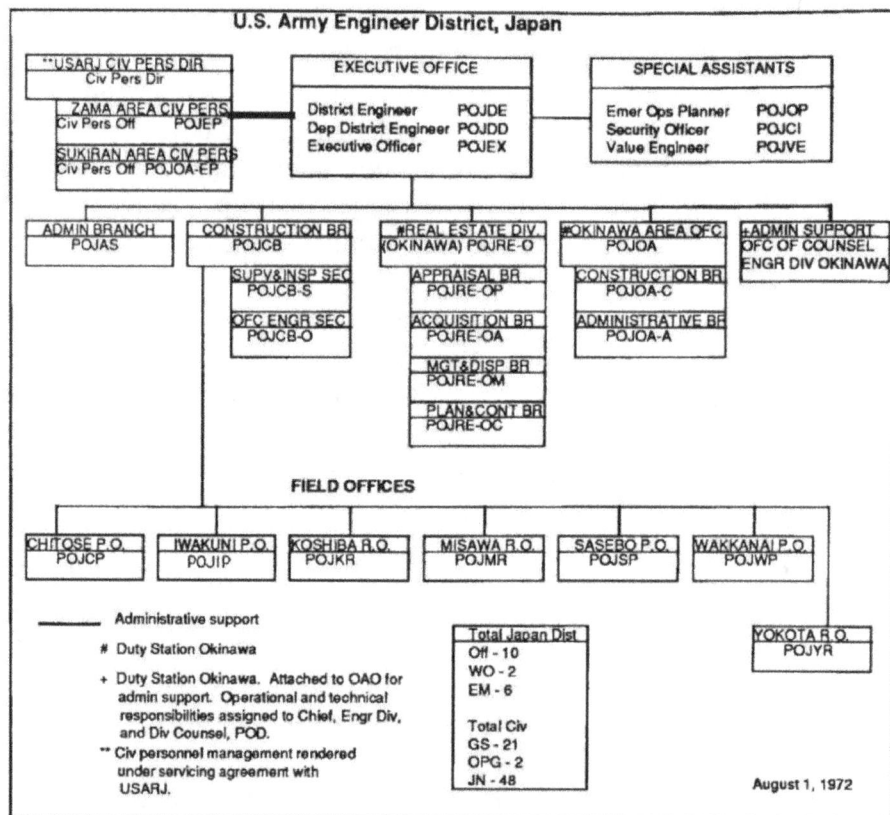

Colonel Edward M. Willis
Japan Engineer District's First
District Engineer
June 1972 - September 1975

Office. Under the construction branch there were four project offices and three resident offices. The district engineer had no contracting authority; POD was responsible for contracting and, in addition, provided support in the area of design and engineering.[5]

In the beginning it seemed that the reversion construction would take off quickly and some work related to Naha actually did began prior to reversion. The Japanese government was anxious to have the American Navy P-3 aircraft removed from Naha's air base as soon as possible. Preparations were underway for Ocean Expo '75, a world's fair type of exposition, and the government wanted to use Naha as an international, civilian airport. The P-3s would be transferred to Kadena Air Base but replacement facilities had to be built prior to the transfer. Procedural problems developed during negotiations delaying construction at Kadena. Colonel Willis soon concluded, as had the American negotiating team which drafted the original reversion agreement with Japan, that the Japanese would not launch a major construction program consistent with the needs of the United States bases on the island without prodding. Getting the program started and keeping it on schedule proved to be linked with internal Japanese politics. Three military services, the Army, the Navy and the Air Force, had to decide what the Japanese government should build, where they should build it and how.[6]

Facilities at Kadena Air Base for the Navy's P-3's were the first reversion construction projects.

Once the difficulties related to Naha and Kadena Air Base had been resolved, a crash program had to be instituted in order to finish the construction on time. In addition, reversion construction not related to the P-3s was delayed until 1973. JED's non-reversion workload at the time was under $10 million. These delays caused serious concern; manpower requirements could not be firmly established with so many program unknowns.

While the level of construction during the district's first year remained low, the district's work with the real estate program on Okinawa continued to occupy the attention of over 17 staff members. Settling all claims related to real estate that the United States had returned to owners just prior to reversion was one of the biggest tasks. Another program was established to process over 4,000 ex-gratia claims against the United States. These claims were for private land or facilities used by U. S. forces which had been damaged during the Occupation. Damage was described as physical damage or the inability of the landowners to use the land as it had been originally used. Farm land covered by concrete is an example. This program resulted in 3,900 meritorious claims and occupied the real estate division's time through the summer of 1977.

A third program was the real estate trust fund established in 1959. Frequently ownership of the land used by the United States could not be determined or the owner could not be located. Owners died without leaving heirs; heirs were named but could not be found. In all of these cases, rent for the land was paid into a trust fund. If the owner's were located, they would receive fair compensation. Between 1959 and 1970 the fund had been handled by the Government, Ryukyu Islands (GRI) at the request of the U. S. Civil Administration, Ryukyus (USCAR). In 1970, WESTPAC's real estate division became the official manager and, in 1972, that responsibility passed to JED. POD instructed JED to close out that fund by locating all owners to whom rents were due and making payments. This proved to be an extremely difficult task.

The real estate division also settled claims levied against the United States by fishermen's associations on Okinawa. Two of these claims stated that construction for U. S. forces in the Ryukyus had reduced the catch in areas in which the fishermen had exclusive fishing rights. By 1975, both of these claims were resolved and involved substantial compensation to the fishermen through JED. Problems with construction efforts interfering with fishing rights would plague the district through the 1980s.

The Host Nation Construction Program

Although it was first known as the Okinawa Reversion Related Construction Program and Japan Facilities Adjustment Program, the work the Japan Engineer District began in 1972 for the government of Japan was the start of one of the most successful programs ever managed by the Corps of Engineers in foreign countries: The Host Nation Construction Program. In the years between 1972 and 1990, the government of Japan provided over $3.7 billion worth of construction for U. S. Forces on Japan and Okinawa compared to $500 million the United States Congress appropriated for construction during the same time period. The cost to U. S. taxpayers for the facilities used by members of the Army, Air Force, Navy and Marines is approximately 3 percent of the cost of construction.

Reversion related construction fell under one of two types of programs funded by the government of Japan — the facilities relocation program and the facilities improvement program (FIP did not begin until the late 70s and will be covered later in this chapter). Relocation projects paid for by the government of Japan (GOJ) were in conjunction with the return of facilities and real estate to the Japanese. At the end of the Occupation there were nearly 3,000 bases on Okinawa and Japan occupied by U. S. forces. Under the Reversion Agreement and in conjunction with the Status of Forces Agreement formed at the same time, the United States agreed to return a major portion of the bases to the Japanese in return for construction of new facilities on the bases they retained. These retained bases were furnished to the U.S. forces rent free but the cost of maintaining the forces was the responsibility of the United States. A bi-lateral Joint Committee was established to determine which bases could be used jointly by U. S. and Japanese forces. Facilities furnished under the relocation program by GOJ to U. S. Forces were on a quid pro quo basis — square foot for square foot and function for function.

This was the Host Nation Construction Program in its embryonic state in 1972. Early in the program, JED's engineers dealt with the problems of conflicting design and construction standards as well as safety and environmental standards. They also ensured that the quality of construction met all U. S. standards on projects provided by GOJ for U. S. forces.[7]

The program got off to a late start in spite of the early work done at Naha. It wasn't until the summer of 1973 that GOJ began construction at Kadena Air Base and Futenma Marine Corps Air Station to replace facilities the U. S. had returned to the Japanese at Naha. On mainland Japan, similar construction was planned at Misawa Air Base and Iwakuni Marine Corps Air Station to replace

Colonel John T. Miller
Japan District Engineer
September 1975 - July 1978

The Sagami-ono hospital (right) was replaced with a new, modern facility at Yokosuka Naval Base (below).

bases returned on the northern island of Hokkaido. Program I, originally estimated at $16 million but costing the Japanese over $50 million, was completed in April 1975. The district and the Okinawa Area Office prepared the design criteria and provided surveillance of the construction to insure a quality product. The Japanese contractors resisted American standards in all areas and occasionally used inadequate materials, ignored the criteria and openly resented the surveillance. But, by the end of Program I, JED had made great strides in educating the Japanese contractors and the users were happy with their new facilities which included a refueling system, engine test cell, plane washer, new quarters, roads and utilities for the Air Force. The Navy and Marine Corps projects in Program I included an operations building, high explosive magazine, missile maintenance buildings, shops and hangers. [8]

Program II involved 29 Air Force and Navy projects at Kadena Air Base and included a chapel, gymnasium, NCO mess, theater, warehouses, post office, administrative buildings, roads, a fire station and a high-explosives magazine. Kadena also received 200 units of family housing — the first of 837 units planned for Kadena. Both were underway by September 1975 and completed by 1976 at a cost of $53 million. Runway work and miscellaneous jobs at Futenma Air Station made up Program III; Program IV focused on additional construction on Okinawa and at Misawa Air Base. USAHOMES reappeared at Misawa when 300 of the prefabricated units were relocated from Chitose and Wakkanai Air Bases when they were returned to the Japanese. Program V added another 132 units of family housing at Kadena and 207 at Misawa. [9]

New billeting was provided on Camp Zama for bachelor officers (above) as well as enlisted soldiers (left).

When the U. S. gave up several additional bases in 1977, construction on mainland Japan and on Okinawa was at its peak and the district handled $88 million in relocation construction in that one year. Projects included the relocation of the Army petroleum complex at Naha Port and a new $24.7 million Naval hospital at Yokosuka to replace the one returned to the Japanese at Sagami-Ono. The Sagami-Ono hospital played a major role in support to the Vietnam war— this hospital received the majority of the wounded soldiers who were air evacuated from Vietnam.

A considerable amount of GOJ construction took place on Camp Zama in the late 70s. Zama's Defense Communications System was upgraded and relocation projects resulting from the return of the Sagami-Ono hospital provided a new Naval hospital at Yokosuka, a new health clinic, gymnasium, dining center, veterinary clinic, bowling alley, a closed circuit television center, and modernized BOQs and BEQs at Zama. [10]

New facilities on Camp Zama included (clockwise) a medical/dental clinic, enlisted dining facility and gymnasium.

As the decade drew to a close the district was still plagued with problems with the Japanese contractors and Brigadier General Hatch, POD commander, noted that "the Japanese firms included the same deficiencies in their designs over and over again". This observation was not the general's alone; JED employees had struggled from the beginning of the Host Nation Program to correct problems and explain differences in American and Japanese ways of doing construction business in an effort to provide the user with high quality, safe, environmentally sound facilities. These problems didn't go away as the program matured; they changed in scope — especially in the environmental area — but differences of opinion, of standards, of quality continued through the 1980s as the two cultures, and their engineers and contractors, worked together.

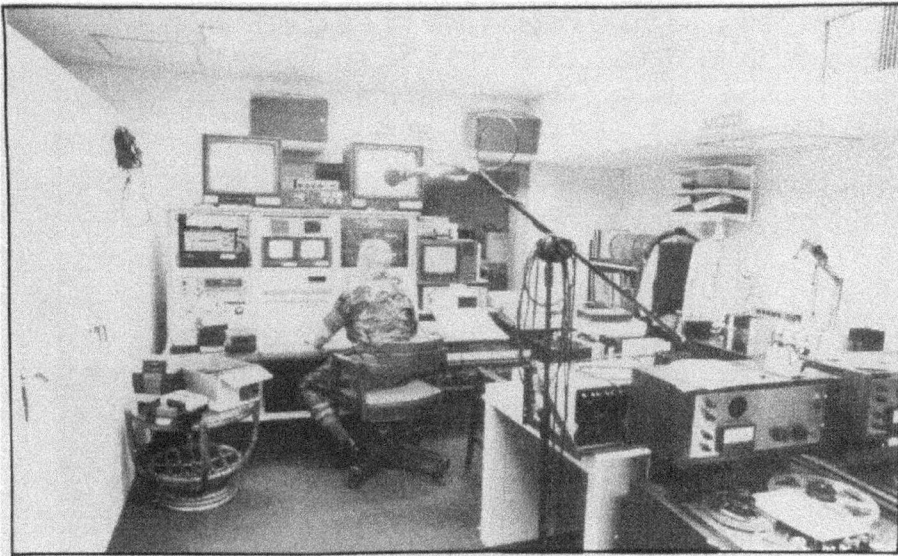

A new closed circuit television studio (left) and bowling center (above) completed the work on Zama.

The Facilities Improvement Program

In 1979, Japan and the United States agreed on a new construction program that promised to keep the Japan Engineer District at a high level of activity for many years to come. Called the Facilities Improvement Program, this plan called for the Japanese government to build family housing and administrative buildings at American military installations throughout Japan without the United States surrendering any land or existing facilities in return.

As a part of the peace treaty which ended World War II, Japan had given up the right to become a military power. However, the Japanese were constantly under pressure from the United States Congress to contribute more to their own defense. The Facilities Improvement Program was developed to allow that to happen. In order to determine how effective this program would be to U. S. Forces, a survey of American requirements was taken. That survey indicated that it would take 15 years at $100 million per year to upgrade U. S. installations to the desired level.

The Japan District renewed its efforts to develop close ties to Japanese officials to overcome their resistance to the district's involvement in the program. JED was pressed to prove its value to U. S. Forces and to reinforce the fact that the Corps of Engineers was the natural agent for efficient management.

There are certain projects that the government of Japan will not fund under the FIP program. Projects that support an offensive posture not funded under this program. Politically sensitive programs — either at the local or national level — are not funded. The Japanese prefer to furnish quality of life projects such as housing, day care centers, clubs and libraries. For the most part, U. S. forces are able to request and receive the types of facilities and facility upgrades they need to maintain readiness and quality of life for the service members and their families living in Japan. Projects that are necessary for the defense of Japan and the U. S. Forces stationed here, not funded by the government of Japan, must be provided by the military construction program.[11]

Highrises on Yokota Air Base.

The Military Construction Program

In spite of the huge government of Japan Host Nation Program and the importance given to getting it started in the early 70s, the military construction program remained an important part of the district's mission to support U. S. Forces in Japan. The size of the program varied from year to year and was at its peak in 1972 when the United States spent $19 million on construction programs. The military construction program from 1972 through 1976 included repair and renovation of the POL storage tanks at Sasebo. JED also supervised construction on Okinawa of the United States Pavilion for Ocean Expo '75. Another interesting project during this period was the overhaul of the power barge *Impedance*. Colonel Edward M. Willis, district engineer from June 1972 to September 1975, considered this as one of the most important accomplishments of the district during his time as commander. A three-deck, self-contained barge built during World War II, the *Impedance* had seen service in Manila Harbor and Pusan, Korea before becoming a part of the island-wide power system on Okinawa. It belonged to the United States Army, but was first operated by the U. S. Army, Ryukyus Islands, and from 1956 until 1970 by the Ryukyus

Power Barge *Impedance* before restoration.

100

Electric Power Corporation, an agency of USCAR. In 1970, responsibility for the barge was transfered to the Office of the Chief of Engineers and, in 1972, USACE assumed ownership. However, the Corps continued to lease the barge to Ryukyus Electric Power Corporation (REPC). When administrative rights over the Ryukyus reverted to Japan, REPC became Okinawa Electric Power Corporation (OEPC), an agency of the government of Japan. Okinawa Electric Power Corporation then assumed operation of the *Impedance* .

In 1972, the United States Army redeployed the *Impedance* to Saipan in the Marianas. Prior to towing it there, the barge needed to be overhauled, renovated and modernized. It was JED's task to oversee the work. After reaching an agreement with Okinawa Electric Power Corporation apportioning costs, the district began work on August 1, 1973 for what was estimated to be an 8 to 9 month job. Problems soon arose; the most difficult to overcome was rewinding the main generator rotor. General Electric performed this time consuming task in the United States. In spite of time delays, the work was completed in the summer of 1975 and the barge was released for new duty in Saipan.[12]

Minor military construction work on Taiwan included repairs to a Navy exchange and an ammunition magazine at Ching Chuan Kang Air Base. At Camp Zama a large construction program provided several new facilities to the community including a new elementary school at the Sagamihara Housing Area and a new high school at Camp Zama built for the Department of Defense Dependent Schools. The high school, which cost $2.8 million, won the Architectural Award of Merit in the 1980 Chief of Engineers' Design and Environmental Awards competition. A satellite communication facility was built for

The $2.8 million Zama American High School won the 1980 Chief of Engineer's Design Award's Architectural Award of Merit. Constructed around an open forum area, the school was DoDDs most modern facility.

Colonel Ralph A. Luther
Japan District Engineer
July 1978 - July 1981

U. S. Army Japan headquarters at Camp Zama. Other MILCON projects varied from a cold storage plant at Yokohama to a flight simulator at Kadena Air Base and a new sewage treatment plant at Misawa.

The decade was ushered out with two major programs for the Air Force at Kadena Air Base. The Commando Nest initiative supported the beddown of a squadron of Air Force F-15 Falcons. The squardon arrived in 1980 to boost United States defense posture in the Pacific.

Commando Eye provided facilities for the Air Force's AWACS — Airborne Warning and Command System. The large E-3A aircraft with a huge radar saucer mounted above the fuselage arrived on Okinawa with the F-15s in 1980. Commando Eye included new shops and additions and alterations to a hanger and maintenance buildings. These two projects exceeded $6 million in construction costs and saw the beginning of a strengthening defense posture that would last throughout the new decade. [13]

Operations and maintenance support (O&M) was provided to the Facilities Engineers (FE) when requested. This organization was renamed the Directorate of Engineering and Housing in the mid-1980s. The program began in 1975 under the Corps' new "One-Stop Service" program. O&M projects consisted of work costing less than $25,000. At the request of service engineers, either the FE or the base civil engineers (BCE), Corps districts would take on minor repairs and additions to existing facilities and similar projects. This relieved the base engineers of tasks they often were not sufficiently staffed to accomplish. This program began while Colonel Willis was the district engineer and included such work as POL restoration and the completion of the USAHOMES relocation. [14]

By the time Colonel Ralph A. Luther became the district engineer in July 1978, JED had grown considerably. By the close of the decade, the district had changed from a small Area Office into a dynamic construction agency representing the Pacific Ocean Division and the Corps of Engineers on Japan and Okinawa. The district had not grown much in personnel strength — up from 89 to 105 — but the workload had increased dramatically. At the close of the decade the engineering and design program was at the $215.7 million mark in 1979; construction placement of military and GOJ projects for that year was $98.3 million. The projected workloads for both engineering and construction, $428 million and $451.7 respectively, suggested that the district could become a full-service district within a short period of time and future of JED was very optimistic. [15]

Matsumoto Castle

Matsumoto's 6-storied black donjon (main tower) is unique in Japan and is colloquilly called "Crow Castle" in marked contrast to Himeji's "White Heron Castle." It was completed at the end of the 16th century and is the oldest donjon in Japan. It is also a National Treasure.

Chapter Five
A Decade of Change, A Future of Challenge
1980 - 1990

When Colonel Luther handed over command of JED to Colonel Jonathan D. Nottingham in June 1981, the district was headed for a period of prosperity which would see unprecedented construction at military bases on Japan and Okinawa. The strength of the dollar would fall to an all time low, district manpower would soar to over 325 employees and defense buildups in response to the downing of Korean Airlines 007 in August 1983 would keep the district busy at Misawa Air Base for a major portion of the 80s.

As the decade ended, however, the district would find itself in a struggle to survive as the military services faced the most severe cutbacks since the end of the war in Vietnam and the national debt continued its unimpeded growth. A military construction moratorium, DOD hiring freezes and the possibility of sequestration action became the challenges for Corps management at the beginning of the 90s.

Four Commanders, A Memorable Change of Command Ceremony and a New Home for the District Highlight the 80s

Colonel Nottingham, a 1957 graduate of the United States Military Academy, received his Master of Science degree in civil engineering from the University of Michigan. Prior to commanding the Japan Disrict, Nottingham was the assistant director of Civil Works for the Great Lakes and Upper Mississippi River, Civil Works Directorate, USACE.

He saw the district grow in both personnel and in capabilities. The district almost doubled in size during his tour as commander. A public affairs office was established and he initiated the publication of the district newspaper. He brought computers to the district and paved the way for the future of information management. Colonel Nottingham signed JED's first contract after the district received contracting officer authority and saw the compeltion of the Misawa runway project. With the signing of an historical agreement between JED and the Japan Civil Aviation Bureau, the district was allowed, for the first time, to serve as the agent for both U.S. forces and a foreign country.

Known for his fondness of Japan and its people, Colonel Nottingham aggressively promoted the Corps of Engineers and the work of the district to its Japanese counterparts. He strengthened relationships with all of the district's partners on Japan and Okinawa. Marine Colonel Robert Carney of U. S. Forces Japan became an important advocate of the district during Colonel Nottingham's command. [1]

Colonel Jack H. Clifton replaced Colonel Nottingham as JED's commander on July 9, 1984. A graduate of Ohio University with a Master of Science Degree in Mechanical Engineering from the University of Missouri-Rolla, he came to the district from an assignment as the deputy division commander, Missouri River Division. He'd also served as the executive assistant to Lieutenant General Morris, Chief of Engineers. Colonel Clifton placed a high value on the methods used in the district to tell the rest of the Corps and its partners on Japan what JED does in the Far East. He recognized that the complicated host nation program, already a huge source of work and income to the district, was neither easily explained nor understood. He spent three years concentrating on the complexities of the program and fostering the relations forged by Colonel Nottingham with members of the

Colonel Jonathan D. Nottingham
Japan District Engineer
June 1981 - July 1984

Colonel Jack H. Clifton
Japan District Engineer
July 1984 - July 1987

Defense Facilities Administration Bureaus (DFAB) and the Defense Facilities Administration Agencies (DFAA).

In addition, Colonel Clifton supervised the design phases for JED's new headquarters building, leaving Japan just prior to the ground breaking. He saw the start of the Hario Family Housing project, one of JED's biggest construction efforts, and cut the ribbon on an unprecedented number of quality of life projects on Japan and Okinawa for U. S. forces and their families. He left the district on June 11, 1987 to fill the position as chief of staff at the division head-quarters at Ft. Shafter. In a ceremony held that day at the Camp Zama Community Club, Colonel Clifton passed command of the district to Colonel Jerry M. Lowrance. [2]

Colonel Lowrance came to Japan from a tour as deputy division engineer at the Ohio River Division but, even in Japan, he was never far removed from his home in Texas and his alma mater, Texas A&M where he was the distinguished military graduate. He held a MS in Engineering and Construction Management. Colonel Lowrance expressed concerns about two areas in the district during the first month of his command. Information management and logistics offices were not doing well throughout the Corps and he wanted to ensure that both of these functions in JED were fulfilling their vital roles within the organization. His belief that automation and communication held the key to success in management made him a strong advocate for the information mangement office and he helped to increase its image and performance during his time as commander.

Colonel Lowrance viewed himself as a hard, demanding leader. "If the boss isn't hard, no one else will be!" And, when asked what legacy he wanted to leave behind after his tour was over, he expressed a desire to make JED the district in the Corps of Engineers where everyone in the Corps really wanted to be assigned.

Unexpectedly, Colonel Lowrance left the district only eight months after he arrived, opting for an early retirement and a position in Texas. Due to the suddenness of Colonel Lowrance's departure, Colonel Clifton returned as the interim district engineer while USACE selected a new commander for JED. [3]

On July 19, 1988, Colonel Leon R. Yourtee III, a graduate of the United States Military Academy's Class of 1964, officially became JED's seventh district engineer. Colonel Yourtee's graduate degree in Nuclear Engineering was awarded from the Massachusetts Institute of Technology in 1970. He came to the district from USACE's Resource Management Office where he served as deputy director. Before that, he was the director of program analysis and evaluation for the U. S. Army Strategic Defense Command.

Brigadier General Robert H. Ryan (left), Commander, U.S. Army Corps of Engineers, Pacific Ocean Division, passes the engineer flag and command of the Japan Engineer District to Colonel Jerry M. Lowrance.

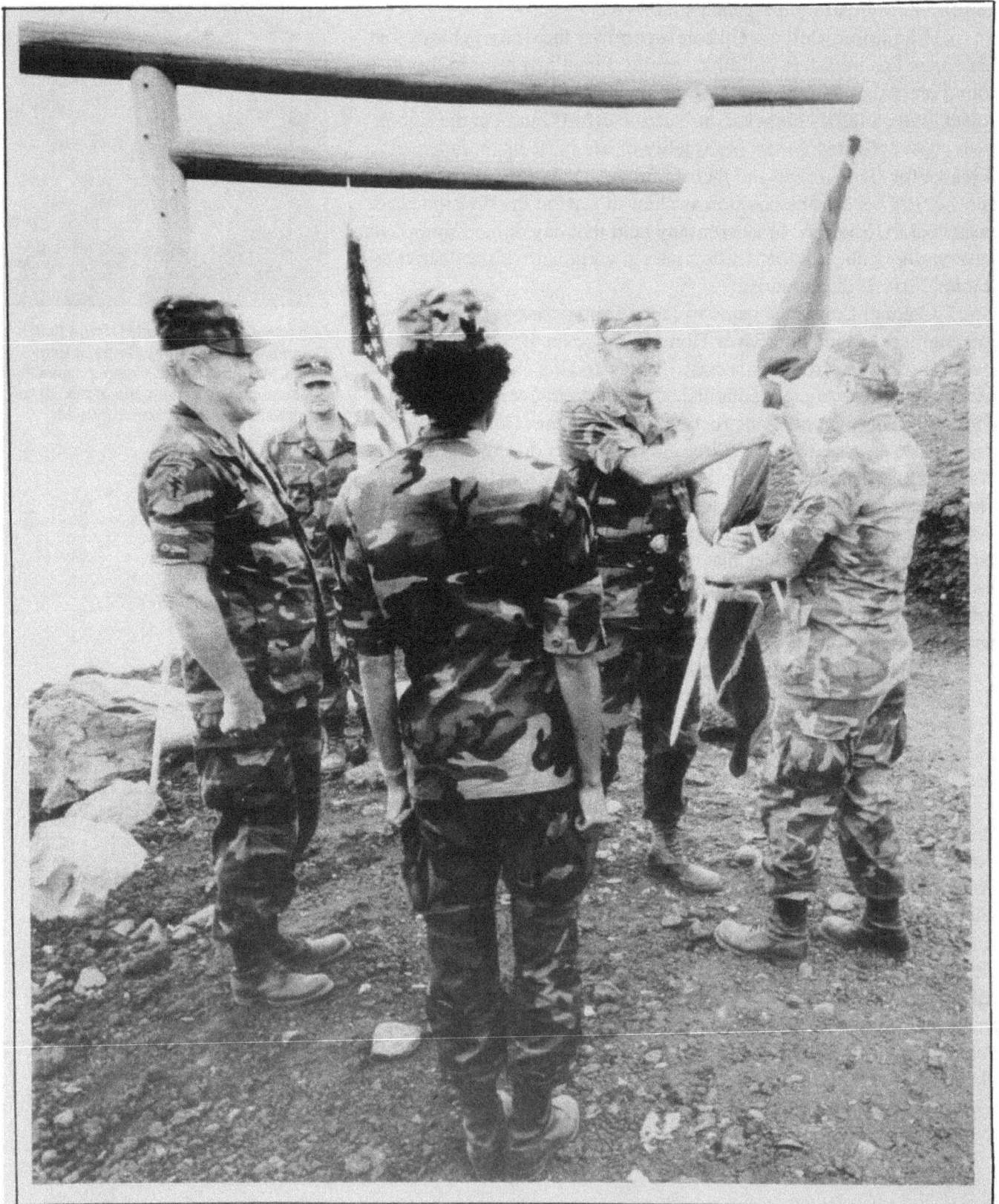

At his change of command at the top of Mt. Fuji, Colonel Yourtee, right, accepts the flag from Brigadier General Williams while (R-L) Captain David Hoffman, Colonel Jack Clifton and Staff Sergeant Andrea Clarke (front) look on.

Colonel Yourtee inherited a district which had reaped enormous financial benefits from the host nation construction boom. There was money available for travel, training, conferences, and people. But JED's financial future, along with that of the Department of Defense, was rapidly changing. By the end of his first year in Japan, Colonel Yourtee was faced with a financial disaster as construction income fell to $1.6 million below the estimated amount. His background in resource management, coupled with his insistence on corporate management within the district, resulted in a solution to the problem which had no adverse affect on any employee and which prepared the leaders of the district to face the lean years ahead.

In addition, he succeeded in getting the district's property book moved from POD to JED, hired a property book officer and completed a 100 percent inventory of all JED property within his first six months.

Colonel Yourtee's change of command ceremony was one of the most memorable milestones in the history of the district. Held at the top of Mt. Fuji, Japan's highest and most celebrated mountain, the ceremony was filled with significance for all of the participants. Climbing the 12,295 foot mountain is a religious pilgrimage for many Japanese. The climb is not an easy one and takes perseverance and physical strength. To pass the Corps flag on such a revered spot was a first for the district and unique to the Corps of Engineers.

Participating in the ceremony were Brigadier General Arthur Williams, Commander, Pacific Ocean Division, Colonel Jack Clifton, outgoing district engineer, Captain Dave Hoffman, Yokosuka Project Office Engineer, Staff Sergeant Andrea Clarke, Admin NCO and Colonel Yourtee. Almost all of the military personnel assigned to the district made the climb and POD's command sergeant major travelled from Korea to participate in the ceremony. A total of 75 people joined in the climb; spouses and children joined their JED moms and dads in the trek up the mountain. The event was covered by the Armed Forces Radio and Television's Far East Network and was featured in their evening news program. Although a second, more formal change of command ceremony was held on July 19 at the Camp Zama Community Club, district employees will always feel that Colonel Yourtee took command of JED at the top of Mt. Fuji.

Another significant milestone during Colonel Yourtee's tour was the dedication of JED's new headquarters building on August 18, 1989, at Camp Zama. Two Japanese construction companies, Tada Kensetsu and Fukuda Gumi, began construction on the joint venture project in April 1988. The headquarters, a two-story reinforced concrete structure, gave the employees of JED over 51,000 square feet of floor space and allowed all JED employees at Camp Zama to be housed under one roof as opposed to the former three building ar-

The dedication of JED's new headquarters building included a centuries old Japanese Shinto ceremony. The ceremony is conducted by a Shinto priest who drives all evil spirits from the building and ensures its safety for the new inhabitants. Chief Priest Yamamoto from the Zama Shrine conducted the dedication ceremony. An open house for residents of the community and family members of district employees was held after the dedication.

rangement. The project was funded by the government of Japan at a cost of $6 million.

In his eloquent dedication remarks, Mr. Shushiro Asano, Deputy Director, Yokohama Defense Administration Bureau, drew a poignant parallel between a Japanese and an American fable when he expressed his happiness for the engineers that, after providing quality of life projects for all members of the U. S. forces, were receiving a new facility themselves. The Japanese story of the dyer receiving his dyed clothes, so much like the American story of the shoemaker and the elves, was a part of Mr. Asano's dedication remarks: "There is a western proverb about the barefoot shoemaker who made shoes for everyone else but himself. In Japan, there is a proverb about the dyer's white clothes. The story is about a dyer who always dyed other people's clothes yet none of his clothes were dyed. I am filled with

joy to see that our partners who use this building have finally received their dyed clothes." [4]

JED gets Contracting Officer Authority

An agreement and two important contracts signed during the early 80's paved the way for the district to handle its increasing workload. The Facilities Improvement Program (FIP) document was signed in 1981 by Colonel Luther, representatives of U.S. Forces Japan and the Japanese government. [5]

On September 11, 1982, Colonel Nottingham signed the first construction contract by the district under his contracting officer authority marking JED's development into a full-service district. Prior to the district receiving contracting officer authority for the district engineer and the deputy district engineer, this authority rested with POD. Although the decision was made to grant CO authority to JED in 1981 because of its expanding workload, it wasn't until September 1982 that the first contract was signed.

A second historically important contract was signed by Colonel Nottingham on October 2, 1982 as the culmination of an agreement which began in the summer of 1981. TDA domestic airlines wanted to increase its flights in and out of Misawa Air Base which allowed the commercial airline use of the military runway. The Japanese government asked JED to manage the design and construction of runway improvements necessary to increase traffic at the base. POD provided assistance in devising a way that JED could legally perform work for a foreign nation.

Above, the new headquarters. Below, from L-R: Colonel Thomas Bruns, Commander, 17th Area Support Group, Colonel Leon R. Yourtee III, Commander and District Engineer, and Mr. Shushiro Asano, Deputy Director, Yokohama Defense Administration Bureau, cut the ribbon on the new JED headquarters.

Colonel Jonathan D. Nottingham signs the first locally awarded construction contract at JED for a temporary lodging facility at Iwakuni Marine Corps Air Station. Amount of the contract was $1.4 million. From left to right: Mr. Sadao Tokimori, President, Tokimori Kensetsu Co., Ltd., Nottingham, Mr. Yoshi Nishida, President, Matsumoto Kensetsu Co., Ltd., and Mr. Tsuneo Ichikawa, Chief, Procurement and Supply Division. The contract was joint venture between the two Japanese construction firms.

Colonel Nottingham stated that the significance of this agreement was that it enabled the Japanese government to fund a project that would incidentally benefit the U.S. military without having to use money from the limited and politically sensitive funds of Japan's defense budget. [6]

The Organization in the 80s

In 1980, the district functioned with 130 people. There were no computers and the district did not have an office of counsel, public affairs or executive secretary. The executive assistant was also the emergency manager and the safety officer was also the value engineer. The chief of administrative services was dual-hatted as the security manager. These offices fell under the heading of "special assistants."

In addition to the support staff which included the financial management office and the procurement and supply division, engineering and construction divisions completed the organizational structure.

Under the engineering division there were five branches: estimating branch, military branch, technical review branch, facilities support branch and the Okinawa Liaison Branch located on Okinawa with the area office. Construction division included the office engineering branch, supervision and inspection branch and contract admin branch. Responsibility for the projects fell to the assistant chief of construction for the Honshu Area who supervised the Iwakuni, Misawa, Yokosuka and Zama project offices. The Okinawa Area Office included an administrative branch, a U.S. construction branch and a GOJ construction branch.

A message dated August 18, 1982, from Colonel Alfred J. Thiede, POD Division Engineer, approved the district's first major reorganization. The reorganization (POD 25-1) added 69 civilian and Japanese national spaces to the organization. Major changes in the reorganization authorized the formation of the Southern Resident Office at Camp Zama and the Northern Resident Office at Misawa. All project and field offices, except on Okinawa, were placed under one of these resident offices. The procurement and supply division received a substantial increase in spaces due to the new contracting responsibilities and an office of counsel was established with the same justification. In addition, authority was given for expansion of five people to to the one-man ADP center which was created in February 1982. [7]

Minor restructuring from 1983 to 1985 provided for public affairs, safety and value engineering offices to separate from special assistants. In addition, name changes and internal reorganizations affected the financial management office, the procurement and supply division and the safety office. They became, respectively, the resource management office, contracting division, and the office of safety and occupational health. In August 1987, a separate office was established for emergency management/security and law enforcement. The position was filled in November 1987.

In August 1988, the office of admin services became the logistics management office. This reorganization incorporated the functions of the old OAS and the logistics office in IMO. Two branches — the travel branch and the supply branch — as well as the library and mailroom made up the new LMO. Responsibilities included arranging travel for employees on official duty, maintaining supplies for the daily operation of the district, and control of the JED property book which had been maintained by the division until this reorganization. One hundred percent property accountability was the first task assigned to the new LMO. [8]

The biggest potential reorganization efforts of the decade came in conjunction with the implementation in the Corps of Engineers of Life Cycle Project Management. The changes began in JED in 1989 and were accomplished in early 1990. The program was established under USACE's Initiatives '88 to provide comprehensive management during the Corps involvement with a project — planning, engineering, construction and operations — through either an individual project manager or a project management team.

The reorganization of both engineering and construction divisions was based on the principles of project management as well as the projected amount of future military and host nation work.

Engineering's host nation and military branches were consolidated to create the project management branch. Project managers were assigned both U.S. funded and FIP projects in an effort to allow maximum flexibility and efficient use of resources to decrease workload peaks. Project management teams were assigned responsibility

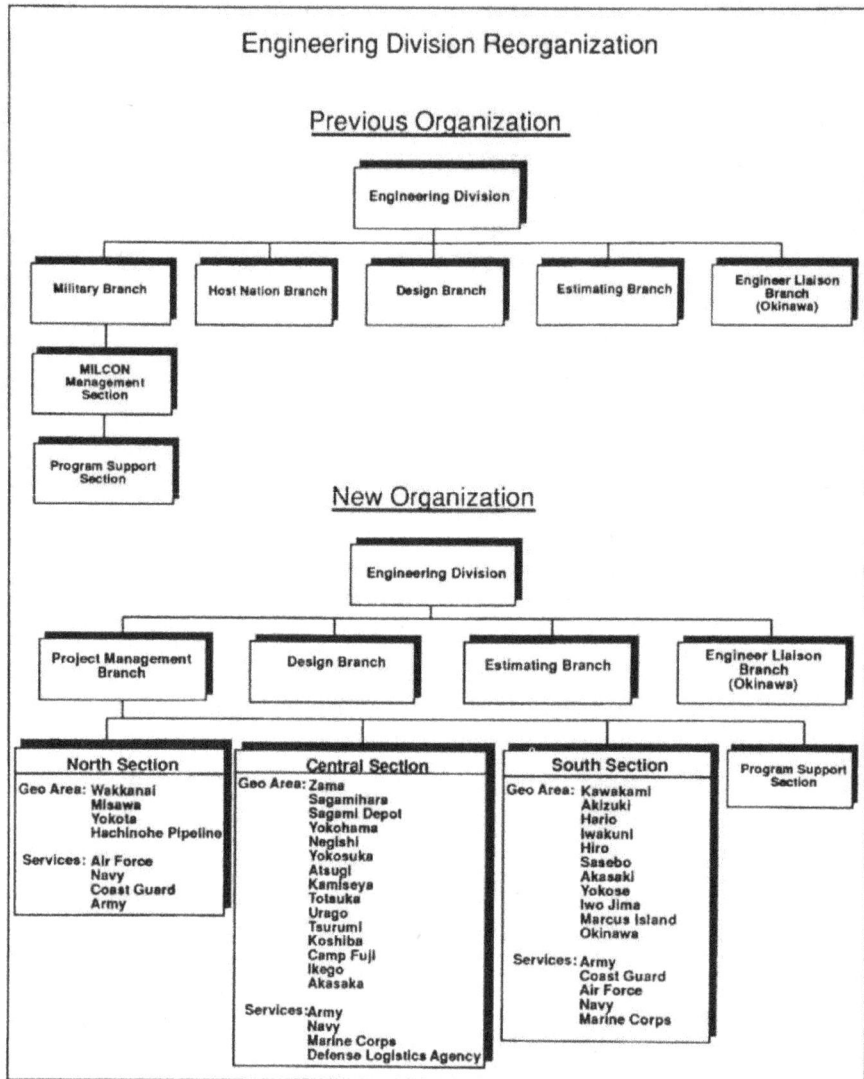

Engineering Division Reorganization

Previous Organization

Engineering Division

Military Branch | Host Nation Branch | Design Branch | Estimating Branch | Engineer Liaison Branch (Okinawa)

MILCON Management Section

Program Support Section

New Organization

Engineering Division

Project Management Branch | Design Branch | Estimating Branch | Engineer Liaison Branch (Okinawa)

North Section
Geo Area: Wakkanai
Misawa
Yokota
Hachinohe Pipeline

Services: Air Force
Navy
Coast Guard
Army

Central Section
Geo Area: Zama
Sagamihara
Sagami Depot
Yokohama
Negishi
Yokosuka
Atsugi
Kamiseya
Totsuka
Urago
Tsurumi
Koshiba
Camp Fuji
Ikego
Akasaka

Services: Army
Navy
Marine Corps
Defense Logistics Agency

South Section
Geo Area: Kawakami
Akizuki
Hario
Iwakuni
Hiro
Sasebo
Akasaki
Yokose
Iwo Jima
Marcus Island
Okinawa

Services: Army
Coast Guard
Air Force
Navy
Marine Corps

Program Support Section

for MILCON, O&M and FIP projects for specific geographical areas and installation engineers, enhancing JED's installation support to all partners by providing a single element of contact and enhancing communication and customer satisfaction.[9]

Construction division's reorganization, like engineering's, placed increased emphasis and awareness on project management. Absorbing the office engineering and contract admin functions previously performed in the Southern Area Office (SAO) and combining the old construction division's office engineering and contract admin branches into a project management branch were the first steps in setting up the reorganization.

The program and control section of the program management branch, formerly the office engineering branch, coordinates all placement, budget, income and expense activities between the field offices and other offices within the district and maintains staff responsibility for all operating budget activities.

The project administration branch, formerly the contract admin branch, is responsible for all contract administration actions as well as contracting officer modifications generated by the field. In addition, this branch assumes day-to-day contract admin functions for the Yokota and Kanagawa project offices as well as the Southern Area Office, freeing the field of admin burdens and creating an operating construction division at the headquarters.[10]

Quality assurance responsibilities fall under the project quality branch and includes offering quality assurance guidance to the field offices. The host nation unit focuses on host nation projects from design through construction completion. The construction evaluation unit

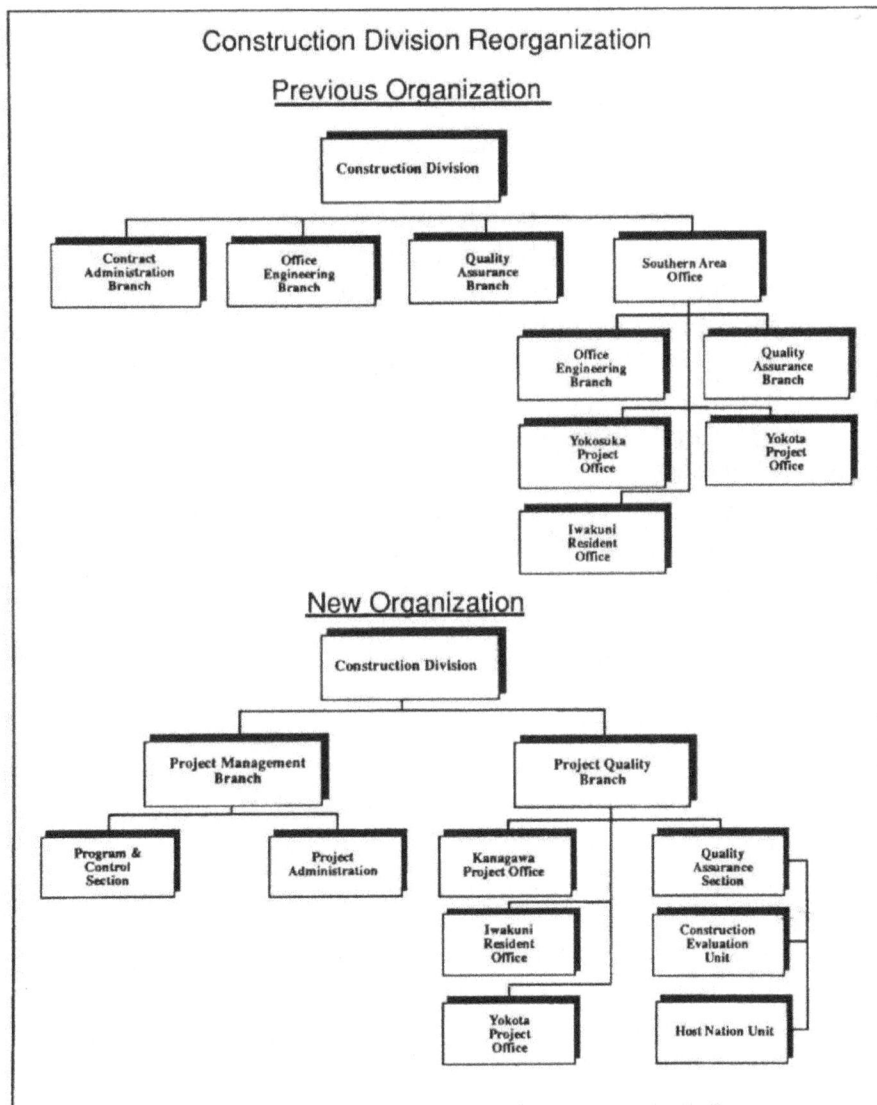

Construction Division Reorganization

Previous Organization

- Construction Division
  - Contract Administration Branch
  - Office Engineering Branch
  - Quality Assurance Branch
  - Southern Area Office
    - Office Engineering Branch
    - Quality Assurance Branch
    - Yokosuka Project Office
    - Yokota Project Office
    - Iwakuni Resident Office

New Organization

- Construction Division
  - Project Management Branch
    - Program & Control Section
    - Project Administration
  - Project Quality Branch
    - Kanagawa Project Office
    - Iwakuni Resident Office
    - Yokota Project Office
    - Quality Assurance Section
    - Construction Evaluation Unit
    - Host Nation Unit

provides staff direction to the field on U.S. funded construction projects.

The reorganization of construction division reduced the Zama manpower spaces from 71 to 59 and the operating construction division is structured to share common project management control mechanisms with engineering division.

Changes to the Support Staff

The 80s brought extreme fluctuations in the dollar affecting all of the district's construction programs. In 1972, when the district was established, the exchange rate averaged 310 yen to the dollar. In 1980, the exchange rate fluctuated between 195 and 240 yen to the dollar. At the beginning of 1986, the rate was still a healthy 222 yen to the dollar. By the end of the year, the rate dropped to 153. For the first time a post differential allowance was paid to civilians on Japan and on Okinawa. The allowance grew during the next two years as the dollar continued to plunge. The low rate in 1987 was 138; in 1988 it was at its lowest at 121 to the dollar.

On October 1, 1986, the Department of Defense reactivated the Foreign Currency Fluctuation Construction Defense Act (FCFCD), initiating budget exchange rate accounting for MILCON and family housing appropirations for the Army and MILCON for the Air Force. One year later, Air Force family housing and construction for the Navy and DoDDs were added; on August 1, 1987 the DoD Special Representative (DODSPECREP) were included in the budget exchange rate accounting system.

Paying additional allowances to the civilian workforce was only a part of the fiscal problem for JED. In 1986 a severe loss in S&A income resulted because income was earned on placement valued at the budget exchange rate of 322 yen to the dollar. However, expenses were captured at the actual rate.

Although the dollar gained some strength during 1989 and 1990 — a high of 150.5 in 1989 and 140 on September 1, 1990 — S&A problems remained severe for JED. The main reason for the high rates at this time was the drop in work placement. During June 1989, five special Program Budget Advisory Committee (PBAC) meetings were held to create action plans to solve a $1.6 million deficit in construction S&A accounts.

Measures taken to reduce spending between June and the end of FY89 were severe. Construction division personnel maximized leave usage during the fourth quarter. Nine construction employees were transferred to engineering division for the balance of the year. A hiring freeze was implemented; training, travel and the purchase of non-essential equipment and supplies were cancelled. The commander instituted a policy requiring his signature on all travel orders, training requests and purchase requisition orders. The budget office held formal budget training classes in conjunction with the formation of the FY90 budget.

The strategies to reduce spending were the most severe in the existence of JED; the prosperity that JED had enjoyed was clearly over as employees wrestled with an uncertain future.

Manpower cutbacks accompanied the declining work placement figures. Manpower strength had climbed during the 80s to support the growing workload. Year-end strengths over the 80s were 130 in 1980, 140 in 1981, 184 in 1982, 213 in 1983, 262 in 1984, 305 in 1985, 322 in 1986 and 331 in 1987. In 1989 Colonel Yourtee requested a POD manpower survey to recommend suggested manpower strengths for the district in light of its declining workload and orientation toward a host nation district. The survey was completed in November and the recommended ceilings were 293 employees if the district retained its military construction and operations and maintenance workload and 199 if the host nation work was its only source of income. On November 1, before the survey results were final, POD decreased JED's civilian authorization from 336 to 321.

At the end of FY88, JED's manpower strength was at 337. Fifteen of these were military personnel. By December 1989, JED's strength was down to 316, five below POD's new authorization for the district. As 1990 brought serious defense cutbacks and new hiring freezes within USACE, the district ended FY90 with 271 employees. Additional cuts were planned for FY91.

Over the decade, the value engineering program grew in proportion to JED's expanding workload. From 1983 through 1989, over $8 million was saved through the program. In 1990 the value engineer officer assumed the collateral responsibility of assistant chief in the safety and occupational health office. This was not an unprecedented action. Until August 1984, Mr. Masayasu Saito held the position as both JED's safety officer and the value engineering officer.[11]

At that time, Brigadier General Robert M. Bunker, POD Commander, informed JED that a requirement for a full-time VE officer at the district level predicated on the following factors would necessitate hiring a separate district safety officer: (1) direction from USACE to consider upgrading the part-time VE position to full-time in order to realize maximum benefits from the VE program; (2) POD VE directive to raise the VE savings goal from 2 percent to 5 percent of the program amount. As a result, a GS-11 safety officer position was created in the district and was filled in November 1984.

Sam Bradley, JED's ADP coordinator and Lydia Inks, data transcriber, take a peek at a part of JED's new computer.

To publicize the program, 600 copies of the second edition of the JED publication "VECP Makes You Additional Profits," written by Mr. Saito in 1979 in Japanese, were printed and distributed in December 1984. In addition, concentrated VE orientation briefings were given to JED contractors, improving their understanding and participation in the program. With the significant increase in the projected workload in 1985, a value engineering committee was formed in late 1984 to conduct VE studies on MILCON projects. Due to these efforts, JED's value engineering program exceeded the POD imposed goal from 1984 through the end of the decade.

The ADP center saw the most growth during the 80s; from one person when it was established in February 1982 to 13 employees in 1990. JED's first mainframe computer, a Harris 500, was installed in the district's ADP center in November 1982. At that time there were eight computer terminals in JED and it would be a another year before the first ten Wangs were delivered. By 1987, Zenith PC's were installed throughout the district and Macintosh computers were becoming a familiar sight in many offices. The ADP center had become a full-service information management office and, over the next three years, the office was involved with the formation of JEDESS data base and the Common Data Base Directory, converting existing software programs on the Harris to the VAX, designing and establishing a district-wide network and implementing the first records management program at the district. All of these efforts were in preparation for the purchase and delivery in 1989 of the district's new Digital VAX 6310 computer.

Attrition and hiring freezes took a toll on IMO's manpower and by 1990, the office was staffed by 13 employees, down from their peak of 17 in early 1989. The future for IMO holds the possibilities of computer time-sharing with FED and the division as well as becoming the major IMO training center at Camp Zama. [12]

The Projects in the 80s
The Northern Area Office

Captain Bruce Porter, project engineer in the early 80s at the Misawa Project Office, was fond of stating the incongruities of his realm: "Misawa is the only place where the Air Force runs the ground operations, the Navy brings in the planes and the Army brings in the ships." His staff of eight serving Misawa Air Base and its 3,000 residents was building for the base's future but they had no idea how quickly the base would grow, rendering many of their projects inadequate to support the massive buildup during the upcoming decade. As the construction program grew throughout the decade the office was upgraded to a resident office in 1982 and became the Northern Area Office in August 1984. The staff grew from eight employees in 1980 to 27 in 1984 and 32 employees by mid-1985. The program justified a lieutenant colonel to fill the position as area engineer and Major (P) Leonard Hassell, currently the chief of staff at POD, became the Northern Area Engineer in July 1984. When he was promoted to the rank of lieutenant colonel in August 1984, Lieutenant General Joseph K. Bratton, the Chief of Engineers, and Brigadier General Robert M. Bunker, then POD commander, pinned on his new rank insignia at a promotion ceremony held at Camp Zama.

As the 80s began, Misawa Air Base had the two-fold mission of electronic security functions on the strategically located base on the northern tip of Honshu and operating the base's airfield.[13]

JED's project office was involved in providing quality of life facilities for the residents of the air base. Two of the early projects were the Robert D. Edgren High School and the Misawa Chapel. The $5.13 million school opened in April 1984, less than two years after the ground breaking. It replaced a 30 year old structure never intended to serve as a school. Before the new school opened, high school athletes used the base gymnasium; the new 45,114 square foot facility provided the teenagers a gym of their own.[14]

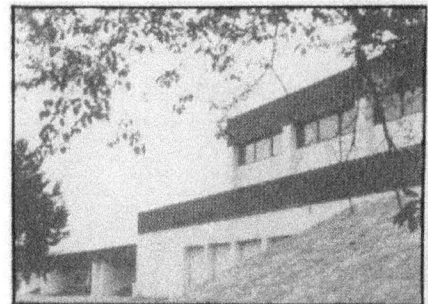

These two photos show the new Robert Edgren High School on Misawa.

Misawa's interdenominational chapel was entered in the 1984 Chief of Engineers' Design Award competition for its unique architecture. It replaced a Quonset hut used for worship services. Work on both of these projects, along with the new child care center constructed at the same time, presented special challenges. Extremely severe

winters in 1983 and 1984 made construction on these facilities difficult. Over 20 feet of snow fell during the winter of 1983-1984 completely covering the school at one point. Construction on the interior of the school continued, however, and the snow cover created insulation against the sharp wind even though contractors could walk completely over the building without touching it.[15]

Most winters at Misawa are cold and snowy (above), but the winter of 1983-1984 was even worse than normal affecting construction on the new high school, chapel (right), and child care center (below).

The greater part of the buildup at Misawa was described in the Air Force's Commando Port Facilities Master Plan, August 1983, which identified Commando Port projects proposed for funding in both the GOJ and MILCON programs. Commando Port was the name given to the beddown of two squadrons of F-16 tactical fighter aircraft which added 4,000 military and dependent personnel to the base.

By 1985 several major projects for Commando Port had been completed. These included the alteration of aircraft hangers, maintenance facilities, squadron operations areas, munitions storage igloos, a new commissary and the South Area fire station. In addition to these projects, a portion of the massive North Area housing project was opened and work was beginning on high rises to add additional housing at Misawa.

At 2:56 p.m. on April 1, 1985, Colonel Mike Ryan, USAF, touched his F-16A's landing gear onto Misawa's runway and the beddown had begun. That same day, three F-16s, one addition F-16A, and one F-16B arrived at the base. On July 4, the 13th Tactical Fighter Squadron of the 432nd Tactical Fighter Wing was activated. It soon received its full compliment of 24 aircraft. By the time the aircraft landed, construction placement for the beddown contributed heavily to JED's overall construction placement program: 45 percent of the MILCON work and 23 percent of the district's host nation work.[16]

By 1986, the number of NAO employees had increased to 33. The construction management effort continued to focus on Commando Port. Air Force and Navy construction in the Munitions Storage Area was filling in most of the base's unoccupied space with the Navy work being in support of its own Naval Air Facility and Mobile Mine Assembly Group (MOMAG) missions. Row upon row of protective munitions Stradley Arch Igloos, with regularly spaced above ground storage magazines could be seen in various stages of construction from clearing and grubbing the "wooded footprint" to painting the finished product.

The North Area Housing complex was taking on a lived in look with tall steel skeletons turning into highrise apartments and 2, 3, and 4 bedroom townhouse units stretching out in artistically balanced large radius paths ending in typical American cul-de-sacs. By the end of April there were 811 GOJ constructed townhouses and ten senior officer's quarters. [17]

One of the richest archaeological finds in Japan was unearthed during 1986 on the site of the North Area highrises. Contractors discovered 4,000 year old pieces of pottery at the construction site. The Aomori Prefectural Buried Cultural Asset Investigation Center stopped construction on the site for a year while its archeologists reclaimed the artifacts from two different periods in Japanese history. Six ancient housing sites from the Heian Period (active over 1,000 years ago) were found. It was the first time Heian housing sites had been discovered in the Misawa area. Each house, about 3 square meters and 50 centimeters in depth, had a kitchen with a duct to the surface of the ground for ventilation of smoke.

In the same area, remains from the Jyomon Period (4,000 years old) included 30 boxes of straw-rope patterned pottery and stoneware along with 35 storage sites and pitfalls for hunting. Dubbed the "Ruins of Odanainuma", the excavation area covered 3.5 acres. [18]

Above: Area Engineer Lieutenant Colonel Leonard Hassell with one of the 4,000 year old pots found early in the digging process. Left: Methodical, laborious, painstaking. . . and enormously rewarding to archaeologists all over the world. The ruins of Odanainuma are considered an extraordinary find.

The 48 hardened aircraft shelters include six flow through shelters which allow the F16s to run in one end and out the other. The shelters (below) allow maintenence crews to work inside in a heated environment rather than outside. The jets can also be refueled and loaded with weapons inside the shelters rather than outisde in revetments. The huge doors of the shelters (above) can be opened in under two minutes and closed in the same amount of time.

Several more projects were constructed under the Commando Port initiative during the last three years of the decade. They included a fire protection system for the flight hangers provided in Phase I, a $20 million Singer Link flight simulator and two underground JP-4 (jet fuel) storage tanks. Phase III included more jet fuel storage tanks. Maintenance buildings were constructed to support the three maintenance squadrons which arrived in 1986 with the Tactical Fighter Squadron.

All of the operational/maintenance facilities were funded by the U. S. government and cost $166 million dollars over the life of the program. The government of Japan funded quality of life projects provided, in addition to housing, a new base exchange garage, gym, consolidated personnel buildings and a 50,000 square foot supply facility, a library, BEQs and BOQs, and a new hush house. During Phase II of Commando Port, GOJ began funding some of the maintenance facilities including 48 hardened aircraft shelters which cost $2.2 million each. Construction of these shelters, the last of the Commando Port projects, will be completed in 1995. By that time, Japan will have invested $475 million in projects for Commando Port. [19]

In spite of the enormity of the program, the Misawa Project Office maintained a large construction program outside the Commando Port umbrella. A $23 million secure Permanent Capability Facility dubbed Ladylove was built for the Electronic Security Group at Misawa's Security Hill. Another large, difficult project was the upgrade of the base's runway. The $2.5 million project included crack repairs to the entire runway and overlaying two to three inches below finished grade, repairing cracks and overlaying the entire surface with two 1.5 inch asphalt concrete lifts and establishing a crown. The majority of the work was done in the middle of the night because the runway was never shut down. The NAO provided quality assurance on a 24 hour per day, seven day per week schedule at both the runway and the contractor's laboratory.

Other major projects completed during the decade included new $2.2 million water towers for the base and the $2.5 million North Area Support Complex which provided the 1,800 residents living in North Area housing a beauty and barber shop, cafeteria, laundry and dry cleaners, video rental store and mini-mart. A $6.7 million passen-

Above: One of the Commando Port projects was the upgrade of Building 911. Shown here during the upgrade, the building was straffed during World War II by Navy Hellcats. The close-up shows the bullet holes in the steel structure.
Left: Nine stradley arch ammunition igloos and a munitions preload complex were completed in May 1989 under a $129 million MILCON project. The complex included two preload buildings, one missile assembly building, one bomb assembly building, and 17 holding pads surrounded by revetments (shown here).

The Misawa runway was never completely closed during construction in 1988. Commerical traffic, including TDA shown above, Japan Self-Defense Forces and the American F-16s kept flying.

ger terminal project provided a 1,294 square foot terminal building, a freight terminal, exterior storage and maintenance areas.

In 1989, NAO saw the completion of a new base exchange and the beginning of a project for the Air Force Systems Command. The new AAFES exchange mall, an $11 million project funded by the Army and Air Force Exchange Service included the exchange and 20 vendors under one roof. In addition, the mall included five fast food vendors. The 92,000 square foot facility opened in March.

A project for the Deep Space Tracking System (DSTS) began early in the year. The DSTS is a satellite tracking facility designed to detect, track and catalog man-made objects in space by monitoring satellite transmissions to determine their positions. The facility at Misawa will be one of only three in the world — the others are located at Griffiss Air Base in New York and the Royal Air Force Feltwell in the United Kingdom. All three locations were selected for their ability to provide global deep space coverage. Deep space is defined as an altitude of three miles.

The original base exchange (above) was constructed during the early 1950s and wasn't nearly large enough to meet the demands of the base. The new post exchange, which opened its doors in March 1989, included under one roof a larger exchange store, and 20 other concessions including a video tape rental, florist, bookstore, barber, and five fast food restaurants.

Construction of the Deep Space Tracking System, shown below, doesn't look very interesting, but the project was very fast track. The structures themselves didn't have any special requirements, but the electrical and mechanical systems inside were very complex.

Included under the quality of life projects was the Military Airlift Command's new passenger terminal (right). It replaced an old wooden structure (above) built in 1956 as the base chapel. But the biggest contribution to quality of life for Misawa residents was the new housing including these highrises (below) in the North Housing Area.

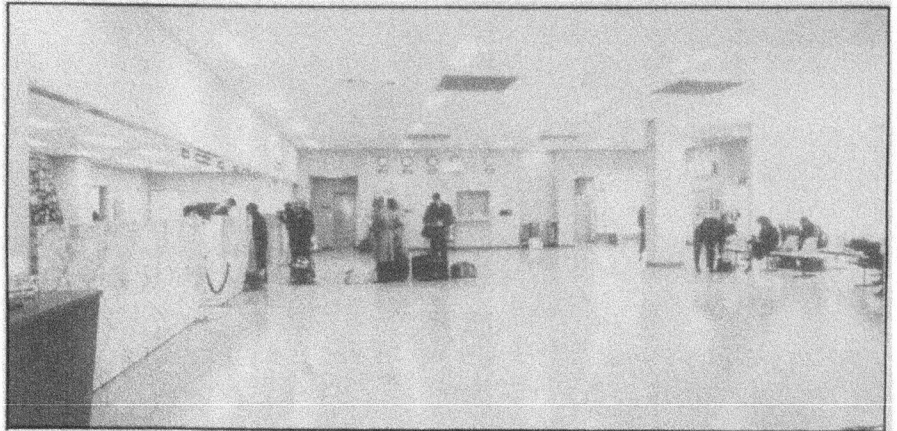

Residents of the North Area have a new elementary school to accompany their new homes.

Phase I of the DSTS, designated Project Ringo, began in May and was completed in August. It included the demolition of 11 existing storage buildings and clearing and grubbing of the site. Phase II included the construction of an operations building, a support building, an entry control point, a radome (antenna), parking lot and covered walkway. The $17 million research and development project will be completed in early 1991. [20]

Sollars Elementary School became too small for the children at Misawa almost as soon as it was built. Not only did the school receive a $10 million addition in 1989, the base received another elementary school. The government of Japan funded a new, two-story elementary school in the North Area. It provides 17 classrooms, two kindergarten rooms and four special requirements rooms. In addition, there's a learning center which includes the library and audio-visual center and a gymnasium. The height of the basketball goals are adjustable and adults at Misawa can use the gymnasium when school is not in session.

One of the NAO's most interesting projects on the horizon is the construction of a new hospital. Misawa's existing hospital consists of several buildings built between 1948 and 1957. The deteriorating condition of these buildings reflects a medically unacceptable condition. The government of Japan will construct a new hospital/dental clinic which will provide 25 beds and 24 dental chairs. The bed capacity can be increased to 233 during contingencies and, during peacetime, the hospital will serve the normal inpatient and outpatient requirements. For inpatient care now, residents of Misawa are flown to the hospitals at Yokota Air Base and Yokosuka Naval Base in central Japan.

At the end of construction, a separate MILCON project will harden the facility. If necessary, the second floor can be evacuated and the basement will serve as a self-contained, blast resistive retreat and as an active triage/treatment center. A contamination control unit will

The Sollars Elementary School (left), originally constructed in 1948, received several upgrades over the years, but no major additions until 1989. Included in the addition are a kindergarten wing, cafeteria, gymnasium (above) and admin building.

also be provided under this project. The hospital is due for completion in late 1993.

When Major Bruce Fink arrived at Misawa in May 1989 as the new area engineer it wasn't his first experience in Japan. He was born at the Sagami-Ono hospital in 1956. His father, who would later become the POD commander, and Colonel Yourtee's father were both stationed on the Kanto Plain; Lieutenant Colonel Yourtee at Yokohama Engineer Depot (Sagami) and Captain Fink at Zama. Just as Major Fink's father led the Pacific Ocean Division into the austere

The new hospital will replace this structure built in the early 1950s.

Runway work continues on Misawa with a selective slab replacement project (right). The project replaces portions of the runway to eliminate the safety hazards associated with deteriorating asphalt and concrete. An ongoing project has been to upgrade the steam system on Misawa. This photo (above) shows the header pipes in the boiler plant.

decade of the 70s, Major Fink faces similar challenges at the district's northernmost outpost at Misawa.

Kanagawa Project Office

This office, co-located with JED headquarters, has undergone more change over the years than either the Northern or Okinawa Area Offices as it evolved to meet the challenges placed on it. In 1980, the office was designated the Zama Project Office. In August 1982, the Southern Resident Office was formed with field offices at Zama and Atsugi and project offices at Iwakuni, Yokota and Yokosuka.

On February 13, 1985, the resident office was upgraded to an area office and kept that status until the 1990 reorganization of construction division. At that time, the office was redesignated the Kanagawa Project Office.

Zama Project Office

Lieutenant General Alexander Weyand, Commander, U.S. Army Japan/IX Corps, and Amy Dziuban, an elementary school student, cut the ribbon on the Arnn Elementary School on November 19, 1982.

The Zama Project Office managed all of the quality of life projects that have enriched the lives of U.S. forces and their dependents on the Kanto Plain. Projects in the early 80s included the three-phase project to replace the wooden structure that served as an elementary school until it burned in 1976. The new school opened in August 1982. The school was named after Major John Arnn who died in Vietnam in 1965. Major Arnn was devoted to helping others and was particularly concerned with the needs of orphans and children. He walked over 2,000 miles and climbed Mt. Fuji 27 times to raise money

The townhouses (left) were the first new housing on Zama in several years and helped alleviate a serious housing shortage. The new child care center (above) served the entire Zama community and was located at the Sagamihara Housing Area. Its grand opening in 1983 was held in conjunction with a Christmas party.

for a new orphanage, Garden Of Light, in Kyushu. [21]

Eighty-four new townhouses funded by the government of Japan opened on Camp Zama in February 1983. The project cost $17 million. Prior to the opening, housing was critically low on the base. In addition to new family quarters, a new 38 unit BEQ was turned over for occupancy at the same time. [22]

A new $1.2 million GOJ child development center opened its doors at Christmas 1983. The 9,500 square foot center consolidated three existing structures.

Late in 1984, JED was called upon by the State Department to assist in Japan's EXPO '85. This unique opportunity was one of the few times the district had worked for another agency under the Corps' then Federal Engineer Program. Serving in an advisory capacity, four of JED's engineers, John Pinkham, Haruo Nagano, Kiyoto Fujita and Katsuhiro Murai, joined with the United States Information Agency project managers to assist in the design of the administrative office area of the U.S. National Pavilion and to provide technical support in reviewing designs for the remainder of the facility. EXPO '85 ran from March 17 through September 16 and brought together technological advances from many nations. Over 20 million visitors attended the science exposition which promised to "chart man's future course."[23]

Camp Zama was the recipient of the Army Community of Excellence Award for small posts overseas in 1989 due largely to the construction of quality of life projects and several new administrative offices which were constructed from 1985 to 1989.

One of these is Zama's most popular facility, the Camp Zama golf club house. A ribbon cutting for the 4,770 square foot club house was held on June 23, 1986. Designed by Taisei Corporation, the

The roof of the U.S. Pavilion resembled a giant sailing ship. The theme of the pavilion was "Dwellings and Surroundings, Science and Technology for Man at Home."

A $250,000 MILCON project, completed in 1988, added the administration and starter booth, pro shop, locker rooms and meeting rooms (right) to the main golf course clubhouse (above).

The completion of Zama's new exchange with Burger King, (above) brought the first "fast food" restaurant to the base. The photo below shows the new exchange (center of the photo) as well as the old wooden structure (left) it replaced. To the right of the exchange is a new library/ education center completed in July 1987.

structure is an adaptation of Dr. Etsuro Suzuki's famous dome structure. Suzuki, a past board member of Taisei, pioneered the development of the dome and has lectured on this type of architecture in the United States. The $461,000 project was paid for with non-appropriated funds. In the first year that income from the golf course was used to support the Camp Zama's morale, welfare and recreation fund, the golf course made over $800,000. An addition to the initial project completed the facility and added a new starter's box, a pro shop and employee locker rooms.[24]

Construction of the new AAFES exchange, a $5 million GOJ project, began in March 1987. Its 49,000 square feet hold the main retail store, a convenience store, Baskins Robbins, Burger King, Anthony's Pizza, a merchandise processing and receiving area, unloading dock and administrative offices. The exchange opened its doors just before Christmas 1988.

Construction projects at Zama's Kastner Army Airfield were funded by GOJ, MILCON and O&M funds. The government of Japan

provided a new hangar — a 32,791 square foot, two-story facility large enough to hold all of the unit's Blackhawk helicopters. The hangar was completed in February 1988 at a cost of $4.2 million. GOJ also funded a new $495,250 fire station and replacement fuel oil storage tank, at the airfield, enhancing safety for the pilots, crews and aircraft.[25]

MILCON projects at the airfield included a 15,000 gallon underground fuel storage tank and a new 7,433 square foot, $1.5 million operations building.[26]

GOJ built a new building for the 294th Military Police Company Provisional ending their previous occupancy of one of the wooden structures built for the Imperial Army Military Academy.

The new hangar (in the right of the above photo) dwarfs the hangar it replaced (left of the photo). The fuel storage tank, fire station, operations building and control tower surround the airfield. The new hangar could accommodate all the battalion's Blackhawks (left) greatly reducing the time required for maintenance.

Completion of this $1.3 million facility in May 1988 paved the way for construction of JED's new headquarters building on the site of the old PMO offices.[27]

A telephone exchange, a new 33,000 square foot, $4.7 million headquarters building for the 500th Military Intelligence Brigade and a $1.9 million headquarters for the 1104th Signal Brigade provided better working conditions for many of Zama's military personnel and civilians.

The new building (below) for the Military Police consolidated the MP Station, Provost Marshall's Office, vehicle registration and pass office in one location. It also replaced an old wooden structure that dated from World War II (above).

131

Located in the 33,690 square foot Education Center, are a library, media center, admin offices for the Academic Training Division, classrooms for the University of Maryland, Central Texas College and the University of Oklahoma.

Zama's new child care center (right) allowed the child development program to expand and include full-time programmed care for infants. The new building for the 500th MI Brigade (below) includes a SCIF area.

Additional projects at Zama during the 80s include a new commissary at the Sagamihara Housing Area, renovations to the Zama chapel, and a new education center with a library and classrooms for adult education opened in the summer of 1987.

Projects completed in 1990 included a new child care center, bank and a new middle school which is connected to the award winning Zama High School and a new Visual Information Center for the U.S. Army Japan and 17th Area Support Group.

Work in progress at the beginning of FY91 includes new townhouses and a sewage treatment plant at Sagamihara and two highrises and a transient billet on Zama.

Atsugi Field Office

The projects managed by the Atsugi Field Office over the last ten years have greatly enhanced the quality of life for sailors and Marines at this small naval air facility on the Kanto Plain. Currently one construction inspector mans the field office; there were two inspectors assigned to the office in 1980 when it was opened in conjunction with the construction of Atsugi's highrise apartments.[28]

In the early 80s several GOJ projects were completed at the air facility. Two nine-story highrise apartment buildings, as well as new townhouses at the base, were completed in November 1981 along with supporting projects such as steam and electrical supply lines, a telephone distribution system, and an addition to an existing boiler plant.

In addition to the badly needed housing, a new post exchange was completed in February 1983. The $2 million GOJ facility included a snack bar, Baskin Robbins ice cream shop, florist shop, video rental and optical shop.

These highrises (above) were completed in the early 80s. The 90s will bring more housing and highrises to the base. The new post exchange (left) at Atsugi was a welcome addition to the base.

By the summer of 1983 a four-story BEQ and two additions to the elementary school were turned over to the Navy. The elementary school upgrade provided a kitchen, facilitating a new hot lunch program, and four new classrooms including a Japanese culture room with traditional tatami mat floors.

In 1984 a new GOJ funded enlisted dining facility costing $912,000 opened its doors to the sailors and Marines. The facility provided a seating capacity of 300 and 7,198 square feet filled with new furniture, chillers, a flight rations room and a large kitchen.

The new dining facility was completed in 1984.

133

Environmental projects in 1983 included a $4.5 million hush house designed to reduce noise pollution on the base and a third sewage treatment plant for the air facility.

Hush house (right) and new P-3 hangar (below) were just two of many projects completed at Atsugi during the 80s.

In the mid to late 80s, the Atsugi Field Office began large projects in support of the air facility's flight mission. Included in these projects was a maintenance hangar for the Navy's P-3 Orions completed in the summer of 1990. The hangar includes two maintenance bays equipped with overhead cranes and an attached two-story admin building which includes a computer room, briefing room, library, communications center and operations office.

A ribbon cutting was held in August 1989 for a $10 million Aircraft Intermediate Maintenance Department (AIMD) building. The two-story, steel-framed structure provides 69,500 square feet for 72

The AIMD (above and right), one of the largest buildings on Atsugi, includes an X-ray room, jet engine maintenance shop, film processing room, paint shop, welding shop, avionics repair shop and battery room.

separate rooms. These include a wide variety of speciality shops like X-ray, tool, jet engine maintenance, film processing, paint, engine parts storage and administration shops, all located on the first floor. The second floor houses a screen room, avionics repair shop. battery room, production control room, quality assurance and training and conference rooms. The AIMD facility was funded by the government of Japan.[29]

Additional Atsugi projects completed in the 80s include a new gate guard facility with sleeping quarters for the Japanese employees who man the front gate, a vehicle pass section and a brig to detain drunk or disorderly drivers at the base. A special services center for arts and crafts and other classes opened in the mid-80s.

Above: Gate guard facility. Below: A new medical/dental clinic provides space for expanded care for the sailors and Marines and their families at the air facility.

As the 90s begin, Atsugi is busy with two new nine-story high-rises. A growing population has forced a majority of personnel assigned to Atsugi to seek quarters off base. The new housing, scheduled for completion in the spring of 1991 and early 1992, will provide two and three bedroom apartments for the Navy families.

Camp Fuji

Like Atsugi, the Camp Fuji Field Office was established to supervise the construction on one major project — a new $11 million base camp for the Marines stationed at the foot of Mt. Fuji. The primary mission of Range Company, Camp Fuji, is to provide a live fire training base. It is one of the few bases outside the United States where the Marines can fire virtually all weapons in their arsenal including tanks, small arms and artillery. Training areas for these exercises cover 34,000 acres. While the number of Marines permanently stationed at the base camp is only 90, the population can swell to over

1,500 as units from the United States and Okinawa spend up to twelve weeks at a time training.

The new construction was prompted by a tragic fire at the camp in 1979. Typhoon Tip, a major typhoon which swept over the Kanto Plain, overturned several barrels of fuel stored above ground. The fuel spilled, ran downhill through the area housing the Marines and ignited. One Marine was killed and 41 seriously injured by the fire that ripped through the camp.[30]

Construction began at the base camp in May 1981. Marines began moving into the new GOJ furnished facilities in April 1983. Construction at the new camp provided the Marines with BEQ's which house 90 men in 3-man rooms with a bath in each room, a BOQ, messhall, guardhouse, administration building, fire station, roads and water, electricity and communications system. A POL tank farm should ensure that a fire like the one that overtook the Marines never happens again.

By July 1984, additional construction was underway for six open bay BEQs, a medical/dental clinic, a larger messhall and head-quarters building, a PX and a club. In addition, there's a new boiler plant, an ammunition storage facility, a cold storage facility and racquetball courts. All of the construction was completed before the decade drew to a close.[31]

Prior to Typhoon Tip, Marines training at Camp Fuji could call quonset huts (above) home. The new headquarters/administration building (right) was one of the first buildings completed after Typhoon Tip. Since Camp Fuji is one of the few Marine Corps bases outside the United States that allows live fire, the ammo igloos (below) were a needed project.

The new BEQs can be seen in the center of the photo. Immediately in front of the three story buildings are the new dining facility and medical/dental facility. Behind the BEQs is the huge training area.

Yokota Project Office

Prior to 1971, the Yokota Project Office had a thriving workload and nine employees to manage the projects. By 1974, however, the situation had changed and the office was closed. It reopened in March 1980 with five employees.

One of the first large projects of the decade was the MILCON funded Yokota West Elementary School. At the time it was constructed the $7.2 million school was one of the largest U.S. funded projects on the island of Honshu.

From start to completion, the school progressed on schedule due to a good network analysis and the school was turned over to the user on September 2, 1983.

Clearing the site for the school included the removal of over 120 trees to a nesting area for the duration of construction. Yokota West Elementary School was designed by Onuma-Wood, the same A-E firm that designed the award-winning Zama High School. Takenaka and Mabuchi construction companies were the contractors on the joint venture. The Japanese crane, a symbol of happiness in Japan, decorates the inside and the outside of the school.[32]

Tsutomu Mita (Inspector, Yokota Project Office) visited with some new friends in the Oriental Garden in the school's cultural center.

The beautiful Yokota West School (right) is home to 500 lucky elementary students. The Yokota East Elementary School (below) received a $2.5 million addition in September 1983. The addition provided 11 new classrooms.

The opening of a $4 million incinerator at Yokota in April 1984 provided significant environmental and energy conservation benefits to the residents at the base. The incinerator replaced the process of burying waste disposal by burning all of Yokota's waste except for glass and rubber. The resulting ash, a fraction of the size of the original waste, is stored in one of the 24 ash cells located beside the incinerator. Each ash cell takes approximately five years to fill and is then permanently sealed. There is sufficient room at the site to provide ash cells to serve the base for 20 years.

The incinerator is equipped with a heat exchanger to generate heating steam for three of the tower apartments which house 210 Yokota families.

Yokota's incinerator saves energy and enhances the environment at the air base.

Although the theory behind the heat recovery system is not new, extremely modern technology was necessary to locate and monitor the heat recovery system in the incinerator facility. Funded by the government of Japan, the incinerator was built on property that served for years as the landfill for burying all of Yokota's waste products.[33]

Pacific Stars & Stripes Bookstore.

A ribbon cutting was held in July 1984 to mark the grand opening of the Pacific Stars & Stripes Bookstore at Yokota. Work began on the $200,000 project in May 1983 and was completed on June 29, 1984. The bookstore, located next to Yokota's banking facility and the main exchange, has 1,900 square feet and provides ample room for a wide variety of books and magazines. Until the store opened these items were located in a crowded corner of the main store. The contractor on the non-appropriated fund project was NEC Overseas Marketing.

A $20 million Defense Communications System Reconfiguration (DCSR) project was officially turned over to the 1956th Communications Information Systems Group in September 1984 ceremonies held at Yokota Air Base. The Yokota Project Office served as coordinator on the government of Japan project which began in March 1983.

The efforts of 19 contractors and a total of 482,000 man-hours went into the completion of the three-level, 66,000 square foot facility. Among these contractors were Ito, Ishihara and Rokugo, J.V. for architectural work, Toshiba Plant Engineering Company, Ltd., and Shin-Nihon Kucho for the mechanical work.

The most unique design feature on the facility was a special shielding in the basement area to minimize the emission of radio waves originating in the building. In order to ensure proper welding

During construction of the Communications Center, a sample of the welding techniques used on shielding was located on the site. Mr. Mita, left and Captain Steve Arn, inspect the sample.

techniques on this shielding, a sample was provided on the site for the contractors to study and duplicate.

A highlight of the ribbon cutting and turnover ceremonies came when Colonel Jan P. Huggins, Commander, 1956th Communications Information Systems Group, presented a special award to Mr. Tsutomu Mita, Yokota Project Office Inspector and GOJ coordinator on the project. He commended Mr. Mita for his outstanding work and dedication in the timely completion of the Defense Communications Systems Reconfiguration project.

The project was built under the GOJ's facility relocation program. In return for North Camp Drake at Asaka and major portions of Fuchu Air Station, the government of Japan agreed to construct a major communications facility at Yokota and a microwave facility at Fuchu. The Yokota Project Office was responsible for both portions of the project. The contract also provided for installation of two 1,500 kw generators installed in March 1985, a rectifier and a wide band equipment device at Fuchu, 150 parking spaces adjacent to the Yokota facility and fencing and landscaping.

While the work schedule was hectic and construction was hampered by the most severe winter weather Japan has seen in several years, the contractors stayed on schedule. The extra care and effort put forth by the contractors resulted in an accident free construction period.[34]

Runway repair has been an important mission for the project office over the years; the most recent work was done in 1987. Special challenges accompany each job at the runway due to the fact that it is a vital military airlift command center in the Pacific and cannot ever be completely closed to air traffic.

An aerial view of the Yotota runway shows the huge blocks.

The runway looks like a huge checker board, with each block measuring 20 feet by 25 feet. Blocks of concrete were broken, dug up, and replaced with new concrete. Several blocks that had been temporarily restored with asphalt were also scheduled for repair.

Like the runway at the Misawa Air Base, Yokota's runway can never be completely shut down so much of the work was done at night.

In all, 553 of these blocks were replaced under the contract. The original contract called for the repair of 396 blocks, but as the work progressed, the contractors found that more and more of the blocks needed to be replaced. Some of the original blocks were 30 to 40 years old.

Once the old blocks were removed, a base course, consisting of 2 feet of gravel, was laid. Then, the concrete was placed, resulting in a 13 inch thick wearing surface. Approximately 24 hours are needed to remove the old concrete and place the new. Another two to three days are required to allow the concrete to cure completely.

This repair work was the completion of major repairs to the runway that began in the fall of 1986 under an Air Force funded OMAF contract. During a 60-day closure of the runway at the beginning of the project, 465 blocks were replaced leaving 88 for the shorter duration monthly runway closures.

Maeda Road Construction and Taisei Road Construction companies were the contractors for the $5 million joint venture project. The repair work on the runway did not go unnoticed or unrewarded. For his efforts on this sensitive and important project, Don Tutor, project engineer, was named PACAF Civilian Project Manager of the Year by the Air Force.[35]

Other projects in the 80s in support of the air base included housing, airfield support facilities, work for the 5th Air Force Command and the DoD Special Representative. And a project on a tiny speck of an island in the Pacific kept the Yokota Project Office busy. The end of the decade saw an increase in both U.S. and GOJ funded work. Between 1986 and 1988 the workload increased almost 500 percent.

Included in the workload increase are two new highrises for Yokota residents. The 70 unit buildings will help alleviate the housing shortage on Yokota. One building will feature two bedroom units and the other, three bedroom units. New housing also included 11 senior officer quarters. Again, the new quarters, the first new SOQs in many years, were built to ease the housing situation.[36]

These new highrises provided the first new housing on Yokota in several years.

A high visibility, high priority project on Yokota was a hydrant fueling system. The 9,000 linear feet of stainless steel pipe that now runs under the apron and taxiway of the Yokota runway enables the planes to refuel directly from the fuel pipeline.

GOJ provided a vital support project to the hydrant fueling system by building a 100,000 barrel fuel storage facility. The new $6 million tank replaces three smaller tanks and significantly increases fuel storage capacity.

The Department of Defense Special Representative, headquartered at Yokota, got a completely new facility in December 1988. The $5.4 million structure presented special requirements for the folks at Yokota because of the strict security requirements that had to be met.[37]

A $6 million MILCON project to upgrade the 5th Air Force Command Center and improve command, control and communication capabilities was completed in April 1990. Like Commando Port in Misawa, this project was prompted by the KAL 007 incident.

The renovation work included upgrading the lighting system and interior finishes, providing additional electrical controls, replacing the existing fire sprinkler system and constructing an electrical support building. Phase I of the project was completed in June 1988 and involved approximately 35 percent of the interior upgrade work as well as the completion of an exterior cable distribution system and pneumatic tube system. Phase II was a 200 calendar day "no work" period designed to give the using activity the opportunity to relocate operations. In Phase III reconstruction of the central basement area and portions of the first floor was completed. Contributing to the construction difficulties was the fact that the building is also home to Headquarters, U.S. Forces Japan (USFJ). While USFJ offices were not included in the renovation, employees of USFJ and 5th Air Force continued to occupy the building during all phases of construction.

Contributing to the construction difficulties at the 5th Air Force Command Center was the fact that the building is also home to Headquarters, U.S. Forces Japan (USFJ). While the USFJ offices were not included in the renovations, employees of USFJ and 5th Air Force continued to occupy the building during all phases of construction.

Marcus Island, a triangular shaped island covering three-fourths of a square mile (740 acres), is the site of a United States Coast

Marcus Island is a small triangular shaped island over 1,000 miles from anywhere. The grand opening of the new administration building (below) was held on September 21, 1990.

Guard Long Range Aids to Navigation (LORAN) station, one of the most recent projects managed by the Yokota Project Office. The LORAN Station has a 700 foot antenna for radiation of the synchronized LORAN pulses. All ships and planes equipped with LORAN-C receivers can use these signals for precise navigation when two or more pairs of signals are present. Marcus' LORAN Station provides one leg of a star configuration of stations throughout the northwest Pacific that includes similar sites on Iwo Jima, Hokkaido, Guam and Okinawa.

The geographic location of the island — 1,020 miles southeast of Yokota (over 1,000 miles of that the Pacific Ocean) — created several challenges for the employees at the project office. Because the island is so isolated, the only visitors to the 24 Coast Guardsmen and 30 sailors from the Japanese Maritime Self-Defense Force on the island, come once a week on a C-130 supply plane. In addition, the salt water and exposure to the elements have taken their toll on the facilities.

The new one-story, multi-purpose building of reinforced concrete, completed by Kajima Corporation in September 1990 at a cost of $3.8 million, included officers' and enlisted men's quarters, dining hall, kitchen, guest rooms, classroom, administration rooms such as the commander's office, dispensary, mailroom, and recreation room. The kitchen will include dry and fresh food storage and a walk-in refrigerator and deep freeze.

As with the old building, the roof of the new building was constructed as a water catchment system. The administration and barracks building as well as the tennis court serve as a 32,000 square foot rain water catchment area — the only source of fresh water on the island. The rain water is transferred to 30,000 gallon holding tanks where it's purified and channeled as needed. The placing of concrete increased the need for fresh water and the contractor developed a method to collect water along the 1,380 meter runway.

Other challenges included monitoring the project and handling problems from 1,000 miles away. Transporting the bulk construction materials to the remote island was also difficult. Ships can off-load at Marcus but only make the trip twice a year. For the rest of their supplies, including food and mail — and construction materials — they rely on the weekly flight from Yokota.[38]

Yokosuka Project Office

The Yokosuka Project Office managed a thriving construction program in the 1980s. Early in the decade, several GOJ quality of life projects provided much needed facilities to this shore community.

The Yokosuka Officers'-Chief Petty Officers' Club (O-CPO) opened in early 1983. The two story design provided a kitchen and separate dining areas, game rooms and joint-use party and meeting rooms on the second floor. The club has its own swimming pool. One of the meeting rooms has Japanese style walls and a wooden beamed ceiling.

O-CPO Club, Yokosuka Naval Base.

The Marine Corps Barracks, a major command at the naval base, got a new headquarters/billet building unique to the entire Corps. The Yokosuka City Police have an office in the building allowing easy coordination between the host nation and the Navy security police. The barracks has its own pistol range, recreation center and weight room. The top floor houses the Marines assigned to the barracks.

A new MWR facility built at Yokosuka houses a Stars and Stripes bookstore, a deli, a package store and a hobby and craft shop. It is located with the base exchange and incorporates the majority of shopping facilities into one area.

By far one of the most exciting clubs anywhere in the world is the Yokosuka Enlisted Men's Club Alliance which opened its doors on May 27, 1983. The Club Alliance has an interesting history. For years, it was strictly an off-base club for enlisted personnel and their guests. In the early 60s, there was not another club like it anywhere in the world. The club is so famous that it is mentioned in James Michener's novel *Bridges at Toko-Ri* . But, over the years, the club had lost some of its popularity.

The exterior architecture of the Club Alliance serves as a covered pedestrian entrance to the base and houses the Marine Guard and Japanese Military Police.

Under the GOJ relocation program, the government of Japan offered to build a new club in exchange for the land occupied by the old facility. In reaching an agreement, however, it was determined by the user that the new club should retain some of the special characteristics of the old club including an entrance that opened outside of the gates of the naval base. That way, the sailors and Marines felt they could keep the feeling of a private, rather than a military, club.

A three-story facility, the club offers entertainment and recreation facilities that rival any existing club system in the world. The first floor of the building serves a dual purpose. The structure itself houses the new Marine guard gate and serves as the pedestrian entrance to the naval base. The Marine Sergeant of the Guard, the Industrial Security Office and the Civilian Personnel Office are all included on the main floor with spaces separate from the club.

The Club Alliance Disco is also on the first floor. It is an elaborate room decorated by combining shades of vivid red with mirrors and a revolving mirrored ball over the dance floor. A sophisticated sound system, including a control room for a disc jockey, is an integral part of the disco.

The second floor includes the main dining room, the American grill for short order meals and the English Pub and Game Room which features an old world atmosphere, stained glass windows, Kelly green furnishings and pool tables. There is also a well-equipped Video Game Room. The second floor houses the main kitchen for the club.

The Windjammer Ball Room, the Acey/Ducey Lounge, and the Country/Western Bar are located on the third floor. A little bit of Texas, complete with large posters of famous country-western recording artists and barroom type furnishings, makes this bar one of the most popular areas of the club.

The third floor also houses the admin offices, the yen sales facility, television viewing rooms, party rooms, and a laundry facility which serves all of the clubs on the base. The $6.5 million facility has a seating capacity of 1,100 persons and can accommodate seven live bands at one time. [39]

One of the decade's eagerly awaited projects was the GOJ relocation on the Armed Forces recreation center — the Sanno Hotel. Nestled in the shadow of the luxurious Tokyo Hilton, the Sanno Hotel aged somewhat less graciously than its neighbors and had outworn its welcome in the high rent district. On October 6, 1983, the Sanno personnel moved to their new address on Embassy Row in the Hiroo section of Tokyo.

The front gate to Yokosuka is part of the Club Alliance structure.

The old Sanno had an intriguing history despite its rundown condition.

Kanji characters welcome guests to the hotel's Japanese restuarant.

The New Sanno is located in the Hiroo section of Tokyo. Quality construction was provided by the contractors, Shimizu Kensetsu and Obayahsi Gumi Company, a joint venture and the Nikken Sekkei Architectural firm.

The Old Sanno Hotel is rich with history. Completed in 1932, the Sanno was one of the first western-style hotels in Tokyo and was considered one of the most beautiful buildings in the city. Located only a short distance from the National Diet Building (home of the Japanese legislature), it soon became the meeting place for many high ranking officials in the Japanese government.

Perhaps because of this, the Sanno seemed the perfect target in 1936 when a group of young Imperial Army Officers seized the hotel in a planned coup to overthrow the government. A 1983 article in the Pacific Stars & Stripes gives the following account of the takeover:

". . . the rebels killed the finance minister, a former prime minister, and a dozen other anti-military government leaders before surrendering three days later on orders of Emperor Hirohito, in whose name they had revolted. One officer disemboweled himself in the ritual Hara-Kiri before a small Shinto shrine that still stands at the Sanno entrance."

The hotel became known as "Ni-Ni Roku" (2-26) after the February 26 incident and many Japanese still refer to the hotel by that name.

At the end of World War II, the Sanno, one of many surviving structures in Tokyo, was taken over by the U.S. occupation forces dusted off and used to house American military officers and their families. It was later opened to lower ranking officers and senior enlisted men. In 1975, it became a recreation center.

As part of the relocation agreement between U.S. Forces Japan and the government of Japan, the old hotel was replaced by a modern $34 million facility. GOJ gained back some extremely valuable real

148

estate, and the military and civilian patrons who use the Sanno got a new facility.

The New Sanno has the same number of rooms but each room has a private bath. The exterior of the hotel is modern and impressive. There is underground parking for Sanno guests. The inside is beautifully decorated with modern controls to assure comfort and convenience. The front desk includes a sophisticated room control system. When the room key is removed from the key storage panel, that room comes alive with lights and heating or air conditioning so it's ready for the guest when the door is unlocked.

"Twelve Kimonos" graces the lobby area of the new hotel.

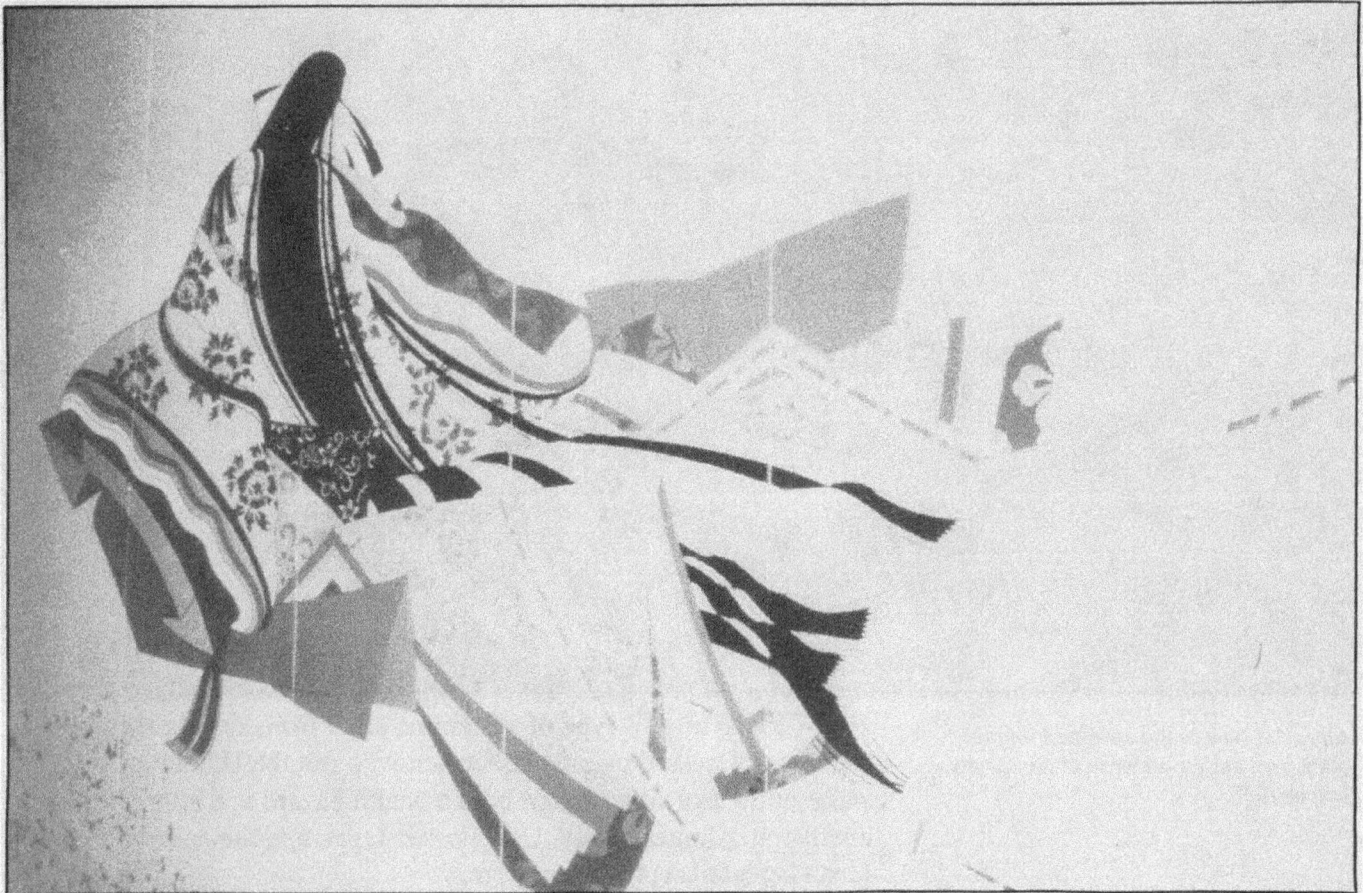

One entire wall of the main dining room is covered by a painted mural of two Japanese women. Across from the elevators on the main floor is another mural — this one porcelain — which is named Iyuni-Hitoe, meaning "Twelve Kimonos." It is a portrayal of a famous Japanese girl in 12 kimonos of the type worn in Japan over 1,000 years ago.

The hotel took 27 months to build and was completed on schedule. It has been booked consistently since the day it opened and serves a vital function for all U.S. forces in Japan.[40]

149

Environmental work at Yokosuka included a new ship-to-shore sewage collection system and a sewage treatment plant. In November 1981, work began on the system and by March 1982 the second phase of the project, the sewage treatment plant, was underway. On May 20, 1983, a Shinto ceremony and ribbon cutting marked the official opening of the treatment plant and the successful completion of these extremely complex and sensitive projects.

An aerial view of the sewage treatment plant as it appeared while under construction in 1983.

Plans for this type of system resulted from environmental concerns expressed by area fishermen who felt the U.S. ships dumping waste in the bay area created both a health hazard and a threat to their livelihood. Consequently, U.S. Forces Japan and the government of Japan began plans for the system.

A unique aspect of the design is based on the fact that the sewage from U.S. ships is salt water borne. Japanese engineers had little or no experience with salt water borne sewage. A study team, made up of representatives from the Naval Public Works Center, the Japanese government, and Nihon Koei Company, an engineering consulting firm, traveled to Pearl Harbor to examine an existing system. Plans for the Norfolk and San Diego systems were studied as well.

An incredible amount of cooperative effort went into the planning and execution of the system. Seven contractors, working simultaneously, were needed to complete the project on time. The construction was designed and supervised by Nihon Koei Company, an international architectural engineering firm headquartered in Tokyo.

Most of the construction, especially for the ship-to-shore system, was done along the waterfront. The biggest problem to come up during construction was in this area. The base is a very old Imperial Navy Base and some water lines and live power lines were not clearly marked in the old drawings. In a very confined area, the contractors were dealing, not only with power lines, but with steam, compressed air lines and salt and fresh water lines. Adding sewage lines to this already overly crowded area was extremely difficult. There were some power and telephone outages and broken water lines during the waterfront stage of construction.

The ship-to-shore system consists of pipelines which receive ship sewage that has been collected and held in the ships' holding tanks during transit within Tokyo Bay. During in-port periods, all the ships' sewage is pumped into the shore system for treatment. The system is designed to handle a variable flow as opposed to a continuous flow required by most systems. When ships are in port, the system must be able to handle an extremely heavy flow which is not required at other times.

The sewage treatment plant has several unique design properties. The plant relies on bacteria for treatment of waste and bacteria are not tolerant to changes in the salinity of the water. Designing a treatment plant for salt water borne sewage from ships and fresh water sewage from facilities on the base was very difficult. The system is designed to have minimum fluctuation of salinity levels so that the high standards for quality and safety of the discharged effluent can be maintained.

Because the majority of Japanese residents living in the bay area depend on the fishing industry for their livelihood, the sewage treatment plant was an extremely welcome facility. Few construction projects have as great an impact on the environment and on the quality of life of the people they serve as the $16 million treatment plant.[41]

By 1984, several more GOJ projects were open for the residents of Yokosuka. Towers 9 and 10, nine-story, 48 two-bedroom unit highrises, were completed, providing housing for couples and one-child families.

A $2.7 million dining facility provides 18,670 square feet of gleaming white tile, waterfalls and Japanese gardens and seating for over 600. A separate dining room for E-7s and above, a patio for outside dining, lots of glass to let the sunlight in and air conditioning to keep the sun's heat out make the dining facility popular with the users. The reinforced concrete structure was designed by Mabuchi Kensetsu of Tokyo.

Like many bases in Japan, housing at Yokosuka is a critical concern. The above photo shows an overview of the highrises and townhouses on the crowded base.

151

The new personnel support facility on Yokosuka.

Admiral Togo (above) and the traditional Japanese garden (right).

A personnel support facility (PSF) was turned over to the Navy on April 19, 1984. The three-story, $5.1 million building provides 55,121 square feet of space to the banking facility, Navy Relief, Navy Finance, the Red Cross, Navy Campus, the University of Maryland, Central Texas College, and the University of Southern California. Court rooms for the staff judge advocate, a community center and one main processing area where personnel can have IDs made, apply for passports and visas, file travel vouchers and in- and out process are also located in the building.

Special design features include an attractive and functional layout and wheel chair access for handicapped patrons to every part of the building. There is also an elevator in the facility, unusual in GOJ constructed buildings. Construction began on the PSF in April 1983 and drew much community interest as it neared completion. Both the dining facility and PSF were funded under the GOJ facilities improvement program.

A ribbon cutting ceremony was held at Yokosuka Naval Base on August 21, 1984 to officially open the new Unaccompanied Officer's Personnel Housing (UOPH) facility built for the Navy by the government of Japan. The new building houses unaccompanied officers as well as transient officers and visitors to the base. There are 62 apartments in the 43,958 square foot, three-story structure. Each apartment has a well-equipped kitchen, a living area, a bedroom, and a private bath. Located on the site of the old officer's club, the new building is reinforced concrete — a total of 6,000 tons of concrete.

By far the most outstanding feature of the facility is the Togo Room, the $14,000 VIP quarters named for Admiral Heihachiro Togo, Admiral of the Japanese Naval Fleet. Admiral Togo was born in Japan

152

in 1847 at Kyushu. He studied in England and served for two years in the British Royal Navy before being appointed to the Imperial Japanese Navy. In 1906, with Admiral Togo as commander-in-chief, the Combined Fleet annihilated the Russian Fleet in the Russo-Japanese War. The admiral died in 1934.

The original Togo Room was built in his honor in 1928 and was tediously moved to its new location in the UOPH. Material salvaged from the palace of His Imperial Highness Admiral Prince H. Fushimi, destroyed by the great earthquake of 1923, was used in the original structure and was moved to the new Togo Room.

Complete with an authentic Japanese garden, the quarters are furnished with antique rosewood pieces and artifacts belonging to both Fushimi and Togo, including a samurai sword and headdress. The smell of Japanese white cedar, used in the entry way and walls of the quarters, along with the sounds from waterfalls in the garden, create an atmosphere of peace and tranquility and provide VIP visitors with a uniquely Japanese experience. In the spring of 1985 a second wing opened adding 52 additional apartments to the UOPH in Phase II of the project. [42]

The last half of the decade brought an abundance of new, highly sophisticated construction to the Yokosuka Project Office. One of Yokosuka's biggest projects in the 80s was the construction of utility tunnels which began in March 1987 and is scheduled for completion in 1992.

Phase I of the work used the open trench method to complete 1701 feet of tunnels with an average size of 12.5 feet high by 10 feet wide. This process of digging up streets and sidewalks caused major disruptions to base traffic — pedestrian and vehicular alike.

Ground was broken for Phase II of the tunnelling work on October 1, 1988 and will add 1,114 meters of tunnels to the network. To prevent any further disruptions to the already chaotic traffic conditions, the government of Japan opted to use the shielded tunnel method (boring).

Featured in the boring method was the Slurry Shield Tunnelling Machine — a 95-ton piece of equipment that is capable of advancing 6 feet per hour or of moving 27.7 cubic meters of earth per hour. Super hard bits attached to the cutter rotate clockwise and counterclockwise to scrape the soil. Excavated soil is pumped out of the machine with slurry that acts as a vehicle to carry the cut earth to a treatment plant. In the treatment plant, the mixture is separated into slurry and muck and the slurry transferred back to the tunnel face for reuse.

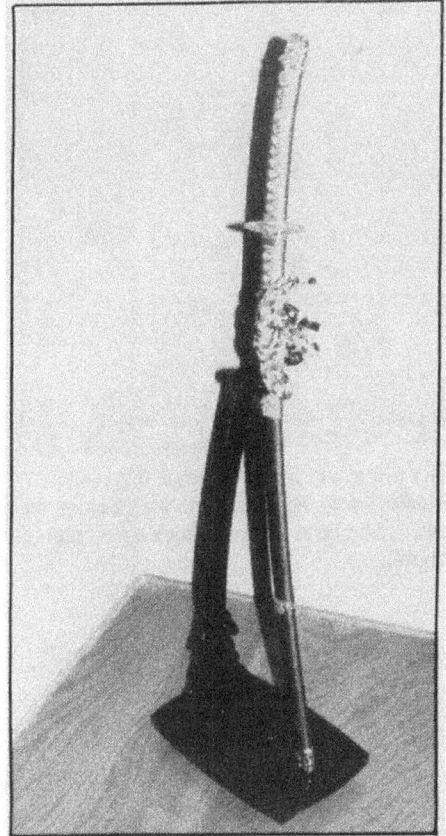

The sword (above) and headdress (below) grace the Togo Room.

The photo at the right shows the Slurry Shield Tunnelling Machine as it begins its job. The photo above shows a completed tunnel.

When completed in 1992, Yokosuka will have a network of underground tunnels covering 2.2 miles that will carry all utilities except steam and sewer to each of the ships berthed at Yokosuka. The $15 million project was funded by the government of Japan and was a joint venture between Zenitaka-Dainippon-Asakawa companies.[43]

A $6.4 million parking garage/administration building for the Naval Supply Depot was completed in March 1988 and provides 251 parking spaces.

A $20 million Naval Supply Depot general purpose warehouse located adjacent to the parking garage was completed in July 1990.

The new NSD warehouse (left) is one of the largest buildings on the base.

The three-story structure provides 65,794 square feet of storage space for admin offices, a mechanical room, and general, dry, humidity controlled, security and medical storage areas. Previously, NSD relied on pre-World War II warehouses for storage. Making room for the warehouse and parking garage involved cutting into a hillside and moving over 27,000 cubic meters of earth.

Prior to the completion of the trash incinerator facility in October 1988, all trash generated on Yokosuka had to be transported to an off-base incinerator. The $19 million facility burns all waste products from the base and has a plastic reduction capability for non-burnable waste.

A high visibility project at Yokosuka was the new electrical distribution system. The $2.2 million MILCON project provided four permanent and one relocatable substation for berth 12 — home of the U.S.S. Midway — and drydock 6 the largest drydock in the Pacific. The project completed in December 1988 also included the addition of two pier electrical outlets. Prior to the upgrades, electrical power was provided by temporary substations.

Interior of the trash incinerator at Yokosuka.

Security was enhanced at the Urago ammunition storage area, 5 miles north of Yokosuka, with a project to add 37 security lights and a perimeter security fence. The $500,000 improvements were completed with GOJ funds under the Facilities Improvement Program.

The Tsurumi Oil Depot received an improved drainage system and an oil leakage detection system during 1988 under an GOJ initiative. The Tsurumi area is operated by the U.S. Navy but provides storage space for all the services. The $3 million project provided for oil detection and oil separation to control accidental spills.

155

Yokohama North Dock.

In addition to the locations already mentioned, the Yokosuka staff also provides support to the 19 organizations assigned to Yokohama North Dock.

Building 219, the home of AAFES Yokohama Transportation Center, was one of Yokosuka's few OMA projects. The $190,000 repairs to the office building, completed early in 1988, included replacing roofing, gutters, windows and doors to include security screens on the storage area.

Similar repairs were completed in May 1988 on another building at North Dock — building 347, home to the Directorate of Engineering and Housing sub facility engineer, and the cargo operations division of the 334th Transportation Detachment.[44]

When Secretary of Defense Dick Cheney toured the Far East in February 1990, he stopped at Yokosuka Naval Base where he saw several district projects. Among those he visited were the harbor master pier and the new Yokosuka Nile C. Kinnick High School.

The harbor master tradition was rekindled at Yokosuka when the government of Japan began construction on a new harbor master pier in August 1989. In the years before the Vietnam conflict, harbors were controlled by a harbor master and the job was an important one at Yokosuka. The harbor master worked out of a three-story building on a floating steel pontoon pier originally constructed in 1935. The pontoon pilot lived on the top floor of the building and the bottom two floors were used by the harbor master. Oilers, tugs, water barges and other small craft berthed along side the pier but, since no larger craft could dock there, it was never considered a berthing pier.

During the Vietnam conflict, the harbor master organization was replaced by the port control. The port control began numbering the berths at Yokosuka with the submarine berths and continued in a clockwise rotation. Since the harbor master pier wasn't a berthing pier, a number wasn't assigned and the name remains to this day and, at least until the new pier is completed, it will continue to be referred to as the harbor master pier.

Dredging for the new pier began in July 1989 and was completed by August. Approximately 52,000 cubic meters of dredged material were disposed of in the Pacific Ocean near the Marianas Trench to avoid interference in the local fishing industry. The dredging resulted in an area 230 meters long and 190 meters wide. The depth of the area is 11.6 meters or 38 feet. Dredging on the area surrounding the construction site was completed in January 1990. This phase of the construction cost $3.7 million.

With the ground breaking ceremony on August 30, 1989, the first pile was driven and construction began on the new harbor master pier. Completed in November 1990 at a cost of $7.7 million, the pier

Secretary of Defense Dick Cheney was briefed by Captain Bill Weed of the Kanagawa Resident Office on the progress of the Harbor Master Pier.

is 170 meters long and 27 meters wide and is used to dock Frigate class ship which include some of the largest ships at Yokosuka. The previous steel pontoon pier was only 20 meters wide and provided a total of 130 meters of berthing space making it too short to accommodate the current types of ships at Yokosuka.

Construction of the permanent concrete pier included open type piles supporting a platform structure that allowed water to flow underneath, mooring lines, anchors and bumper guards.

TOA Kensetsu Kogyo Co., Ltd. was the contractor for the dredging portion of the project; Goyo Kensetsu, Toyo Corporation and Saeki Kensetsu built the pier in a joint venture.

Yokosuka's new high school replaced an old, converted 1934 barracks building. On November 4, 1989, the day of the school's annual homecoming game, the ribbon was cut on a new, modern facility furnished by the government of Japan. For 50 years the aging building served the naval base. In the final phase of the new high school project, the building was torn down.

The construction of the new $22 million Kinnick High School was the result of close coordination between the school's department heads and Onuma and Onuma, the architectural company. The department heads' committee produced a list of features they felt would create the best atmosphere for promoting secondary education. Their ideas included a cafeteria run by the Navy Exchange, new furniture and fixtures, computer capable classrooms, business lab, science lab, drama room, shops, art room and band room, each designed for their specific purposes, and an oversized gymnasium. In addition, the committee felt central air throughout the structure was a necessity.

The new library at Kinnick High School.

The old Kinnick High School has been demolished after 50 years of use at the base.

To accommodate these requests, Onuma and Onuma came up with a design of a complex of six buildings to be built around the existing school. That structure was torn down in the final phase of construction and the area landscaped into a courtyard in the center of the new facility.

One of the six buildings contains the library and cafeteria; another the main classroom building. There is a shop and gym building, an administration building, a music and drama building and an air conditioning and heating building. The school was completed prior to the 90-91 school year. [45]

Iwakuni Resident Office

The arrival of Iwakuni's F/A-18 Hornets in 1987 provided the impetus for a build-up of base facilities.

The Iwakuni Resident Office is located on Iwakuni Marine Corps Air Station in southwestern Japan. Steep mountains crowd toward the sea behind the flat slice of coastal plain making the area one of Japan's most beautiful.

Although the construction workload in the early 80s was sufficient to support a project office, a significant increase in workload in the mid-80s was directly related to the beddown of the Marines F/A-18 Hornets on July 12, 1987. Housing and operation support facilities for the air station continues to keep the resident office employees busy into the 90s.

Construction of the DoDDs Matthew C. Perry School, a $6.5 million facility for children in grades 1-12, was the largest project at the air station when construction began in December 1981. Kajima Kensetsu Company, contractors on the MILCON project, finished the school for the 1983-84 school year. BEQs, BOQs, mid-rises, townhouses, a fuel tanker mooring, a hush house, a sewage treatment plant, dining facility, and a new transient billet — the Iwakuni Hostess House — were all completed between 1983 and 1986.[46]

The Hostess House replaced an old, condemned building dubbed the "Hostage House" by Iwakuni residents. The September 30, 1983 opening of the MILCON funded, 15,000 square foot, $1.2 million facility marked the completion of a historic event for JED. The contract for the Hostess House was the first contract awarded by the district after the district engineer received contracting officer authority.

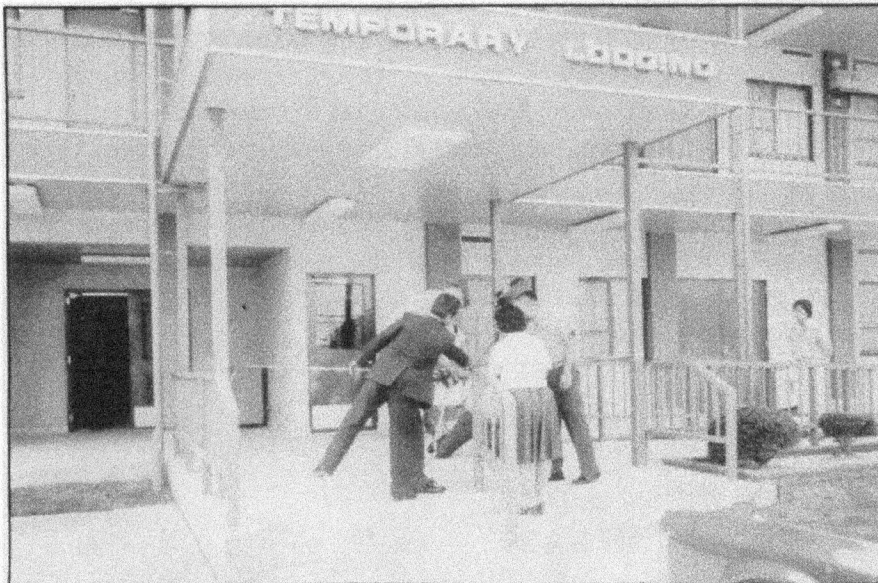

Designed by Pacific Architects and Engineers, the Hostess House (left) was constructed in a joint venture, by Tokimori Kensetsu Company, Ltd., and Matsumoto Kensetsu Company, Ltd. The rooms (below) were a welcome addition to the base.

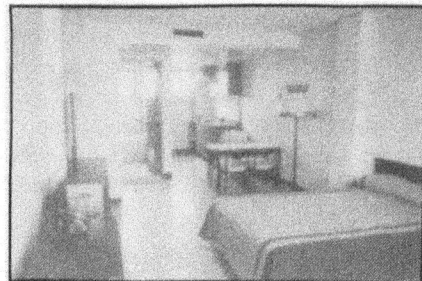

All of the soldiers stationed at Akizuki's Kure Pier #6 are there on unaccompanied tours. After years of being overlooked in terms of quality of life facilities, the soldiers got a new headquarters and new barracks in the mid-80s compliments of the government of Japan. Included in the project which enhanced the lives of the Kure Pier residents were recreation facilities and a new handball court, tennis courts and exercise rooms along with larger living quarters.

By 1987 several facilities for the F/A-18 Squadron VMFA 115 were completed or nearing completion. Two MILCON projects that directly supported the aircraft were an operational trainer facility — a building that will house an F/A-18 flight simulator — and the van pads.

The simulator serves VFMA 115 but also serves carrier based F/A-18s and is important for several reasons. Not only is it the first of its kind in the Pacific, it will also provide invaluable training for the pilots. The simulator is basically the cockpit of an F/A-18 attached to a computer that provides flight information to simulate situations such as daylight and night landings and in-flight emergencies.

By taking training out of the actual cockpit, the simulator saves maintenance and fuel costs, and provides training unavailable to the pilots in the actual jets. Work on the simulator began in September

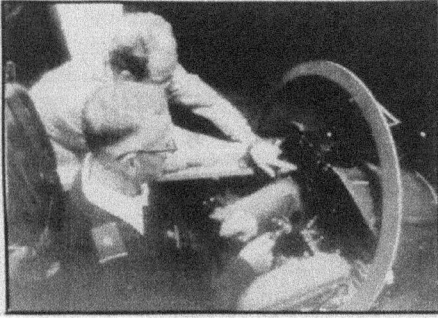

Brigadier General Arthur Williams, Commander, Pacific Ocean Division, got a first hand look at the simulator during his visit to JED in March 1988.

Freedom Bridge, Iwakuni.

1986 and was completed by Takahashi Soshoku Co., Ltd. October 31, 198 at a cost of $842,000.

Also important to the F/A-18 squadron was the completion of the van pads — paved asphalt/concrete areas with utility hookups including electricity, water, compressed air, computer and telephone conduits. Miles of utility lines run several feet underground to support the vans.

The van pads accommodate up to 400 fully mobile, self-contained vans (except for power). The vans house equipment costing anywhere from $35,000 to $1 million. This equipment is used to repair aircraft components. Construction on the van pads began in November 1985 and was completed in June 1987 by Sumitomo Construction Company, Ltd. at a cost of $5.4 million.[47]

Another project completed in 1987 was Freedom Bridge. In December 1985 construction on the bridge over the Monzen River began and on October 2, 1987, Freedom Bridge was officially dedicated and opened to traffic.

The bridge connects the Monzen Housing Area to the air station. Prior to the completion of the $6.1 million bridge, Monzen residents had to drive approximately one mile on Japan Route 188 to reach the base. That one mile commute could take anywhere from 10 to 30 minutes depending on the time of day and traffic conditions. With the completion of the bridge, the trip takes two minutes.

160

The bridge alleviated traffic concerns and at the same time improved base safety by decreasing response time for emergency vehicles. In addition, school children no longer have to walk or bicycle along the heavily travelled highway.

The 802 foot (244.5 meter) GOJ-funded structure was constructed of post tensioned reinforced concrete girders. Due to the large size of the concrete girders, (40 and 44 meters), they were fabricated on the construction site and then moved on rails to be placed on the piers. A total of 132 piles, each 30 meters deep, and five piers provide support for the bridge. With a width of 30 feet, the bridge is designed to handle vehicle, pedestrian and bicycle traffic.[48]

On July 4, 1988, the ribbon was cut on Phase IA of one of the district's most ambitious projects — the construction of the Hario Housing Area. Until the completion of the housing area, Navy families stationed at Sasebo Naval Base lived on the Japanese economy in very small apartments or houses. They now have western-style housing plus a complete new city. The area provides wide open space for children to play — a luxury Japanese children do not share. And some of the things most of us take for granted — television and telephones — are now only a reach away. American television in Japan is available only on cable provided to military bases; Japanese telephones can cost up to $600.00 and are cost prohibitive for most families living off-base.

Construction began on the government of Japan project in October 1986 and approximately 100 contractors began simultaneous construction on a myriad of new facilities that now serves as home base for navy personnel and their families.

A new commissary at Iwakuni, completed in 1986, replaced a wooden structure. The new store offers 30,000 square feet of shopping and warehouse space as well as computerized checkouts, wide aisles and deli.

An overview of the new facilities at the Hario Housing Area.

Main entrance to the Hario Housing Area.

Highlights of Phase IA's $70 million facilities include:

•A nine story highrise consisting of 68 two-bedroom units and a child care center,

•Twenty-two townhouse buildings consisting of 52 two-bedroom units, 74 three-bedroom units and eight four-bedroom units,

•A gymnasium with basketball and volleyball courts, men's and women's locker rooms equipped with sauna and whirlpool baths, weight lifting room, exercise room and separate bathhouse for people using the swimming pool,

•A community support facility with Navy exchange, barber, beauty and dry cleaning shops, open mess, bank, post office and game room. The second floor of the building has a youth center, mini theater, library, office, classrooms and craft shops,

•A public works/communication support facility that accommodates the housing office, telephone exchange, FEN radio and television, battery rooms, maintenance shop and warehouse,

•An elementary school for students in grades kindergarten through six with office space, teachers' lounge, cafeteria, 10 classrooms, host nation room/culture room, library, conference room and nurse's office,

•A recreation area with a lighted softball field and tennis courts,

•A fire station.

Phase IA of the construction also included drainage, sewage and water systems, a steam distribution system, electrical and communication systems, fuel tanks, sewage treatment plant, water supply facility, boiler plant, roadwork and landscaping. Phase II will add

162

more housing as well as an expansion of the utilities and is scheduled to begin during 1991. The most recent project at the $200 million housing area is a recreation center. [49]

The district's longest running project has been the restoration of seven POL storage tanks at Yokose for the Navy Fuel Detachment. Originally built for the Japanese between 1937 and 1943, the tanks posed a threat to the environment and local fishermen when they began leaking aviation fuel into the water.

Yokose, with a total fuel storage capacity of 2.7 million barrels of petroleum, is the largest of three fuel storage areas on the island of Kyushu. Akasaki Depot has a total capacity of 1.2 million barrels and 1.3 million barrels can be stored at Iorizaki. In addition to providing fuel for U.S. Navy ships at Sasebo Naval Base and jet aircraft sta-

This aerial view of Yokose shows the seven tanks in various stages of completion.

Katsumi Harauchi was the project engineer on the Yokose tanks for 53 years. He died in 1990. He saw six of the seven mammoth tanks completed for the second time.

The workers in this photo show the scale of the tanks.

The interior of Iwakuni's new exchange.

tioned at Iwakuni Marine Corps Air Station, these three storage areas also service ships from Okinawa and Korea.

Katsumi Harauchi, electrical construction inspector for the tanks when they belonged to the Japanese navy, started working on the tanks in 1937 and spent the next 35 years working as a project engineer at the Navy Fuel Detachment (NFD), Sasebo. In his position at NFD, Harauchi reviewed tank designs and supervised necessary maintenance and repair work. Four months prior to his scheduled retirement from NFD, Harauchi transferred to the Corps of Engineers, bringing with him his extensive knowledge and experience in tank construction and operations.

The existing concrete tanks were adequate for storing the crude, heavy fuels of the past but needed to be rebuilt to properly and safely store the more refined, volatile, thinner fuels of today. The funding — an average of $10 million per tank — is provided under the facilities improvement program as a GOJ environmental initiative.

Harauchi saw a great improvement in safety and construction methods on the new tanks. Approximately 400 Japanese prisoners taken from Japanese jails built the original unreinforced concrete tanks using bamboo to vibrate the concrete. Today, the common electrical method of vibrating concrete is used.

The new tanks, which are literally being built inside the old tanks, are steel-lined, post tensioned reinforced concrete with fuel transfer pumps and lines. The reconstruction of the tanks involves removing the existing structural steel framing and roof slab of the original tanks. A 1.5 meter space separates the original and new walls and will be used for inspection purposes. To maintain the original fuel capacity, the new tanks are being built higher than the old ones. Each of the seven new tanks has an interior diameter of 279 feet with an exterior diameter of 288 feet. The 39 foot high tanks have a capacity of 380,000 barrels of 15,960,000 gallons each. Tanks one through six are completely renovated; tank seven will be completed by the end of 1990.[50]

Work completed by the Iwakuni Resident Office in the late 80s or under construction in 1990 includes two GOJ funded sonar dome/propellor pits at Sasebo for maintenance to the props of the giant ships berthed there, a new $1.8 million vehicle maintenance facility, a new medical/dental clinic, three microwave towers to enhance communications throughout Japan, and a $20 million addition to Sasebo's Harborview Club.

At Iwakuni, a $9.9 million base exchange funded by GOJ incorporates all retail outlets on the base providing one-stop shopping for the residents. A new 53,000 square foot medical/dental complex will replace a 1936 facility and construction of the final 20 new ammu-

Seaside Grill in the Harborview Club (above). And, the medical/dental clinic (left) at Sasebo Naval Base. The new clinic at Iwakuni (below) replaces the one with the scalloped tile roofs in the bottom photo. The original clinic was built during the 1936-1941 time frame with additions tacked on seemingly at random.

nition igloos by 1991 will complete a MILCON project at Kawakami that will provide 61 new storage igloos for all branches of the armed forces. This environmental project greatly enhances safety at the site.[51]

A new vehicle maintenance shop (above) and ammunition igloos (right) at Kawakami.

Okinawa Area Office

The early 80s saw a boom in quality of life projects for members of the armed forces stationed on Okinawa as well as support facilities for the Commando Nest F-15 beddown initiative discussed in Chapter 4. This increase in workload coincided with the end of Major Larry Ryan's tour as area engineer. Lieutenant Colonel Jerry Berry followed him as area engineer from October 1986 through August 1989. He was followed by Lieutenant Colonel Larry Talley.

The most important of the quality of life projects in support of Commando Nest was housing. With housing shortages at ten military installations on the island and 32,000 personnel in need of base housing, the task was immense and lasted throughout the decade and into the 90s. Facilities varied to meet the needs of each of the four services and ranged from fully-equipped BEQs and BOQs to highrise apartments.

Extensive reconstruction of the Kadena Officers' Club uncovered sprayed-on asbestos encapsulated on gypsum board. The asbestos was removed by taking out the entire wall units. Termites and a gutted kitchen added to the complications on the project but the club was turned over to the user in December 1981 in time for holiday celebrations.[52]

The NCO club on Kadena was renovated along with the officers' club (left). This picture (below) shows new kitchen appliances.

A GOJ funded junior-senior high school with an olympic-sized swimming pool and a child care center, both at Kadena, were projects completed in the early 80s. The child care center was the combination of a GOJ funded relocation project and a U. S. funded project added at the end of the GOJ construction to increase the size of the facility. With the combined square footage, the $657,000 center was large enough to accommodate the needs of the air base. The center opened in November 1983.[53]

Completion of the Stearly Heights Elementary School on time for the first classes of the 1984-85 school year took heroic effort by the contractor, Kobuka Gumi.

Typhoon Holly, a super-typhoon that struck the island in mid-August, cost the contractor five precious days of paving time. In spite of Holly's wrath, Kobuka Gumi persevered and the company's huge trucks rolled away from the completed school at 4 a.m. on August 27, 1984 — just four hours before the first bell on opening day. The $6

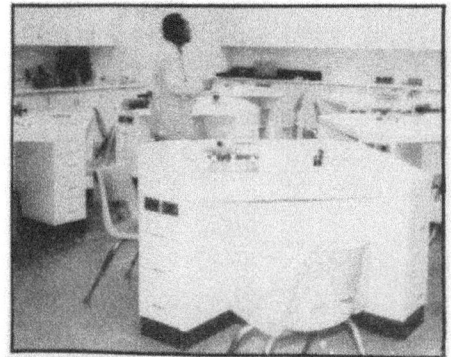

Inside Kadena's Junior/Senior High School (above), the Stearley Heights Elementary School (left) and a new child care center on Kadena (below).

167

million DoDDs school, funded by the government of Japan under its facilities improvement program, provided 56,800 square feet of space for the 650 elementary students entering the new school. In June 1984, a $2.1 million BEQ opened at Camp Buckner for personnel from the signal battalion. Before the barracks was completed, these personnel were spread out over several bases on the island.

Projects in support of Commando Nest included Kadena's first hush house completed in 1981. At that time it was the only noise suppression facility in the world for large aircraft. Hardened aircraft shelters provide protection for the Falcons against typhoons and, if necessary, hostilities. Fifty weather shelters for the F-15s were completed by 1983 and provided protection from the corrosive environment on Okinawa for the sophisticated aircraft and their electronic components. Until construction of the shelters, inclement weather often stalled repairs. The ground support crews servicing the aircraft benefited from the protection as well. [54]

Hardened aircraft shelters (above), weather shelters (right) and hush house (below) helped the airmen assigned to Kadena go their jobs in the early 80s.

An engine maintenance repair shop turned over in 1983 incorporated some of the most sophisticated construction ever done in Japan. Completely windowless, the facility's work areas are slightly pressurized to help keep out dust and humidity. The temperature in the engine repair areas can deviate no more than 2 degrees and the humidity no more than 5 percent. Precise electrical power is essential. The combined talents of the facility designers, the OAO staff, the contractor and the user were needed for the completion of this complex project.

Marines march past old NTA Headquarters building (left). The old television room is shown in the photo above.

The North Training Area (NTA) on Okinawa is a permanent home to some of the toughest Marines in the Corps. They're the men who train over 200 young Marines several times each year at the NTA's 12-day intensive survival training course which includes rappelling and extensive land navigation.

Before the government of Japan built a completely new $4 million camp, the Marines existed with Quonset huts and dusty, often muddy roads.

The new camp, completed in 1984, provided the men of the NTA with paved roads and a new headquarters building, a water treatment plant, sewage treatment plant and lighted tennis and basketball courts. In addition, the Marines got an officers' club, an enlisted men's club, a fully equipped medical facility, classrooms, a dining facility and new living quarters.[55]

A tank vehicle maintenance shop at Camp Schwab, a new base exchange at Kadena, a $5 million dispensary for the Marines at Camp Kinser and work at the Chimu-wan Tank Farm at Camp Courtney kept the office busy through the mid-80s.

A deserted home at Makiminato (above). A water tower (right) sits atop Sugar Loaf Hill -- site of one of Okinawa's most devastating battles during World War II. Sugar Loaf Hill was part of the Makiminato Housing Area.

The return of Makiminato Housing Area to the Japanese government in 1987 signified the end of the GOJ relocation program. In 1954, the Okinawa Engineer District provided permanent facilities for U. S. forces on Okinawa at Maki. The Makiminato Elementary School and 1,181 sets of family quarters, a commissary, fire department, post office and an officers' club were soon constructed for servicemembers and their families assigned to Naha Port and the Machinato Service Area, known today as the Marine Corps' Camp Kinser.

Most of the facilities to replace those given up at Maki were constructed on Kadena Air Base. Four mid-rises and 751 family housing units on Kadena, plus an additional 221 units on Camp Lester house former Maki residents. Another DoDDs school, Bechtel Elementary, was completed in the mid-80s for elementary school students

Housing such as these standard design townhouses (above) and highrises (right), both on Camp Kinser, were replacement housing for Makiminato.

Okinawa Expressway.

at Camp McTureous elementary school at Kinser completed the quid-pro-quo relocation construction.[56]

In 1987, the district joined forces with the Japan Highway Public Corporation (JHPC) to relocate military facilities, making way for a new major highway on the island.

The JHPC, in its first venture with the district, completed construction on a 32 kilometer addition to the Okinawa Expressway that opened for traffic in October 1987. This addition to the highway runs from Ishikawa to Naha and completes the 57.6 kilometer highway that runs north and south through the center of Okinawa.

The highway cuts through several U. S. installations: Kadena Ammunition Area, Camp Shields, Kadena Air Base and Plaza and Kishaba Housing on Camp Foster.

Because U. S. forces gave up portions of their facilities, JHPC built new facilities as part of a relocation program. Construction of 104 family housing units, 3 senior officers' quarters and a community center on Camp Courtney, which replaced the units lost at Foster, began in October 1984 and was completed in October 1985. A new

USO and transient airmen's quarters were completed at the same time on Kadena Air Base.

The total cost of the JHPC highway and the relocations totalled $1 billion; the relocations amounted to $54 million. JED was the administrative agency and Nishimatsu Construction Company was the contractor on these and several other relocation projects associated with the massive highway project. A 14,420 square foot warehouse at Camp Zukeran and a 4,000 square foot small ammunition storage facility at Camp Henoko were both completed in August 1987 at a total cost of $2 million. A 6,000 square foot ammunition storage facility at Kadena Ammunition Area was the final project of the relocation program. The $77 million igloos were completed in the spring of 1989.[57]

Typhoons are commonplace for the residents and the construction crews on the island. Often they delay construction; sometimes they destroy it. Typhoon Dinah, the strongest typhoon to hit Okinawa in since 1966, uprooted trees, knocked down fences, downed power lines and caused widespread power outages before moving up the western coast of Japan in September 1987.

U.S. facilities were not immune to Dinah's wrath as she dumped 10 inches of rain on Kadena Air Base and 107 mph winds caused extensive damage to several sites. A portable school building was damaged when a section of bleacher seats was thrown into the building. A 75-pound metal ventilation hood was blown off the roof of Kadena's Amelia Earhart Intermediate School into the school parking lot and several bleachers at a baseball field complex were flipped onto playing fields.

Dinah did serious damage to Pier Bravo on Okinawa (above) before moving on to Sasebo where she halted construction on an enlisted mess (right). Portions of a seawall at Sasebo were also washed away

Pier Bravo after construction completion.

Of immediate concern to the Okinawa Area Office, however, was the damage done to Pier Bravo at White Beach. A big chunk of the pier was literally washed away and the remainder of the pier suffered structural damage.

Dinah gave the Iwakuni Resident Office its own headaches when she struck the Sasebo area on the island of Kyushu. Construction on an enlisted mess came to a complete halt as workers surveyed the damage and began to clean up the site. Portions of a seawall were also washed away. When Dinah swept across Iwakuni, she was the third largest typhoon to hit the area in recorded history but the area escaped the widespread damage suffered on Okinawa.[58]

In spite of the damage done to the pier during the storm, the project was completed and turned over to the user in February 1989. It was a complicated project from the beginning. There were no as-built drawings and the contractor, Kokuba Gumi Company, Ltd., was required to open the pier, determine the existing conditions and then proceed with the repairs.

The $5 million project included construction of a new peripheral bulkhead complete with concrete pile caps, tie rods, a concrete retaining wall, mooring bit, steel pipe piles, steel sheet piles, rubber fender systems and a reinforced concrete deck. A new POL line and lighting package completed the project and it is now used to off load fuel to neighboring tank farms as well as to unload supplies for the Military Traffic Management Command.[59]

173

Among the quality of life projects at Courtney were the post exchange and commissary complex (above), the high rises (right) and senior officer quarters (below).

The Marines at Camp Courtney continued to receive new facilities throughout the 80s. Along with new four-bedroom homes, five senior officers' quarters were constructed on the base. The cost of the new housing totalled $2.3 million and occupancy began in May 1989.

Quonset huts acted as storerooms on Courtney before the completion of a 50,000 square foot warehouse. The $5 million facility is one-story, reinforced concrete and contains office space, a sprinkler system and parking area as well as the storage area.

A new gymnasium on Courtney provides racquetball/volley ball courts, basketball courts, weight and exercise rooms, saunas and a scuba facility. The $3 million project was completed in May 1988.

A new library and hobby shop was completed in July 1988. The $1.7 million facility is actually divided into two wings — a 7,000 square foot library and an equally large center for arts and crafts enthusiasts.

New construction on the base also includes a new shopping complex with a post exchange, commissary, gas station, bank and post office. All of the new facilities were funded by the government of Japan.[60]

Marines at Camp Butler got a new ground support shop, a maintenance shop and a heavy gun shop.

The area office's work at Chimu-wan Tank Farm began in the early 80s in response to a huge fire at one of the tanks that gravely endangered the lives of many residents in the surrounding town. The early work included an elaborate computer operated foam fire protection system. By 1987, major restoration was needed at the tank farm that supplies gasoline and jet and diesel fuel to all military services on Okinawa.

Chimu-wan consists of three separate tank farms with a total storage capacity of approximately 840,000 barrels. Tank Farm Number 1, the largest of the three, got two new 100,000 barrel tanks under a GOJ contract completed in April 1988. Construction began on Tank Farm Number 2 in March 1988 and was completed in early 1990. The $11.8 million project involved the demolition and replacement of two existing 40,000 barrel underground tanks with two 100,000 barrel tanks. The tanks have a steel lining on the inside and are encased in reinforced concrete. They are then buried underground and equipped with a fire protection system.

The GOJ funded contract was a joint venture between Nihon Kokudo Kaihatsu/Aoki Kensetsu, Fiji Denki Koji, Taisei Setsubi and Ryuyu Tsushin Koji.[61]

Asbestos removal remained a major environmental concern throughout the 80s and one of the most important asbestos removal projects was for the Department of Defense Dependent Schools. Kubasaki High School on Camp Foster is one of the oldest schools in Japan and, besides serving the students who attend school in the facility, Kubasaki hosts large sporting events each year which draw

Chimu-wan's fire protection system (above) allows foam to be sprayed on a fire from computerized controls located at a central system. The photo at the left shows the interior of one of the tanks and the photo below shows a tank under construction.

students from throughout the Far East. Under an O&M project funded by DoDDS, the asbestos was removed from the gymnasium area in time for the 1989 High School Boy's Far East Basketball Championship competition.

The 1989 High School Boy's Far East Basketball Championships were held in the asbestos free Kubasaki High School gymnasium.

The $5.9 million, two phase project involved the removal of asbestos containing materials from the school's cafeteria and gymnasium and replacing existing carpeting, insulation, doors, ceilings, piping, mechanical equipment, lights and cabinetry. During Phase II, the same type of work is being done in the auditorium, the classroom building and the administration building. The contract completion date is scheduled to coincide with the beginning of the 1991-92 school year.[62]

The new bowling center on Camp Foster (above) features computerized scoring (right).

The new bowling center on Camp Foster is a $3 million project and is one of the first projects designated under the Life Cycle Project Management Program in the district. The facility is huge; over 22,000 square feet provide room for 20 computerized bowling lanes, a kitchen, bar and lounge area, a restaurant, pro shop, lockers and a game room. A wet fire protection system and specialized humidity control features are unique additions to the project.[63]

The 150 bed U. S. Navy Hospital at Camp Lester is undergoing a $2.3 million life safety upgrade scheduled for completion in 1992. The work consists of removing the existing fire detection system and asbestos and installing a new sprinkler system. The hospital will remain open during the upgrade and the five phases of scheduled construction will take special coordination between the district, the contractors and the user. The hospital has served the armed forces on Okinawa since it's construction in 1958 under the supervision of the Okinawa Engineer District.[64]

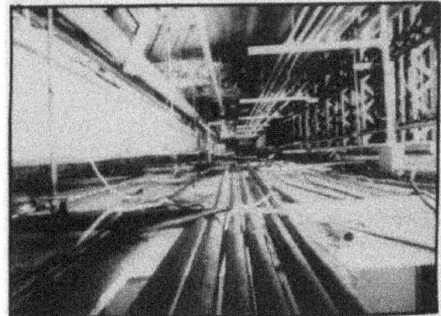

This photo shows the wiring and pipes for the hospital upgrade.

The concrete weather shelters replaced corroding metal shelters.

By the late 1980s, Okinawa's weather had taken its toll on the aircraft shelters built at the beginning of the decade for Commando Nest. The replacement of 50 aircraft shelters is an ongoing project at Kadena Air Base in support of the 18th Tactical Fighter Wing. Eighteen bays have been completed and construction began in July 1990 on ten more. The final 20 will be completed by the mid-90s.

A $5 million MILCON project is underway to upgrade the aircraft fueling system at Kadena. Current work on the project includes two 5,000 BBL underground fuel tanks, vertical turbine pumps, generator-control buildings and the stainless steel piping required to provide fuel to the various aircraft parking areas.

Additions to the operations building and maintenance hanger on Futenma Marine Corps Air Station were recently completed. The operations building houses the personnel who provide flight operations for the base as well weather and radar observation. It was completed in May 1990.

Renovation work on the maintenance hanger includes upgrades to heating, air conditioning, lighting, insulation, fire protection, storm drainage, the electrictal distribution system and new utilities connections. The two-story addition will be used for adminstation offices, training, maintenance and storage. [65]

A new $26 million noise suppressor facility was completed in December 1989 at Kadena Air Base. The hush house provides the latest in safety and engine test technology for the mechanics who service the F-15 Falcons. The reinforced concrete building contains four engine test cells complete with an overhead crane and fuel supply system. Engines from F-15s, F-16s and F-4s can all be tested in the cells. Four different engines, or any combination of engines, can be tested simultneously. To test the noise suppression capability before the hush house was turned over to the Air Force, four engines were tested and the decibel, or noise level, reading was taken outside the building. All readings were under 70 decibels. Normal city noise registers between 60 and 65 decibels. Hearing protection is required for sounds above 85 decibels. The decibel level is low because the hush house is able to isolate vibrations from the engines. [66]

Kadena's noise suppressor was one of the biggest projects on the base in terms of money and overall size. The high tech electronics inside allow the jet engine mechanics to closely monitor the engines (above and right).

The combat training village under construction.

Twenty-five thousand Marines on Okinawa spend the majority of their time in combat training. In addition to those stationed on the island permanently, Okinawa serves as a temporary duty station to train Marines from Hawaii and the United States. Until now, however, the Marines have not been able to train for a combat situation in a populated, congested area. When the Combat Training Village at the Camp Hansen Central Training Area was completed in March, the Marines gained an urban environment.

The village, the only one of its kind in the Western Pacific, consists of six mock buildings — a church, primary school, restaurant, bank and two two-story apartments — and includes a central roadway, plaza, alley and sewer complete with manholes.

The site of the village was carefully located within the 20,000 acre, non-live fire training area. It has road access from two different sides of the village and a helicopter landing zone is nearby. Both of these fetures are necessary to get the Marines in and out of the village and allow for a variety of tactical situations from a hostage rescue to a full-scale invasion.

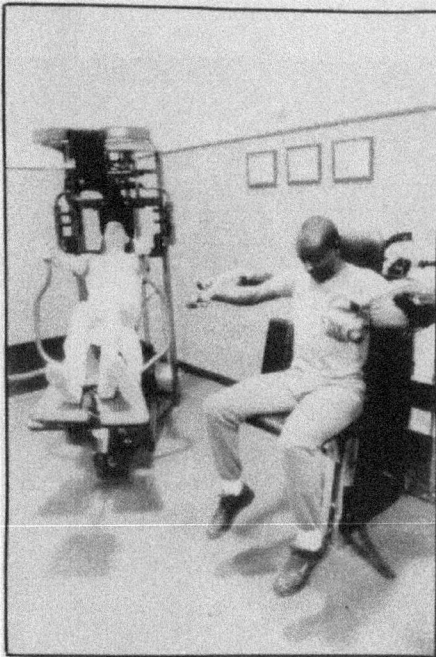

Risner Athletic Complex features a well-equipped Nautilus Room.

Construction of the village presented some unique challenges to the contractors. Each building is equipped with grappling hooks to allow for climbing and rappelling. The windows are all sized differently and one of the archways is too small for an adult to walk under. All of these irregularities are designed to teach the Marines to expect the unexpected.

The construction program on Okinawa during the 80s included many other quality of life and support projects to all services living and working on the island. Two of the most welcomed of these were the Risner Athletic Complex at Kadena and the Chibana Sports Complex. The Risner Athletic Complex is the largest in the Air Force. The $7 million GOJ funded facility includes 13 regulation racquetball courts and two exhibition courts, exercise rooms, weight rooms and state of the art exercise equipment for the personnel stationed at Kadena Air Base. Chibana is the largest recreation area anywhere in the world. Covering over five acres, the complex features an Olympic-sized swimming pool, four softball fields, a skating rink, two tennis courts and a six-hole golf course. There are bath houses and two large playgrounds with new equipment, a large soccer field and plenty of parking. The facility, built on the edge of Kadena Air Base, is very close to the Army personnel stationed at Torii Station and the Marines at Camp Shields and Camp McTureous. The GOJ funded complex cost $5 million.

Recent construction for the Army at Torii Station includes rennovation of a dining facility and a $1 million vehicle maintenance shop constructed for the Special Forces troops stationed there.[67]

Vehicle maintenance shop at Torii Station.

Housing, including BEQs, BOQs, highrises and townhouses, at virtually every base on Okinawa, was a major initiative during the 1980s. These townhouses at Camp McTureous, scheduled for completion in 1991 will provide homes for 450 families and are the last homes under construction for military families on Okinawa.

Conclusion

Between February 18, 1946 when the Okinawa Engineer District was established and the beginning of fiscal year 1991, the Corps of Engineers in Japan has played an integral part in rebuilding Japan and in providing a support base during wars in Korea and Vietnam and the current conflict in the Middle East. Now, as Communism fails over and over again throughout the world, as East and West Germany find renewed strength and growth in unification, and North and South Korea work toward unification themselves, the mission of the Japan District is taking on new dimensions.

The environment all over the world is sending a clear message to each of us. Infrastructures — in every country in the world — are failing. The United States Army faces an uncertain future in a new world that, for the most part, embraces peaceful solutions to serious problems. The Corps of Engineers faces its own uncertainties. We cannot continue to be the preeminent public engineering agency in the world if we do not learn how to become more cost effective and relevant to the needs of our partners.

The Japan District has met challenges head on; this work is a record of many of the challenges the district has met and overcome. But it will be faced with some of our most difficult hurdles as this decade continues. Many of those are the same that the Corps faces in all of its districts and divisions; some are unique to the Japan District.

Like the entire Corps of Engineers, JED must finds ways to accomplish the work in Japan more efficiently. The cost of doing business is no less an issue today than it was in 1957 when Brigadier General Davis, POD's commander, sent a message to the Chief of Engineers stating that customers in Okinawa were critical of the district's costs and wanted to see "100 cents out of every dollar spent on design and construction." The Corps seems no closer to finding a satisfactory explanation for our costs than it was then.

Japan's needs have changed as drastically as the country has over the past 45 years. Where the district once rebuilt an infrastructure for the islands of Japan and Okinawa, Japan now needs to attend to problems in that infrastructure. Clean air and water are at a premium in Japan and there are other environmental aspects which concern this host nation. Asbestos, contaminated soils, erosion, noise abatement, the protection of the seas from pollutants and the lack of adequate living space are of great concern to the people living and governing in Japan.

In addition, Japan is undergoing changes in the way they pay for U. S. forces stationed on Japan under the 1952 Peace Treaty. The government of Japan construction program has never provided for maintenance of facilities but, under a new burden sharing program being developed, that may change. If it does, the government of Japan will fund millions in operations and maintenance work now paid for the the United States. In addition, Japan is paying a larger percentage of the salaries and benefits for Japanese national employees working for U. S. forces; in 1992, these employees will be funded totally by the Japanese government. This, too, will result in vast savings to the United States government.

At the same time, the United States government is faced with determining the mission of U. S. forces in the Far East in light of the changing political scene. Base closures overseas already include some bases in Okinawa and the Philippines. As the Department of Defense draws down around the world, one of the Corps' greatest challenges will have direct impact on this district: Is there a continuing need to station U. S. forces in Japan, Okinawa and Korea?

While these big questions are being answered, the Japan District will continue to monitor a huge construction program. Over the years, the labor shortage in Japan has made this task steadily more difficult. Quality construction is harder to provide; timely construction is becoming an impossibility. The military construction moratorium imposed in 1990 has carried over into FY '91; host nation funding has not been adequate to cover costs of quality design, quality assurance and a quality project.

Problems internal to the district focus on its people. The threat of furloughs as FY '91 begins on such uncertain fiscal ground increases the challenges of caring for JED employees personally and professionally. The Department of Defense hiring freeze, as well as an even stricter freeze imposed on the districts and divisions by the Corps of Engineers senior leadership, threaten to erode the technically qualified workforce and dedicated leadership that have been the hallmark of this district for over 45 years.

The strength of this district has always been its ability to face adversity and challenges with vision. During the uncertainties ahead, the Japan Engineer District will continue to provide quality engineering and construction for the United States Army, Navy, Air Force and Marine Corps on Japan and Okinawa in the time honored tradition of the Corps of Engineers. As it has since 1946, *Essayons* —"Let Us Try" — will remain the motto and the guiding principle of this organization.

Footnotes

Chapter One

1. L. Eve Armentrout Ma, Ph.D., "The Man in the Middle: United States Army Corps of Engineers, Japan Engineer District 1945-1982," unpublished manuscript (San Francisco,1984), Chapter 1, pp. 1-3.
2. Erwin N. Thompson, *Pacific Ocean Engineers, History of the U. S. Army Corps of Engineers in the Pacific 1905-1980*, (Honolulu, 1982), p. 170.
3. Ma, "The Man in the Middle," Chapter 1, pp. 4-10.
4. Ibid., pp. 12-14.
5. Grania Davis and Ray Corlett, "Japan Engineer District History: The Historical Background 1945-1972," unpublished manuscript (Tokyo, 1980), p. 23.
6. Thompson, *Pacific Ocean Engineers*, pp. 168-171.
7. Ma, "The Man in the Middle," Chapter 2, pp. 5-6.
8. Thompson, *Pacific Ocean Engineers*, pp. 171-172.
9. Ibid., p. 172 and Ma, "The Man in the Middle," Chapter 2, p. 8.
10. Ma, "The Man in the Middle," Chapter 2, pp. 9-12.
11. Thompson, *Pacific Ocean Engineers*, pp. 173-176.
12. Ma. "The Man in the Middle," Chapter 2, p. 14.
13. Thompson, *Pacific Ocean Engineers*, p. 184.
14. Ibid.
15. Ibid., pp. 184-185.
16. Ibid., p. 185.
17. Ibid., p. 186.
18. Ibid., p. 179.
19. Ibid., p. 181.
20. Ibid.

Chapter Two

1. Thompson, *Pacific Ocean Engineers*, p. 189.
2. Ibid., pp. 190-191.
3. Ibid., pp. 193-194.
4. Ma, "The Man in the Middle," Chapter 2, pp. 20-21.
5. Thompson, *Pacific Ocean Engineers*, p. 198.
6. Ibid., pp. 215-216.
7. Thompson, *Pacific Ocean Engineers*, pp. 285-286.
8. Ellen van Hoften, *History of the Pacific Ocean Division Corps of Engineers 1957-1967*, (Honolulu, 1972), pp. 33-34.
9. Ibid., p. 34.
10. Ibid., pp. 34-35.

11. Ma, "The Man in the Middle," Chapter 2, p. 22.

12. van Hofton, *History of the Pacific Ocean Division*, pp. 34-35.

13. Ibid., p. 25.

14. Ibid., p. 26.

15. Thompson, *Pacific Ocean Engineers*, p. 214.

16. Ibid., pp. 179, 292-293.

17. Ibid., pp. 290-291.

18. Ibid., p. 216.

19. Ibid., pp. 292-293.

20. Ibid., pp. 219-220, 294-295.

21. van Hofton, *History of the Pacific Ocean Division*, p. 104.

22. Thompson, *Pacific Ocean Engineers*, p. 204.

23. Earle Whitmore, *History of the United States Army Engineer District*, Far East, (Seoul, 1976), p. 15.

24. Ma, "The Man in the Middle," Chapter 1, pp. 4-5.

25. van Hofton, *History of the Pacific Ocean Division*, pp. 40-41.

26. Ibid., p. 52.

27. Ma, "American Army Engineers in the Asian Setting: Historical Background and Development of the Japan Engineer district 1957-1984 (San Francisco 1986), Chapter 2, pp. 12-18.

28. van Hoften, *History of the Pacific Ocean Division*, pp. 45-46.

29. Ma, "American Army Engineers in the Asian Setting", Chapter 2, pp. 12-15.

30. Ma, "American Army Engineers in the Asian Setting," Chapter 2, pp. 17-19; Thompson, *Pacific Ocean Engineers*, p. 306.

31. Ma, "American Army Engineers in the Asian Setting," Chapter 3, pp. 9-10.

32. Ibid., pp. 10-11.

33. Ibid., pp. 11-12.

Chapter Three

1. Thompson, *Pacific Ocean Engineers*, pp. 311-317.

2. Ibid., p. 374.

3. Ma, "American Army Engineers in the Asian Setting," Chapter 1, p. 23.

4. Ma, "The Man in the Middle", Chapter 2, pp. 31-32.

5. Thompson, *Pacific Ocean Engineers*, pp. 374-375.

Chapter Four

1. USARJ Information Paper, Office of the Chief of Public Affairs, U. S. Army Japan/IX Corps.
2. *The Morning Star*, Okinawa, May 14. 1972.
3. *Shurei No Hikari,* Okinawa, Reversion Issue, May 1972.
4. Thompson, *Pacific Ocean Engineers*, pp. 353-354.
5. Ma, "American Army Engineers in the Asian Setting," Chapter 1, p. 27.
6. Ibid., pp 27-28.
7. Japan Engineer District Host Nation Construction Briefing, Engineering Division, 1989.
8. Thompson, *Pacific Ocean Engineers*, pp. 375-376, 418.
9. Ibid., p. 376, 417.
10. Ma, "American Army Engineers in the Asian Setting," Chapter 2, p. 10.
11. Japan Engineer District Host Nation Briefing, Engineering Division, 1989.
12. Ma, "American Army Engineers in the Asian Setting," Chapter 1, pp. 32-32.
13. Thompson, *Pacific Ocean Engineers,* pp. 378-380.
14. Ma, "American Army Engineers in the Asian Setting," Chapter 1, p. 34.
15. Engineering and Construction Division Workload Charts, Japan Engineer District Briefing Book prepared for LTG Joseph K. Bratton, Chief of Engineers, June 16, 1983.

Chapter Five

1. *Bamboo Bridge*, June 1984, pp. 1, 8; Ma, "American Army Engineers in the Asian Setting," Chapter 1, p. 39.
2. *Bamboo Bridge*, August 1984, pp. 1, 3.
3. *Bamboo Bridge*, Summer 1987, pp. 4-6.
4. *Bamboo Bridge*, August/September 1988, pp. 8-9.
5. Ma, "American Army Engineers in the Asian Setting," Chapter 1, p. 39.
6. Ibid., p. 41.
7. *Bamboo Bridge*, December 1982, p. 2
8. *Bamboo Bridge*, August/September 1988, p. 12.
9. *Bamboo Bridge*, February 1990, pp. 6-8; Memorandum 14 March 1990, "Subject: Updated Engineering Division Input for JED Historical Report," p. 2.
10. *Bamboo Bridge*, March 1990, pp. 5-7.
11. PR&A, April 1990, Chart 29: Memorandum dated 1 March 1990,

"Subject: History of VE Program 1984 and 1985."

12. Japan Engineer District Annual History Report 1988, pp. 12-13; Japan Engineer District Annual History Report 1989 , p. 16; ONTYME message dated 24 March 1990 from Mr. Sam Bradley to Mr. Michael Fenton outlining the history of JED's ADP office.

13. *Bamboo Bridge*, August 1982, p. 4.

14. *Bamboo Bridge*, June 1984, pp. 1-2.

15. Ibid.

16. Don Bleibtrey, A History of the Northern Area Office, Japan Engineer District 1984 and 1985, unpublished report, pp. 1-6.

17. Don Bleibtrey, A History of the Northern Area Office, Japan Engineer District 1986 and 1987, unpublished report, pp. 3-4.

18. *Bamboo Bridge*, October-November 1986, p. 6.

19. *Bamboo Bridge*, December 1989, pp. 6-7.

20. *Bamboo Bridge*, June 1989, p. 8.

21. *Bamboo Bridge*, February 1983, p. 11.

22. Ibid., pp. 10-11.

23. *Bamboo Bridge*, December 1984, p. 3.

24. *Bamboo Bridge*, September 1986, p. 12; JED Command Briefing, September 1990.

25. *Bamboo Bridge*, December 1987, p. 7.

26. Ibid.

27. *Bamboo Bridge*, May 1988, p. 12.

28. *Bamboo Bridge,* April 1983, p. 4.

29. *Bamboo Bridge*, October 1988, p. 9.

30. *Pacific Stars & Stripes*, October 21, 1979.

31. *Bamboo Bridge,* August 1983, p. 6.

32. *Bamboo Bridge*, October 1983, pp. 1-2

33. *Bamboo Bridge*, April 1984, p. 7.

34. *Bamboo Bridge,* October 1984, p. 4.

35. *Bamboo Bridge*, October 1987, p. 6.

36. *Bamboo Bridge,* December 1988, pp. 6-7.

37. Ibid, p. 3.

38. *Bamboo Bridge*, November 1989, pp. 1 and 6.

39. *Bamboo Bridge*, August 1983, p.4.

40. *Bamboo Bridge*, October 1983, p. 4.

41. *Bamboo Bridge*, August 1983, pp. 1-4.

42. *Bamboo Bridge*, October 1984, p. 4.

43. *Bamboo Bridge*, November 1988, p. 6.

44. Ibid, pp. 8-9.

45. *Bamboo Bridge*, December 1989, p. 12.

46. *Bamboo Bridge*, December 1982, pp. 3-4.

47. *Bamboo Bridge*, November 1987, p. 10.

48. Ibid., p. 16.
49. *Bamboo Bridge*, July 1988, pp. 6-7.
50. *Bamboo Bridge*, December 1982, p. 4; *Bamboo Bridge*, November 1987, pp. 8-9.
51. Command Briefing, September 1990.
52. *Bamboo Bridge*, April 1982, p. 4.
53. *Bamboo Bridge*, April 1984, p. 1.
54. *Bamboo Bridge*, October 1983, p. 5.
55. *Bamboo Bridge*, October 1984, p. 3.
56. *Bamboo Bridge*, September 1987, p. 4.
57. Ibid., p. 6.
86. *Bamboo Bridge*, October 1987, p. 4.
59. *Bamboo Bridge*, May 1989, p. 10.
60. Ibid., p. 6.
61. Ibid., p. 16.
62. Ibid., p. 12.
63. OAO Fact Sheet, January 29, 1990.
64. OAO Fact Sheet, January 15, 1990.
65. *Bamboo Bridge*, July 1990, pp. 4-5.
66. Ibid., p. 6.
67. JED Command Briefing, November 3, 1988.

Bibliography

Manuscripts

Ma, L. Eve Armentrout."American Army Engineers in the Asian Setting: Historical Background and Development of the Japan Engineer District 1957-1984." MS, 1986.

Ma, L. Eve Armentrout. "The Man in the Middle: United States Army Corps of Engineers, Japan Engineer District 1945-1982." MS, 1984.

Public Documents

Thompson, Erwin N. *Pacific Ocean Engineers, History of the U. S. Army Corps of Engineers in the Pacific 1905-1980* . Honolulu, 1982.

van Hoften, Ellen. *History of the Pacific Ocean Division Corps of Engineers, 1957-1967* . Honolulu, 1972.

Whitmore, Earle. History of the United States Army Engineer District, Far East. Seoul, 1976.

Newspapers

Bamboo Bridge   (Japan Engineer District)
Pacific Stars and Stripes (Tokyo)
Shurei No Hikari   (Okinawa)
The Morning Star   (Okinawa)

Miscellaneous

Bleibtrey, Don. "A History of the Northern Area Office, Japan Engineer District 1984 and 1985." Don Bleibtrey was an employee of the district stationed at Camp Zama and at Misawa Air Base. He left the district in 1990 for a position with USACE headquarters. JED history files.

Bleibtrey, Don. "A History of the Northern Area Office, Japan Engineer District 1986 and 1987" JED history files.

Command Briefing, September 1990. The command briefing is a presentation prepared by the JED public affairs office and used to brief

in-coming personnel and visitors to the district. JED history files.
Command Briefing, November 3, 1988. JED history files.

Davis, Grania and Corlett, Ray. "Japan Engineer District History: The
Historical Background 1945-1972." JED history files.

Japan Engineer District Annual History Report 1988. JED history files.

Japan Engineer District Annual History Report 1989. JED history files.

Japan Engineer District Engineering and Construction Division Workload Charts. Briefing Book prepared for LTG Joseph K. Bratton, Chief
of Engineers dated June 16,1983. JED history files.

Japan Engineer District Host Nation Construction Briefing. Engineering Division, 1989. JED history files.

Memorandum. "History of VE Program 1984 and 1985" dated 1
March 1990. JED history files.

Memorandum. "Updated Engineering Division Input for JED Historical Report" dated 14 March 1990. JED history files.

OAO Fact Sheet dated January 29, 1990. Fact sheets are compiled in
the field to use for briefing material. JED history files.

OAO Fact Sheet, January 15, 1990. JED history files.

ONTYME message from Mr. Sam Bradley to Mr. Michael Fenton outlining the history of JED's ADP office dated 24 March 1990. Bradley
was the first chief of the district information management office.
Fenton followed Bradley in that position and remains the chief at the
time of this printing. JED history files.

PR&A Charts, April 1990, Chart 29. This chart is from the April 1990
PR&A briefing book prepared for the bi-annual Pacific Ocean Divi-
sion Program Review and Analysis conferences held in Tokyo and
Korea. JED history files.

USARJ Information Paper, Office of the Chief of Public Affairs, U. S.
Army Japan/IXCorps. JED history files.

Appendix A

Dr. Eve Armentrout Ma bibliography from unpublished manuscript "American Army Engineers in the Asian Setting: Historical Background and Development of the Japan Engineer District 1957-1984."

Published Works
Books:

Allen, G. C. Japan's Economic Expansion. London: Oxford University Press, 1965.

Ayusawa, Iwao F. A History of Labor in Modern Japan. Honolulu: East-West Center Press, 1966.

Beasley, W.G. The Modern History of Japan New York: Praeger Publishers, Inc., 1963.

Bennett, John W., and Iwao Ishino. Paternalism in the Japanese Economy: Anthropological Studies of Oyabun-Kobun Patterns. Minneapolis: University of Minnesota Press, 1963.

Cohen, Jerome B. Japan's Economy in War and Reconstruction. Minneapolis: University of Minnesota Press, 1949.

Corps of Engineers Museum Fort Belvoir, Virginia. Geneses of the Corps of Engineers. Ft. Belvoir: Corps of Engineers Museum, 1966.

Fairbank, John K., Edwin O. Reischauer, and Albert M. Craig. East Asia, the Modern Transformation. Vol. 2 of A History of East Asian Civilization. Boston: Houghton Mifflin Co., 1965.

Fearey, Robert A. The Occupation of Japan, Second Phase: 1948-1950. New York: The Macmillan Co., 1950.

Harasawa, Togo. Nihon Kenchiku Seisanshi (History of Japan's Construction Industry). Tokyo: Naito Tokuji, 1948.

Hoxie, Gordon R. Command Decision and the Presidency. New York: Reader's Digest Press, 1977.

Jurika, Stephen, Jr., ed. From Pearl Harbor to Vietnam: The Memoirs of Admiral Arthur W. Radford. Stanford: Hoover Institution Press, 1980.

Kensetsusho Keikakukyuku. Doboku Kojigyo Chosa Jitsutai Hokokusho, Kenchiku Koji Chosa Hokokusho (Repot of the Investigation into the True Situation of Civil Engineering and the Construction Industry) Tokyo: Kensetsusho, 1961.

Kikuoka, Tomoya. Kensetsu-gyo (The Construction Industry). v. 16 of Shinsan-gyo, shirizu (New Industries Series). Tokyo: Nakai Yoshi Yuki, 1960.

Levine, Solomon B. Industrial Relations in Postwar Japan. Urbana: University of Illinois Press, 1958.

McCune, Shannon. The Ryukyu Islands. Harrisburg: Stackpole Books, 1975.

Martin Edward M. The Allied Occupation of Japan. Stanford: Stanford Univ. Press, 1948.

Mendel, Douglas H. The Japanese People and Foreign Policy. Berkeley: University of California Press, 1961.

Morris, M. C. Okinawa: A Tiger by the Tail. New York: Hawthorn Books, 1968.

Obayashi Gumi (ed.). Obayashi Gumi Hachijyunen-shi (History of the Eighty Years of Obayashi Gumi. Tokyo: Obayashi Gumi shashi henshu I-inkai, 1972.

Office of the Chief Engineer, Gen. Hqts., Army Forces, Pacific. Airfield and Base Development. Vol. VI of Engineers of the Southwest Pacific, 1941-1945. Washington: Government Printing Office, 1951.

Packard, George R., III. Protest in Tokyo: The Security Treaty Crisis of 1960. Princeton: Princeton Univ. Press, 1966.

Reischauer, Edwin O. Japan, Past and Present. 3rd Rev. ed. New York: Alfred A. Knopf, 1964.

Saga, Tadao. Beppu to senryo-gun (Beppu and the Occupation Army). Beppu: "Beppu to senryo-gun" editorial committee, 1981.

Schiffer, Hubert F. The Modern Japanese Banking System. New York: University Publishers, Inc., 1962.

Shiels, Frederick L. America, Okinawa and Japan: Case Studies for Foreign Policy Theory. Washington: University Press of America, 1980.

Thompson, Erwin N. Pacific Ocean Engineers: History of the U.S. Army Corps of Engineers in the Pacific, 1905-1980. Ft. Shafter, Hawaii: U.S. Army Corps of Engineers, Pacific Ocean Division, 1985.

Tokyo-to toshi keikaku kyoku (Metropolitan Tokyo City Planning Bureau). Tokyo no kichi, '77 (Tokyo's Bases, '77). Tokyo: Tokyo-to toshi keikaku kyoku, 1977.

United States Strategic Bombing Survey. The Effects of Air Attack on Japanese Urban Economy, Summary Report. v. 55 of Reports: Pacific War. Washington: Government Printing Office, 1947.

United States Strategic Bombing Survey. The Japanese Machine Building Industry. v. 23 of Reports: Pacific War. Washington: Government Printing Office, 1946.

Uyeda, Teijiro. The Small Industries of Japan. Shanghai: Kelly and Walsh, Ltd. 1938.

Watanabe, Akio. The Okinawa Problem. Carlton, Australia: Melbourne University Press, 1970.

Weigley, Russell E. History of the United States Army. Rev. ed. Bloomington: Indiana Univ. Press, 1984.

Werelius, Barbara A. Preliminary Inventory of the Records of the United States Army Corps of Engineers, Seattle District, Record Groups 77. Seattle: U.S. Army Corps of Engineers District, Seattle, 1974.

Whitehall, Arthur M., Jr., and Shin-Ichi Takezawa. Cultural Values in Management-Worker Relations. Chapel Hill: University of North Carolina School of Business Administration, 1961.

Whitmore, Earle. History of United States Army Engineer District Far East, 1957 to 1975. Seoul: U.S. Army Engineer District, Far East, 1976.

Articles, periodicals, pamphlets and newspapers:

Applegate, Lt. Col. Lindsay. "Electric Power on Okinawa." Military Engineer 311 (May-June 1954): 199-203.

Armstrong, William S. "Okinawa-American Colony." Contemporary Issues 8 (Jan.-Feb. 1958).

Ballon, Robert J. "Lifelong Remuneration System." in The Japanese Employee, edited by Robert J. Ballon. Tokyo: Sophia University, 1969.

Bamboo Bridge. 1982-1985.

Carrigan, Maj. Mark C. "Pipe Line Relocation in Korea." Military Engineer 339 (Jan.-Feb. 1959): 6-7.

Cassoday, St. Col. John B. "Overseas Real Estate." Military Engineer 333 (Jan.-Feb. 1958): 12.

Chang, Paul Timothy. "The Labor Movement." in The Japanese Employee, edited by Robert J. Ballon. Tokyo: Sophia University, 1969.

Cookson, Col. G.M. "Power Production on Okinawa." Military Engineer 345 (Jan.-Feb. 1960): 57-59.

Crandall, Col. Rial S. "The Post Engineer." Military Engineer 353 (May-June 1961): 204-205.

Engineer Update 3, n. 5 (July 1979).

Engineering News-Record 183, no. 22 (Nov. 27, 1969).

"Engineering Scholarships in Okinawa." Military Engineer 315 (Jan.-Feb. 1955): 31.

Goben, Ronald G. "Kammon Highway Tunnel, Japan." Military Engineer 331 (Sept.-Oct. 1957): 346-347.

Guyton, Joseph W., George L. Reed, and Ottis Fowler. "Highways for Okinawa." Military Engineer 414 (July0Aug. 1971): 270-272.

Hands, Arthur D. "Picking up the Pieces: Engineering Aid in Okinawa." Military Engineer 369 (Jan.-Feb. 1964): 31-33.

Hanmer, Maj. Gen. S.R. "Nuclear Combat Missiles. Space." Military Engineer 351 (Jan.-Feb. 1961): 18-22.

Hanna, Willard A. "Okinawa-Ten Years Later." American University Field Service. (Dec. 23, 1955).

"History of Okinawa: 23 — Land Tenure System." This Week on Okinawa 12 (n.d.).

Ishino, Iwao. "The Oyabun-Kobun: A Japanese Ritual Kinship Institution." American Anthropologist 55, n. 5, part 1 (Dec. 1953): 695-707.

Japan Times. 1966-1967, 1972.

Jennings, Corporal Gary. "Post Operations." Military Engineer 311 (May-June 1954): 184-185.

Jones, Lt. Col. Thomas T. "Pipelines in Inchon Harbor." Military Engineer 382 (Mar.-Apr. 1966): 90-91.

Kiernan, Dee. "Jacona—Okinawa's Lamp Lighting Lady." Military Engineer 323 (May-June 1956): 173.

Lane, T.A. "Construction on Okinawa." Military Engineer 419 (Nov.-Dec. 1952): 418-420.

Lutz, M.K. "Military Missiles and Rockets." Military Engineer 343 (Sept.-Oct. 1959): 348-355.

McCollan, Maj. William, Jr. "Raising the Tidal Basin Lock Gates at Inchon, Korea." Military Engineer 298 (Mar.-Apr. 1952): 96-101.

MacEachron, David. "New Challenges to a Successful Relationship." In Japan and the United States, edited by William J. Barnds. New York: New York University Press, 1979.

McGuire, Maj. John H., and Capt. Herbert R. Haar, Jr. "The Construction of Haneda Airdrome." Military Engineer 254 (Dec. 1946): 509-513.

Malevich, Col. Steven. "Nike Deployment." Military Engineer 320 (Nov.-Dec. 1955): 416-420.

Mandel, Lt. Col. Gerson. "Unique Hawk Missile Sites, Okinawa." Military Engineer 375 (Jan.-Feb. 1965): 31.

Morgan, John Davis, Jr. "Engineer Supply in Hokkaido, Japan." Military Engineer 254 (Dec. 1946): 516-518.

Nakayama, Kazuhiko. "Difference in the Degree of Building Damages between Those of Inside and Outside the U.S. Military Bases." Pamphlet. Tokyo: Nikkei Architecture, n.d.

Nesbitt, Lt. Col. Allen. "The New Tokaido Line." Military Engineer 372 (July-Aug. 1964): 234-240.

New York Times. 1967-1984.

Okinawa Engineer District. "188th Anniversary of the Corps of Engineers: Publicity Material." Pamphlet. Camp Kue, Okinawa: Okinawa Engineer District, 1963.

Okinawa Engineer District. "Unit History, 1946-1965." Pamphlet. Camp Kue, Okinawa: Okinawa Engineer District, 1965.

Pacific Stars & Stripes, 1956-1957, 1969.

Phillips, Brig. Gen. Thomas R. "U.S. Civil Administration in Okinawa Intended to be a Model of Enlightened Colonial Rule." St. Louis Post Dispatch. (Dec. 25, 1960.)

Pinckert, W. F. "Okinawa Gets Steam Power Plant." Electrical World. (Oct. 24, 1955): 30-32.

"Precast and Tilt-up Construction, Okinawa." Military Engineer 356 (Nov.-Dec. 1961): 428.

"POL Pipe Lines." Military Engineer 310 (Mar-Apr. 1954): 103-105.

Robertson, Pfc., Jenkins M. "Rebuilding Japan." Military Engineer 323 (May-JUne) 1956): 176.

St. Clair, Col. Harold J. "Nike Construction on Formosa." Military Engineer 243 (July-Aug. 1959)" 282-283.

"Service-1962: Local Post Achievements for Engineerng Programs." Military Engineer 363 (Jan-Feb. 1963): 33-34.

This Week on Okinawa. 9-15 (1963-1969).

"Two Treatment Plants Close Okinawa Sewage Gap." Engineer News Record 187 n. 26 (Dec. 23, 1971): 21.

Uchiyama, Isawu. "Construction Works in Past Decade." Contemporary Japan 24, n. 4-6 (1956): 244-254.

United States Air Force, Kadena Air Base. "Nomination for the 1981 Gen. Thomas D. White Environmental Quality Award." Pamphlet. Kadena Air Base, Okinawa: United States Air Force, 1981.

United States Army Engineer District, Far East. "U.S. Army Engineer District Far East, Corps of Engineers, First Anniversary." Pamphlet. Seoul: U.S. Army Engineer District, Far East, 1958.

United States Information Agency. "United States Pavilion, Japan World Exposition, Osaka 1970." Pamphlet. Osaka: USIA, 1970.

Wise, Robert D. "Training Welders in Okinawa." Military Engineer 376 (Mar.-Apr. 1965): 93.

Yates, Col. E.P. "USAHOMES." Military Engineer 380 (Nov.-Dec. 1965): 414-415.

Yoshino, Toshihiko. "Economic Recovery and Banking System." Contemporary Japan 24, n. 10-12 (April 1957): 570-595.

Unpublished sources

Ft. Shafter, Hawaii. U.S. Army Corps of Engineers. Pacific Ocean Division, Installation Historical Files, 870-5b, MARKS.

Ft. Belvoir, Virginia. (Washington, D.C.) U.S. Army Corps of Engineers. Office of History. Archives.

Congressional Sources

U.S. Congress. Senate. Joint Hearings. Committee on Armed Services, Military Construction subcommittee, and Committee on Appropriations. Armed Services Hearings: Military Construction Authorization — Fiscal Year 1968 on S. 1241 (H.R. 11722). 90th Cong., 1st sess., 1967.

Unpublished manuscripts and letters

Dod, Karl C. "Military Activities of the Corps of Engineers in the Cold War, 1945-1972." Ft. Belvoir, Virginia. Office of the Chief of Engineers. Office of History. Archives.

General Hdqts., Supreme Commander for the Allied Powers (SCAP). "Labor and Agrarian Reform-Part B; Working Conditions." v. 11 in

"History of the Nonmilitary Activities of the Occupation of Japan." National Archives, Washington, D.C.

Gottschalk, Chesney Orville. "The Problem of American Military Bases in Japan." MA thesis, University of California at Berkeley, 1957.

Kaneshiro, Jack H. Letter to Dr. Eve Ma, October 15, 1985. Historical files, POD.

Lansche, Robert L. (Technical Liaison Office, OED). "Steel Overcoats Protect Instruments in Okinawa," 1961. Historical Files, POD.

Loesing, Col. Vernon T. "Corps of Engineers Support in Okinawa," draft article, Jan. 1968. Historical Files, POD.

McCune, Shannon. "The Ryukyus: Islands in a Strategic Location," n.3 in "Ryukyu Islands Project: Research and Information Papers," 1970. Library of the University of California, Berkeley.

Nakashima, Henry S. (Engineering Division, OED). "Integrated Island Water System for Okinawa, Ryukyu Islands." (unpublished manuscript), 1968. Historical Files, POD.

Notes of American Negotiating Team for Okinawa Reversion, Jan.-Mar., 1972. Historical Files, POD.

Office of the Military History Officer, Hdqts. AFFE/8th Army (Rear). "The Far East Command, 1 Jan. 1947-30 June 1957." National Archives and Records Service, Washington, D.C.

Raymond, Lt. Col. Daniel A. (OED). "Design of Small Dams on Okinawa, Ryukyu Islands," (unpublished manuscript), 1961. Historical Files, POD.

Waters, Col. Charles H. "Engineers in the Army of Occupation in Japan." Armed Forces Staff College, 1951.

Waters, Col. Charles H. Letter to Karl C. Dod. 11 Apr. 1976. Historical Files, POD.

Interviews (All interviews were conducted by Dr.Eve Ma).
Alfonsi, Joseph (Chief, Engineering Division, Military Branch, POD, and formerly employee of OED). Ft. Shafter, Hawaii. 18 Apr. 1985.

Ban, Eugene (Chief, Facilities Engineering Support Section, Military Branch, Engineering Division, POD). Ft. Shafter, Hawaii. 9 Jan. 1984.

Bunker, Brig. Gen. Robert M. (Division Engineer, POD). Ft. Shafter, Hawaii. 10 Jan. 1984.

Cheung, Kisuk (Chief, Engineering Branch, POD). Ft. Shafter, Hawaii. 6 Jan. 1984, and 19 Apr. 1985.

Clifton, Col. Jack H. (Commander, JED, June 1985-July 1988). Camp Zama, Japan. 17-24 June 1985.

Cox, Joseph J. (Office of Counsel, POD). Ft. Shafter, Hawaii. 6 Jan. 1984.

DuLong, David (Asst. Chief, Engineering Division, JED). Camp Zama, Japan. 18 June 1985.

Flanders, Everette A. (Chief, Construction-Operations Division, POD). Ft. Shafter, Hawaii. 6 Jan. 1984.

Gerwick, Benjamin K. (Professor of Civil Engineer, University of California, Berkeley, Ca. and President, Ben Gerwick Asso., San Francisco, Ca.). Berkeley, California. 9 Apr. 1987.

Greeson, Gretchen (Chief, Public Affairs Office, JED). Camp Zama, Japan. 18-26 June 1985.

Hayes, Maj. Gen. Thomas J. (former Division Engineer, Corps of Engineers). San Francisco, California. Nov. 1984 and Feb., Apr. 1985.

Higa, Yeiji (Head, Electrical-Mechanical Section, Design Branch, Engineering Division, POD). Ft. Shafter, Hawaii. 18 Apr. 1985.

Houck, Stuart D. (Chief, Construction Division, JED). Camp Zama, Japan. 20 June 1985.

Ichikawa, Tsuneo (Chief, Procurement and Supply, JED). Camp Zama, Japan. 19 June 1985.

Kagimoto, Rick (longtime employee of JED). Camp Zama, Japan. 19-20 June 1985.

Kaneshiro, Jack H. (Deputy Area Engineer, Okinawa Area Office, JED, and longtime employee, JED). Telephone interview. 24 June 1985.

Kimble, Robert L. (Hawaii Resident Office, PO). Ft. Shafter, Hawaii. 18 Apr. 1985.

Luther, Col. Ralph A. (former District Engineer, JED). Ft. Meade, Maryland. 13 Sept. 1984.

Mason, John. (Chief, Southern Area Office, JED). Camp Zama, Japan. 25 June 1985.

Miller, Col. John T. (former District Engineer, JED). Fairfax, Virginia. 9 Sept. 1984; and telephone interview, 9 Oct. 1985.

Moteki, Fujio (Chief, Financial Management, JED and longtime employee of JED and predecessors). Camp Zama, Japan. 18 June 1985.

Nottingham, Col. Jonathan D. (former District Engineer, JED). Telephone interview. 12 Sept. 1985.

Paulson, Prof. Boyd C., Jr. (Prof. of Civil Engineering, Stanford University, Stanford, Ca. and specialist, Japanese engineering techniques). Telephone interview. 27 May 1987.

Richards, Col. Daniel (District Engineer, Far East District, 1959-1960). San Francisco, Ca. 14 March 1984; and telephone interview. 5 Nov. 1984.

Sameshima, Akira (Act. Chief, Technical Engineering Section, Design Branch, Engineering Division, POD, and longtime employee of POD, predecessors of JED). Ft. Shafter, Hawaii. 18 Apr. 1985.

Stiver, Robert (Asst. Chief, Procurement and Supply, Pacific Ocean Division until 1985; earlier, employee of Okinawa Engineer District and POD). Ft. Shafter, Hawaii. 3 Jan. 1984 and 19 Apr. 1985.

Walther, Jack H. (former Chief, Real Estate Division, POD). Telephone interview. 11 Aug. 1985.

Willis, Col. Edward M. (former District Engineer, JED). Telephone interview. 24 Aug. 1985.

Appendix B

Mainland Japan

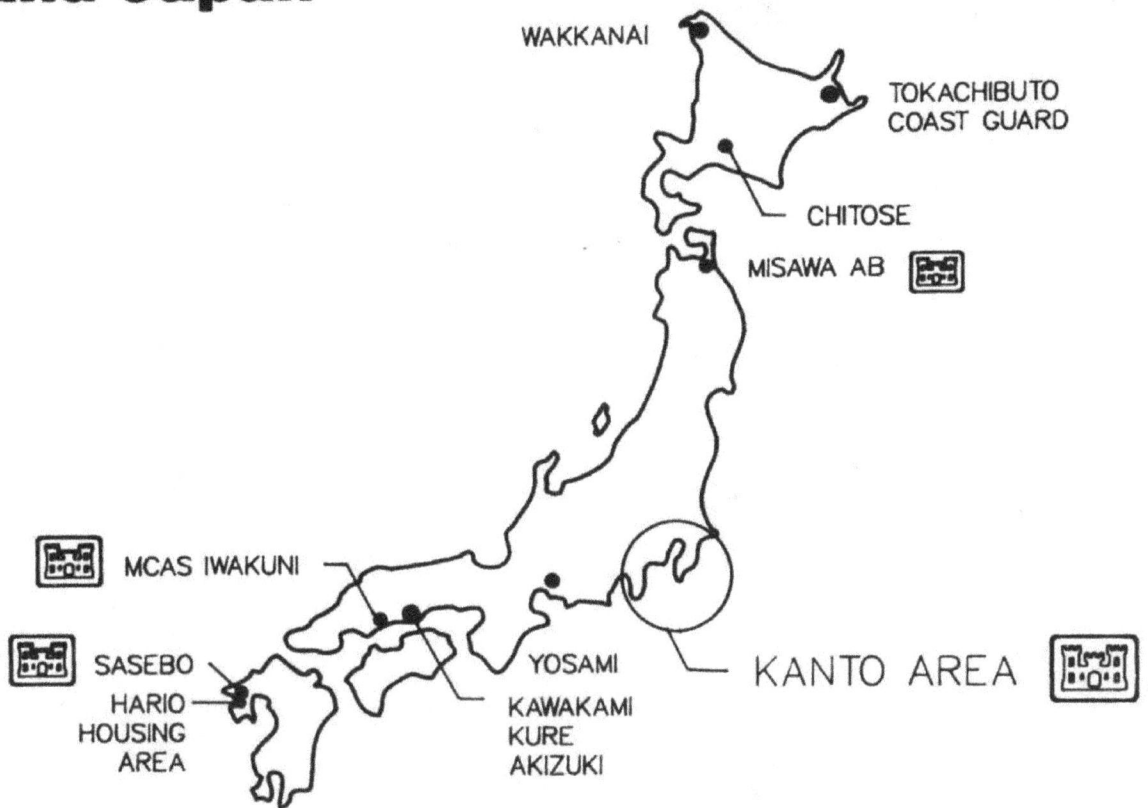

WAKKANAI

TOKACHIBUTO
COAST GUARD

CHITOSE

MISAWA AB

MCAS IWAKUNI

SASEBO
HARIO
HOUSING
AREA

YOSAMI

KAWAKAMI
KURE
AKIZUKI

KANTO AREA

Kanto Plains Area

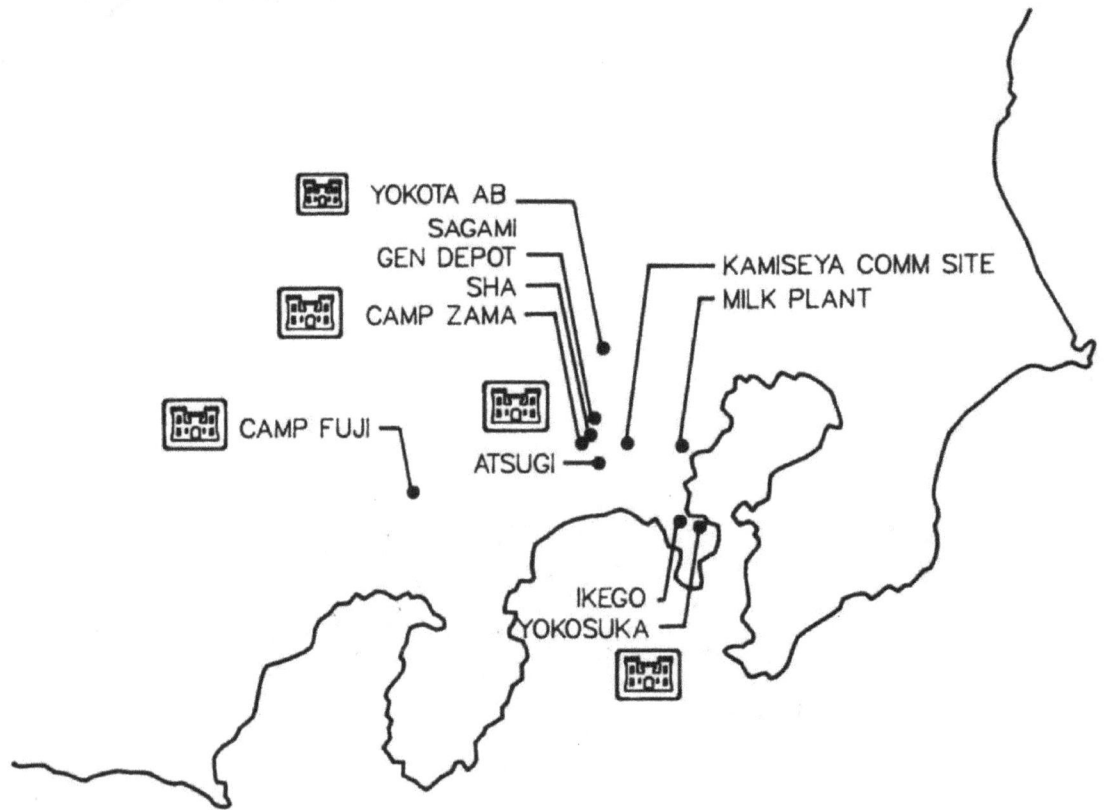

YOKOTA AB

SAGAMI
GEN DEPOT

SHA

CAMP ZAMA

KAMISEYA COMM SITE

MILK PLANT

CAMP FUJI

ATSUGI

IKEGO

YOKOSUKA

Okinawa

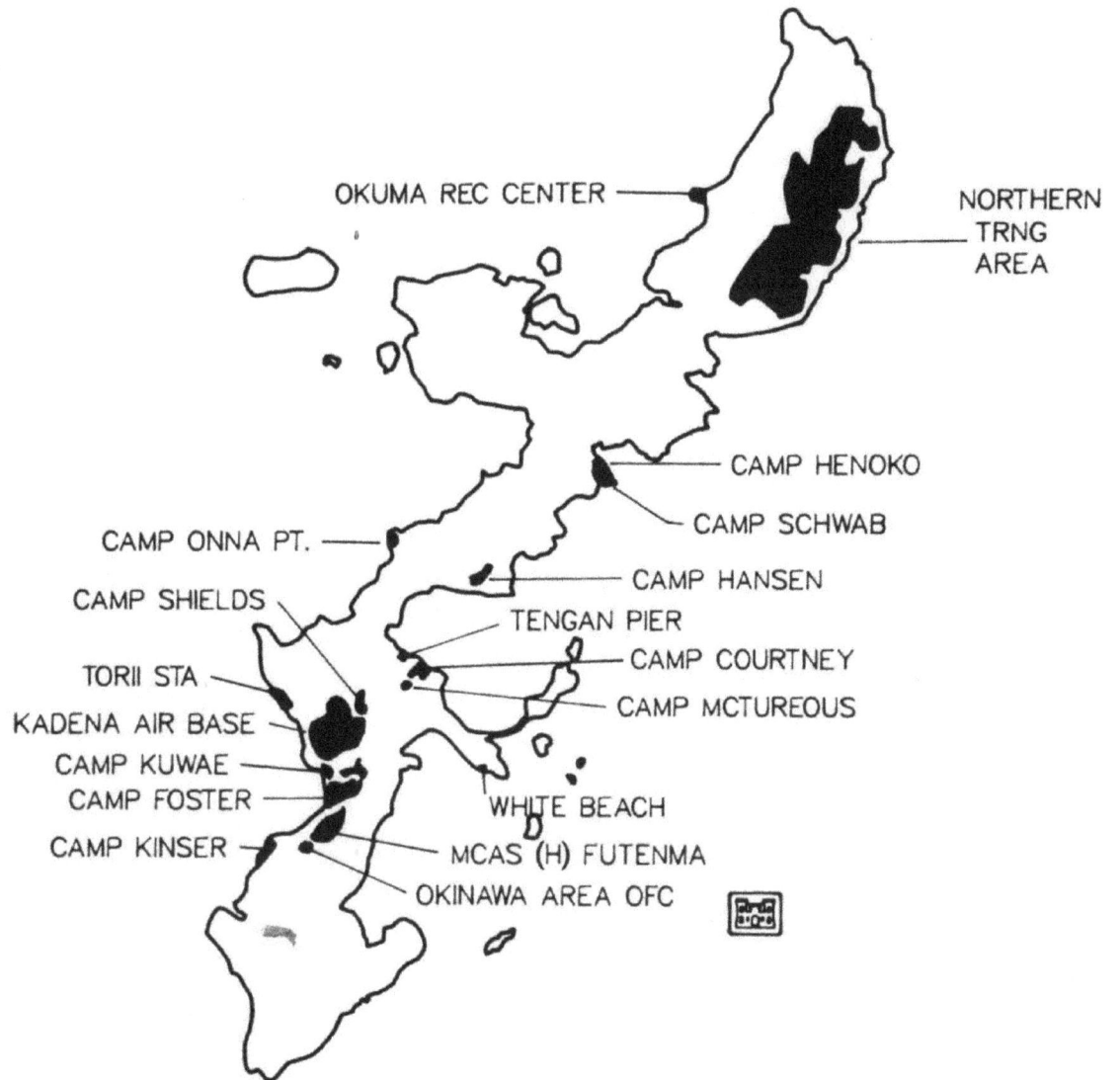

OKUMA REC CENTER

NORTHERN TRNG AREA

CAMP HENOKO

CAMP SCHWAB

CAMP ONNA PT.

CAMP HANSEN

CAMP SHIELDS

TENGAN PIER

CAMP COURTNEY

TORII STA

CAMP MCTUREOUS

KADENA AIR BASE

CAMP KUWAE

CAMP FOSTER

WHITE BEACH

CAMP KINSER

MCAS (H) FUTENMA

OKINAWA AREA OFC